Turtle Dove

Turtle Dove

One Man's Odyssey

JACK M. THOMPSON

To order additional copies of this book, contact:
Xlibris Corporation
1-888-795-4274
www.Xlibris.com
Orders@Xlibris.com
47107

Contents

Dedication

To my grandchildren Adrian, Garrett, Ben, Julia, XingXing, and Ai Mei.

CHAPTER 1

The Boat

Building a log cabin, 700-mile canoe trip, boatbuilding, launching.

Once upon a time a long while ago I decided there were three things I wanted to do:

* Build a real log cabin.
* Paddle a canoe to Hudson Bay.
* Sail my own boat to the South Seas.

(I wonder if others set such grand goals or if they just do whatever seems to make sense at the time. I seem to require a long-range agenda – preferably something to occupy me for the next 10 years or so.)

I was aware that none of these objectives had anything to do with my job as a reporter, or with my wife and four kids. If pressed, I'd probably agree that my goals were self-indulgent – nothing there to make the world a better place or help the poor and downtrodden.

These ideas just floated around in my head until one evening, while I was washing dishes, I suddenly felt as if I were strangling. I've got to get out of here somehow, I thought, and decided to go for Goal Two. I bought some topographical maps and soon my 18-year-old son Andy (commonly known as Ange) and I set off on a six-week, 700-mile paddle from Sioux Lookout, Ontario, to Fort Albany on James Bay, at the southern end of Hudson Bay.

I wrote a piece for the weekly magazine of my newspaper, which titled it *Paddling Through the Generation Gap*. The trip quieted my longings for some time, but eventually the stifled feeling struck again. I located a 27-acre site of beautiful forest in southern New Hampshire and persuaded my wife that it would be a good investment. I prowled the woods and camped out in a tent for a number of weekends and finally selected the proper spot to achieve Goal No. 1: the log cabin.

The site overlooked a valley and a little pond created by beaver dams. Everything necessary for the project – axes and peaveys, chainsaw and block and tackle, rope and lumber and bags of cement and sand – had to be hauled through the woods by hand or by wheelbarrow. Assisted by any poor sucker I could recruit for a day or two, I worked my ass off and loved it. We cut down trees, trimmed off the branches and hauled the logs to the site with block and tackle. The biggest logs, those for the base of the walls, we rated by the number of beers we needed to recover after they were in place. We had one-beer logs, two-beer logs and one three-beer log that took almost a full day.

I thought the finished cabin was a work of art. Everything, except for the rough-sawn planks in the floor and the roof, had been cut out of the woods around us. In the winter I brought my ice skates and glided around the pond, circling the rounded mounds poking through the ice and picturing the beavers inside, warm and snug against the cold. When the ice finally melted I loved to wake up at first light and hear the beavers slapping their tails in the pond – ker – FLUMP! I never actually saw a beaver, though I often saw their wakes in the water as they swam across the pond at dusk.

I used the cabin happily for several seasons. But then I struggled through the snow in the dark one New Year's Eve with a friend to find the woodstove had been stolen. That pretty much took the joy out of the cabin. I sold the place to a rather strange man who went to live there with his aged mother; I never did figure out how the two of them managed the daily trek through the woods, and I never went back to find out.

The shift to Goal No. 3, the boat, was much more gradual. I had been interested in boats for a long time, ever since coming to New Bedford in 1954 for my first newspaper job. I bought an ancient Beetle Cat, a 12-foot catboat much used for kids' races in the area, and set about rebuilding her.

That little boat was the first in a series. There followed a slightly larger sailboat, which didn't sail very well, an iceboat, and finally a 16-foot work skiff modeled after the workboats used by the local shellfishermen. With a 25-horse outboard on her stern she positively flew over the water. I remember our first outing, to see the Tall Ships parade in Newport. With three guests aboard we chugged around the harbor, fresh paint a-gleaming, and heard a congratulatory shout from one of those magnificent vessels: "Nice boat you got there!" I was enormously pleased.

On one of our visits to Block Island I saw a lovely little boat docked in New Harbor. I was struck by her stout bulwarks, her rakish bowsprit and her fat little hull, shaped like a big pumpkin seed. She looked a proper little ship, I thought. I talked to the lady aboard.

"She's a TAHITI ketch," the woman said with evident pride. "My husband built her."

I was smitten. This was the boat for me. But at 10 tons she seemed a bit small. Then I discovered that John Hanna, her designer, had drawn two larger boats with the same lines – the 36-foot CAROL and the 37-foot MOOREA (named after what I later decided was the most beautiful island in the South Seas.)

The CAROL was like the TAHITI, but at 15 tons she had more room for a couple living aboard. I didn't realize that there is a kind of exponential phenomenon in boatbuilding. The 15-ton vessel requires about twice as much work and money as the 10-tonner; the 20-ton boat takes four times as much. Another thing I didn't realize was that building a big wooden boat is not the best medicine for a marriage. A project like this can become an obsession. (Much later I met a fellow wooden boat builder in New Caledonia, who first admired my vessel and then broke into laughter.

"How many years, and how many wives?" he asked. "12, and two," I told him. The other guy said his numbers were better: only 10 and two.)

To a professional boatbuilder the plans probably would seem pretty simple, but to me they were formidable. Fortunately I had Howard Chapelle's book *Boatbuilding*, and it was a godsend. Chapelle taught me about the complexities in the lines drawing of a boat, which is really three drawings in one: first a profile showing the side view of the boat, then cross-sectional views with the hull chopped up into slices like a banana, and, finally, diagonal lines that help the builder reproduce the curves of the vessel.

I had to draw out the lines plan full size on plywood to get accurate patterns of the boat. When the 40-foot drawing was done (some neighbors thought I was constructing a patio in the side yard), I started buying materials, and there were plenty to get. For the ballast keel I needed 10,000 pounds of lead. For the hull I needed tons of wood – big timbers for the keel and deadwood, heavy hardwood pieces for the frames (called "ribs" by the layman), thousands of feet of sawn lumber for planking and decking, more heavy hardwood for the floor timbers, which would support the actual flooring, softwood for planking and interior bulkheads and ceiling (the thinner inner skin), extra-wide heavy slabs for supporting knees.

To fasten all these pieces together I would need bronze rods and bronze plate, copper nails to rivet planking to frames, bronze screws and ring nails to fasten down deck planking.

I wanted to use reclaimed materials where possible, both to save money and because old wood is often better than the new stuff available, and for this I made a lucky find – the scrapyard operated by Nick DiGregorio. Nick was in the demolition business and the fruits of his labor were stored in a huge scrapyard at the rear of his big modern house. He was paid well for the dangerous job of tearing down big old commercial buildings, and then he trucked the salvaged materials to his scrapyard and sold the stuff to all comers – cash only, no checks and no receipts, please.

Nick was about 5 foot 10 and about 5 feet wide and very little of that was baby fat. He loved the idea that I taught at URI and that I was constantly asking him about building materials. "You tell ME!" he would roar in response to my questions. "You're the professor!"

Everything in Nick's domain was huge – cranes, bulldozers, backhoes, generators, trucks and trailers, and his three enormous sons. I felt like a pygmy in the place. The lot was crammed with millions of bricks, timbers and planks, cement and cinderblocks, cable and wire and chain, old bathtubs, even some enormous old steel safes from a bank. Guarded by the proverbial junkyard dog at the end of a long rusty chain (I prayed it would hold every time I drove in there), it was a scrounger's paradise.

I bought a lot of scrap lead from Nick, but even he didn't have enough to melt 10,000 pounds. I put a modest ad in the paper and started entertaining a succession of dubious characters who showed up at the house.

They brought rolled-up sheet lead flashing (I could picture it being peeled off somebody's roof in the dead of night), twisted pieces of old lead pipe, lead melted in old muffin tins, bagfuls of old bullets. I bought it all, no questions asked, and began accumulating a big ugly pile in the side yard.

Meantime I had picked out a huge timber in Nick's yard. It had been part of a 90-year-old mill in Pawtucket and was 40 feet long, 12 inches wide and 14 inches high. This would become the keel, – the real backbone of the boat. Nick said the wood was the finest hard pine, cut a long time ago in the turpentine forests of the South and ideal for boatbuilding. When it came time to cut it I found the wood yellow with resin, as pungent as if it had been in the forest only yesterday.

While all this was going on, I was devouring advice and information – from books, magazines and genuine experts who seemed always willing to talk at length with me. But sometimes, I found, the information could be conflicting.

Pouring the lead ballast keel was an example. I had saved an article in an old boating magazine which described melting lead in a bathtub heated by propane gas. I wanted to use wood as fuel, mainly because there was an unlimited supply of broken scrap wood in Nick's yard. Several people assured me that a wood fire would never get hot enough to melt all that lead. Nick, on the other hand, said it would work just fine. I elected to believe him. But on another part of the problem – the actual pouring of the lead keel – I went with a different expert.

I planned to build a mold of heavy green oak planks, treated with a liquid called waterglass, which would keep the wood from burning. The mold would be sunk in the ground to prevent the molten lead from spreading the sides of the mold. The finished keel would be 18 feet long and 12 inches square in section. It would weigh about 8,000 pounds, with the remaining 2,000 pounds of ballast to be melted into lead ingots or "pigs," to be stored inside the boat in the bilge.

I consulted a professor of metallurgy at URI. He told me, with great authority, that I would need two bathtubs to pour a lead keel of that size. Trying to pour molten lead from only one tub would be "like pouring water on a freezing sidewalk," he declared – the lead would harden into an unmanageable heap before it could reach both ends of the mold.

Bullshit! Nick roared. With only one tub the lead would stay molten plenty long enough to fill the mold, he declared.

I elected to believe the metallurgist – After all, he had a Ph.D., didn't he? So I bought two old bathtubs from Nick's yard and had a kind of downspout welded into the drain holes, to conduct the molten lead into each end of the mold. The flow would be controlled by a valve in the downspout.

The first of two days of keel pouring was cool and drizzly, which proved to be a blessing when we got two enormous wood fires roaring beneath the bathtubs. My volunteer helpers started piling in the pieces of scrap lead until both tubs were full. And then we waited and watched. For some time there seemed to be no results at all. Were the skeptics right about wood fires after all?

But then the pieces started shifting and settling in the tubs, and below them I caught a glint of shiny liquid. It looked like mercury, and it gradually deepened as the fires increased in intensity. Soon we were melting scrap lead as fast as we could feed it in.

Molten lead is weird and beautiful. It shines like liquid silver and it looks as thin as water. But the stuff is so heavy that everything floats in it – dirt, broken concrete, rocks. Especially rocks, of which there seemed to be a great many, apparently stuffed into the twisted lengths of lead pipe to add to the weight. The molten lead was awash with rocks. We had to make a kind of landing net out of heavy mesh wire on a pole to scoop out the stones that were bobbing around in the tubs.

It looked like a scene from Hell – dark skies and a light rain drizzling down, the wood fires roaring and me and my soot-blackened helpers furiously shoveling in wood below and scrap lead above, with all the neighbors gathered around to marvel. One neighbor, a city fireman, ran back to his house and returned with a pair of big asbestos gloves. They were a huge help.

At last we had fed in enough lead to fill each bathtub about two-thirds full; the amount I had calculated would fill about half the keel mold. I planned to pour in two halves – one end of the mold one day and the other half the next. To accomplish this I had built a wooden dam at the center point of the mold.

The big moment was at hand. Donning the asbestos gloves, I opened the valves for each tub and the molten lead gushed out.

But not for long: In one tub the flow slowed to a trickle and then stopped altogether. Meanwhile the other pipe was gushing full tilt, and now I discovered another problem. The molten lead rushed down the mold, knocking my wooden dam all to hell. No "water on a frozen sidewalk" here – the liquid lead filled the entire length of the mold and continued to bubble away merrily while more lead poured in. It looked as if we would be pouring this keel in two halves, all right, but now each half would be full-length, with one atop the other. As I thought about it, this seemed to be a better plan anyway.

I grabbed a big steel cooking pot, a helper took a galvanized pail, and we started bailing molten lead out of the stopped-up tub. It was hot, hard work but it worked. At the end of the day we had the wooden mold just about half full. And it stayed liquid in the mold for a half hour or more. So much for the Ph.D.

Next morning we started the second pour. We used only the "good" tub, and once the fire was blazing we were pouring molten lead out, and dumping scrap lead in, almost simultaneously. The only nagging question now was whether we had enough scrap to fill the mold – I kept worrying about all those rocks that had been hidden inside the pipe.

But we had more than enough. We wound up with the mold full of hot shiny metal and plenty left over. We had to do something with the stuff already melted, so we filled up the galvanized pail with lead, then filled a lot of old coffee cans. When we ran out of containers we dug holes in the ground and filled those.

(Much later, I kept the pail of lead in the boatbuilding shed and sometimes I'd ask a visitor to bring it to me. It was fun watching him try to pick it up. It weighed around 400 pounds.)

While the lead cooled in its mold I started working on the wooden keel. First I had to saw a slice two inches wide off the 40-foot length. I did it with a chainsaw, at the cost of considerable noise and aggravation for the long-suffering neighbors. Next I sunk six broken-off telephone poles (obtained from the phone company) in the ground along a straight line at four-foot intervals and sawed them off evenly, each about 12 inches high, to support the keel and, eventually, the entire boat.

There were to be 10 bronze keel bolts, each an inch in diameter, locking the lead ballast keel and the wooden keel above it together. I drilled the bolt holes in the wooden keel first. Next I clamped the wooden keel atop the lead ballast keel and commenced drilling into the lead, using the wooden keel as a template. The drill bit jammed occasionally, and when it did I found my whole body spinning around, rather than the bit. But it was manageable, even with the occasional body spin. When all 10 holes were drilled to the length of the drill bit I could lift off the wooden keel and complete the holes through the lead.

I bought more heavy pieces of hard pine from Nick. I bought white oak and white pine from a taciturn sawyer in New Hampshire, my supplier during the cabin construction, and hauled it down in truckloads on my pickup. The big knees that would tie the cabin top to cabin sides came from a dead apple tree in the back yard. I chainsawed out enormous slabs and had them planed down in a local woodworking shop. The finished apple wood was beautiful.

I used locust, hard and durable, for much of the interior and for exterior cleats, rub rails and mooring posts. It came from a neighbor's yard full of big unwanted locust trees. I cut down about 20 and spent two days getting them ready to be hauled to another backwoods sawmill about 15 miles away.

Warren Thayer and his son worked there in a big dim open shed, seemingly impervious to the cold. Warren kept an unlit cigar stub between his teeth as he steered snow-covered locust logs into the screaming three-foot saw blade. I watched for several hours, shuffling from one foot to the other to keep from freezing solid. Finally there were enough big yellow planks to load on the truck and haul back home. There were many more trips before I got all that lumber stored in the yard.

Meanwhile I was awaiting a large quantity of white cedar planking from a mill in northern Maine. Almost a year passed before the wood finally arrived. I ordered hundreds of dollars' worth of bronze rod and bronze plating, intending to make my own bolts and even my own bronze washers, by drilling holes in pennies. (I learned that the composition of the American penny was just right to go with bronze bolts and nuts. And they were considerably cheaper than buying ready-made bronze washers.)

Now it was time to start working on the deadwood, the backbone of a vessel. I laid a sheet of clear plastic over the big lines drawing and traced it over with orange grease pencil. Then I cut out the plastic around the orange lines to get a pattern for each piece. With these patterns I marked the heavy pieces of wood, then cut them out with my home-built bandsaw. Wrestling the heavy slabs of yellow pine into the saw was awkward, and I found myself wishing for an extra pair of hands. But I also felt exhilarated – at last I was cutting wood that would become a vital part of the boat.

As the stem and stern pieces were cut I laid them on the big lines drawing to be sure they fit properly. To get a tight fit between two surfaces you rubbed blue chalk on one side, then clamped the pieces together. Wherever there was a high spot on the other surface there would be a tell-tale smudge of blue chalk. You planed that off and then fitted again. Eventually, if your patience held, you had a perfect fit.

With stem and stern pieces bolted to the wooden keel it was time to make the molds. Since this was to be a beamy boat, these molds were big – the widest almost 12 feet across and about seven feet high. It was positively exciting to mount the molds across the wooden keel, supported by diagonal braces to keep each one upright and level across the top. There were 10 molds and when all were in place I suddenly was looking – at last! – at a three-dimensional boat, at least in skeleton form. Now it didn't need a lot of imagination to see it filled out, solid and complete and curvetting over the waves.

There was still a long way to go to reach the curvetting stage, though. Now I had to nail long thin battens, called ribbands, to each frame about a foot apart. These strips followed roughly the lines that the actual planking would take. But like the molds they were only temporary – their sole purpose was to provide a supporting framework to which I could bend the frames. I was learning that this kind of boatbuilding involves a lot of woodwork that doesn't remain in the boat.

With the ribbands all in place it was time to start bending frames. There were to be 120 of them, each a piece of white oak 1 3/4 inches square in section and anywhere from six to 10 feet long. Freshly-cut white oak bends fairly readily when steamed or boiled. Professional boatbuilders use a steam box heated by a boiler. This seemed complicated to me, and I decided I would simply boil the wood. This was where my friend Harrigan and his light pole came in.

Some time earlier Harrigan had been looking for a stove pipe for his new wood stove, long enough to extend well above his roof line. He discovered a downed aluminum utility pole along a superhighway some miles south of his home and decided to liberate it. He borrowed a long ladder and lashed it to the top of his dented little Ford Escort, then waited for the proper hour (dusk, about 5 p.m., during the heaviest commuter traffic – he figured the rush of cars would help to mask The Great Caper.)

But like many plans, easier said then done. The monster pole was heavy as hell. With every ounce of his considerable strength he could wrestle only one end of it up onto the ladder on top of the car. Meanwhile, he found that passing motorists persisted in honking their horns at him as they sped by. Were they encouraging him, or trying to summon the authorities? He didn't know, but the commotion made him nervous.

In the gathering darkness, amid the cacophony of the passing car horns, Harrigan persisted in his lonely struggle. In desperation he girded his loins, took a deep breath, heaved with a final mighty surge of adrenalin, and managed to wrestle the entire pole up onto the ladder. He slumped against the car, convinced that he was having a heart attack. After long minutes of deep breathing he recovered enough to lash the pole to the ladder and set off down the throughway. He drove the six miles back home without incident. Nobody stopped him; nobody even seemed to take a second look at the small private car tooling down Route 95 with a huge highway light pole sticking out each end. He turned into his yard, buried the pole in a pile of leaves and tottered into the house, straight to bed.

The pole turned out to be much too long. This is where I came in. I sawed off the bottom 12 feet, capped one end with a wooden plug (it would be resting on the ground below the fire and shouldn't burn, I figured), propped it leaning against a homemade stand and was ready to start cooking.

Bending frames is a dramatic and exciting part of boatbuilding because you make very visible progress. You need at least three people, a great many C-clamps and double-headed nails, hammers for everybody, a big sledgehammer and a home-made frame-bender with a handle four or five feet long. You also need heavy leather gloves and a cool day, if possible, since the frames are being plucked out of boiling water.

One worker stokes the fire, snags the hot frame out of the tank and hands it up to a worker inside the boat who grabs the steaming frame and forces one end against the keel at the bottom of the boat, using his foot to bend the frame out against the battens running the length of the boat. A second helper pounds with the sledge and twists with the frame-bender to force it down against the battens. Then everybody clamps the frame against each ribband, beginning at the bottom and working toward the top. When the frame is fully in place it is being held by as many as 16 C-clamps.

It all has to be done quickly, before the frame cools. Some frames do break, and these are tossed aside while the job goes on. (Better now than later, is the rationale.) Breakage was most likely to happen in the stern, where a wine-glass curve required severe bends in opposite directions. As the new frame cools it is time to start removing clamps, since you never have enough to clamp the entire boat. As each clamp comes off it is replaced by a double-headed nail pounded through the batten into the frame. (The double head allows you to pound it tight but still withdraw it easily.)

It's hard work but amazingly gratifying – the boat almost seems to leap into shape before your eyes. Since the frames were placed on 6-inch centers, and each frame was almost two inches wide, the boat looked almost solid when all the frames were in. (One friend suggested that I could put one more in between each, then calk them vertically and not have to bother with planking at all.)

Next came the planking. I had decided to use hard pine planks for the first three strakes, starting with the garboards (the lowest of the planks.) These had to have a fearsome twist at both ends, and it took me almost two weeks to get both firmly fastened in place. Things went a little easier as I inched my way up the hull, but still progress was slow.

The planks were fastened to the frames with rivets, heavy copper nails with a rove (a copper washer) placed over the protruding pointed end. Because copper is relatively soft, each nail had to be pre-drilled before I could force it through the hard oak frame. The head of the nail would be countersunk into the planking and a helper would hold it in place with a heavy iron bar while I, inside, fitted a copper washer over the point of the nail, snipped off the point close to the washer, and tapped lightly on the cut end to form a rivet. The process is called "peening." Holding the iron bar against the nailhead on the outside is "bucking." Riveting is not a one-man job, and I had several volunteer buckers. One friend, Dave Cullen, stayed with me for days. We had many deep discussions on a variety of topics as we faced each other, he outside holding his iron bar and me within, wielding my ball-peen hammer.

In the meantime I managed to torpedo my marriage and found myself living on my own. The huge half-finished boat was in our side yard, and I didn't see how I could move it right away. We agreed that I would move out immediately but could return to work on the boat, maybe three days a week.

I moved onto DOWNEASTER, our old boat, and set about living aboard. Three days a week I was in and out of the house to get tools, use the bathroom, etc. I was of course constantly bumping into my now-estranged wife. It was an awkward, embarrassing, and guilty time. Finally it looked as if the half-built boat was strong enough to move. The boat-mover agreed and hauled it to Johnson's Boatyard in Wickford, where I could erect a crude shelter and continue working through the winter. I told Mr. Johnson I thought the job might take five years.

I was in the boatyard store when the truck pulled up. The store clerk stared out in high glee. "WHAT A MOOSE!" he chuckled, obviously unaware that he was talking to the Builder of the Moose. With the Moose installed I constructed a roof supported on poles cut from various woodlots. (Later, I learned that the boatyard crew consistently referred to it as Fort Apache.)

Work proceeded and slowly the hull developed. But as cold weather set in I sometimes found my bare hands freezing to the tools. Even worse were my feet – it seemed impossible to keep them warm. I bought huge oversize boots and stuffed them with extra socks. But I never mastered the art of concentrating on the work and wiggling my toes at the same time.

I had survived most of the winter living on my old boat, also docked at Johnson's Boatyard. But during the worst weather I moved in with a new lady friend in nearby Saunderstown. Life was a lot more comfortable, I found, in a house where the ceiling didn't develop a coating of ice that melted and dripped down on my head when I returned home and got the stove going.

Next summer I decided to move the boat once again – this time to my Saunderstown lady's house and a bigger and stronger boatshed. This one even had heat – a big wood-burning stove that supplied some warmth.

I hired a helper on a half-time basis because it was beginning to look as if the project would never be finished. Bob D'Arcy was young but an experienced shipwright. And he had a sense of humor, which was a major asset. We made a signboard and hung it at the entrance of the new boatshed. *"COCKAMAMIE BOAT WORKS,"* it said. Under the name was a picture of a canoe under construction – the end on the left pointing up, the other end pointing down.

As time progressed I got a new left hip and two other important events occurred:

I married Ellen, my lady in Saunderstown.

I took early retirement from my teaching job at URI.

Now I worked with a new passion, six and sometimes seven days a week. I didn't have to shift gears any more between being a boatbuilder and a professor, and I reveled in it. We completed the planking, the cabin sides, the cabin roof beams, the cabin top, the two hatches (helped by a timely article in *WoodenBoat Magazine.)* Now I started on the interior layout, with cardboard mockups of bulkheads, tables, and bunks. We were planning a multi-purpose house: one designed for living comfortably aboard in harbor, but sometimes battling heavy seas in mid-ocean.

Slowly the interior of the hull took shape: the big V-berth and chain locker up forward with a 50-gallon wooden water tank and hanging locker; then the head, with sink and toilet and storage shelves, a bench and smaller water tank and more hanging lockers opposite; next the main salon with the dining table that converted to a double bed with storage bins underneath and a single settee berth with pilot berth and more storage space opposite; then the galley with sink, propane stove, and refrigerator and the navigation station opposite; finally the engine room with diesel engine now installed.

The cockpit above the engine was made deliberately small, to leave little space for any following sea that might force its way aboard. Aft of that was a lazarette hatch for miscellaneous storage, and, at the stern, an enormous heavy rudder with an eight-foot tiller extending over the cockpit.

All this took several years. Countless details had to be thought about, argued over and completed. Casting bronze fittings for the rudder was just one of those details. For these fittings, exact-size wooden models had to be made, then a suitable foundry had to be located. Bob D'Arcy did the caulking, a formidable job. I guessed the length of all those seams, both deck and hull, would probably run for a mile or so. You could hear the steady ring of Bob's caulking mallet for weeks.

There were a million things still to do. I had so many lists that I had to make a master list of all the lists. There was also the social side of the thing to consider. Several years earlier I had attended a friend's boat launching, and I wanted mine to be equally memorable – after all, it signified both the end of a 12-year project and the beginning of a new undertaking.

I had settled on the name: TURTLE DOVE, taken from Henry Thoreau's Walden:

> *I long ago lost a hound, a bay horse and a turtle-dove, and am still on their trail. Many are the travelers I have spoken concerning them, describing their tracks and what calls they answered to. I have met one or two who had heard the hound, and the tramp of the horse, and even seen the dove disappear behind a cloud, and they seemed as anxious to recover them as if they had lost them themselves.*

My friend Wilbur Doctor was a highly skilled amateur printer, and he prepared a magnificent invitation to the launching. It quoted the Thoreau passage on the first page and then opened to read:

> *Please come to the launching of*
> *TURTLE DOVE*
> *On Saturday, April 23, 1988, at 1:30 p.m.*
> *Johnson's Boat Yard, Wickford*

And followed with the note: *Splicing the mainbrace* (meaning drinks) *to follow at 16 Rose Hill Road, Saunderstown.*

I thought this was elegant. So, swallowing hard, we invited about 200 friends and resolved to get the boat in the water on the specified date, come what may.

The day came – quicker than I had hoped. The boat-mover matter-of-factly loaded TURTLE DOVE aboard his huge truck-trailer, just as if she were any other boat he might move that day. The trailer and its precious cargo slowly pulled out of the boat shed, leaving it hugely empty. I followed close behind, wincing every time the boat leaned even slightly on a curve. The truck turned into Johnson's Boat Yard, where it looked as if all 200 of the invitees were waiting for us.

The truck maneuvered the trailer and its cargo to the launching ramp. It was time for ceremony. I had ordered a special "breakaway" bottle of champagne, encased in netting, which Ellen was to shatter against the stainless steel lower fitting of the bobstay. (I had no intention of denting that lovely wooden stem.)

The crowd, and the boat-mover and his truck and trailer, stood waiting. It hadn't occurred to me that some sort of speech was in order.

"Well," I said, "This is TURTLE DOVE and she represents a lot of work, as most of you know. My wife Ellen has had to live *with* this project for a long time, and now, or pretty soon, I hope, it will be time for us to live *on* it. So let's go ahead and get this thing in the water!"

Ellen, wearing a big smile and holding the champagne bottle in an underhand grip, said in a faltering tone (we hadn't practiced this part, either): "I christen thee TURTLE DOVE!" and swung the bottle against the bobstay fitting.

CLUNK!

The breakaway bottle didn't. Ellen swung again.

CLUNK!

Still no shatter. I had a horrible feeling that striking out three times would be a very bad omen.

Ellen renewed her smile and her grip, braced herself amid encouraging sounds from the crowd, and swung again, full force. There was an enormously satisfying spray of champagne and everybody clapped and cheered. The boat-mover smiled and started slowly rolling the big trailer down into the water.

D'Arcy, Harrigan and I clambered aboard to handle mooring lines, and I anxiously watched the water rising around us. Would the boat just slowly disappear beneath the waves with me standing proudly aboard, as in the old Buster Keaton movie?

Suddenly I felt us move a little sideways. *We were afloat!* A friend in the crowd reached out with a freshly-opened bottle of champagne. I took a huge swig right out of the bottle. It tasted absolutely marvelous. There were no leaks – a tribute to D'Arcy's caulking skills.

The crowd moved out, heading for the now-empty boatshed at home. The mainbrace was waiting to be spliced. And Tahiti was 8,000 miles away.

CHAPTER 2

Waterway

Leaving Wickford, Coast Guard rescue, Inland route to Florida.

1988

Five months later, I hurried into the Wickford Diner. This would be my last visit for some time, I thought. I bought coffee and rushed back across the street, juggling four hot cups. My crew was waiting at the crumbling pier, cramming things aboard and trying to look as nautical as possible. A few friends stood by, hugging themselves and clearly wishing they could say goodbye and get back to a warm bed. It was Oct.4. We were bound for Norfolk, Va., (you never say "going to" – it's wise to leave a note of caution), then on down the inland waterway to Florida, then to parts undetermined.

It was hard to believe we were leaving at last. There had been a hell of a lot of activity in these five months. At the launching in April, the boat was really not much more than a hull and an engine. It needed masts and booms, which were still a-building, rigging, cleats and winches, a stove and the propane tanks to fuel it, anchors and lines, navigational and safety gear. The boat (and the crew as well) needed sea trials to test everything. Somehow, with the help of a lot of people, we had managed to get all that done.

We waved at the little group as we chugged around the turn and out of sight. We were on our way.

There were Ellen and me, my son Chris and my faithful friend Harrigan aboard. Skies were uniformly gray and the wind was northeast, brisk and cold. (I thought unhappily of my sailor friend Redwood, who was fond of saying, "Don't even start if the wind is from the east.")

I was very conscious of the fact that I was now in charge of a large, slow, heavy craft that was still quite unfamiliar. (On maneuvering for the first time toward a gas dock under power, for example, I had come within a few inches of wiping out a gasoline pump as we turned into the dock. I forgot that we were swinging a nine-foot bowsprit out in front of us. And I had suffered nightmares over the prospect of parallel parking the boat in our temporary berth on returning after our first trial run. In a minor miracle, though, we managed to back in very neatly on the first try, which had given me some small encouragement.)

I was still learning how this boat behaved. Under engine power it was slow but steady without any big surprises. It even backed up fairly straight, which was not the case with a lot of sailboats. Under sail, in a moderate breeze with all four sails pulling, the boat moved with real power. She didn't point very high into the wind. (It's called "tacking" – no sailboat can tack directly into the wind. The most modern lightweight racers can sail at 35 to 40 degrees to the wind direction; the best we could do was about 50 to 55. But I was sure we were a lot more comfortable.)

Our first two days at sea were not very comfortable, though. It was dark and rainy and cold, with winds that shifted direction frequently. At one point we found a flicker on board – rather unusual, since flickers are a kind of woodpecker that digs bugs out of the ground. A little later we discovered a pert little yellow warbler hopping around on the deck, so tame that it walked over our shoes and eventually retired below into the captain's cabin. That move proved to be a mistake because Smokey, the seasick ship's cat, was occupying the cabin at the time. Apparently he recovered enough to discover the unfortunate bird. We found only a pile of yellow feathers on the captain's pillow.

In the confused sea we rolled and tossed a lot under sail, making little progress. We started the engine and motored along merrily for a while until the engine gave a few sickly coughs and stopped dead. Paul crawled into the hot cramped engine room and managed to change both fuel filters, which looked pretty dirty. The engine started up and purred happily. We surmised that the rolling and tossing had stirred up some kind of gunk in the old fuel tanks, despite my having had them steam-cleaned and inspected before we installed them.

As our third night approached we sighted what appeared to be high-rise buildings, due west and dim in the gathering darkness. We speculated: were they apartment houses on Cape May, or pilot-houses of passing freighters? Couldn't tell. The wind increased as it grew full dark and soon the knotlog showed us surfing down a breaking wave at a dizzy 11 knots – far beyond the estimated top speed of a heavy-displacement vessel like ours. We pulled down the sails and substituted just the tiny storm jib, which slowed us down drastically. Ellen got on the radio, calling the Coast Guard station in Cape May, N.J., asking help in determining our position. They had disquieting news: weather conditions were deteriorating and we were "strongly advised" to head for more sheltered waters in Delaware Bay.

But we could not sail toward Delaware Bay with our dinky storm jib – we needed the engine. And once again it wouldn't start. Paul crawled back into the pitching engine room and laboriously changed fuel filters once again. Still no start.

The Coast Guard offered a tow. I thought we should stay out on our own, letting the storm carry us on in the general direction of Norfolk. But I didn't argue very strongly – I wasn't at all certain that we were ready to handle a real storm without serious mishap. Finally we asked for help.

For the next three hours we thrashed through the darkness, taking turns at the tiller in the tossing cockpit and trying to keep the boat headed downwind without slewing sideways. The others huddled below in their foul-weather gear, trying to find a secure place to sit without being tossed onto the cabin floor. At about 2 a.m. our Coast Guard radio friend told us the rescue boat should be somewhere near our estimated position. We turned on our masthead strobe light, its bright glare blinking out across the black sea. Within minutes, the radio told us that our rescuers had seen the light and were on the way.

The boat appeared, tossing heavily in the intermittent glare of our strobe. There were three men and a woman aboard, looking bulky and competent in their bright orange foul-weather gear. The rescue boat, no bigger than ours, fought its way alongside. Both boats were rolling heavily as we crashed through the waves. I prayed they wouldn't get too close.

"We're going to throw you a line!" somebody bellowed through a bullhorn. "Pull in the light line and attach the heavy line to your strongest post!"

Easier said than done. The first toss, undertaken by the woman, was short. On the next attempt the rescue boat came even closer, and to my horror at one point was actually directly below our plunging bowsprit. Fortunately, by the time our bow crashed down into the sea the other boat had swung away,

With the fourth toss we managed to haul the heavy line aboard and wrap it around the windlass, the strongest mooring point on the boat. The next six hours were a misery. We couldn't speak directly to the rescue boat – all radio messages had to be relayed through the Coast Guard station on shore. Twice we asked them to slow down because the strain on the boat and on us, as well, seemed intense. We also asked them twice to let out more towline, in an attempt to lessen the jolt as the line went slack and then straightened with a tremendous jerk. We were being towed straight into the storm. One of us stayed in the cockpit, steering in an attempt to keep us headed more or less in line with the towboat, while the other three tried to wedge themselves into someplace secure. Finally everybody just lay on the floor, compacted into a silent suffering mass that at least had nowhere further to fall. Waves crashed over the cabin, and water crept through hatches and portholes. We lay there and suffered, mostly in silence. Progress was agonizingly slow.

When the first sullen gray light of dawn appeared, I got a good look at our rescuers. The sight was disquieting. Far out at the end of what seemed an interminable towline, only occasionally visible in the spray, was this tiny little Coast Guard rescue boat, wallowing along through the spume and looking remarkably helpless. Frequently it seemed to be moving sideways instead of forward.

But conditions improved marvelously as we approached shore. The Coast Guard crew tied us close alongside and maneuvered us to the handsome town dock of Lewes, Del. Our four rescuers looked only a little less beat than we, and we offered them heartfelt thanks. They passed it off as just another night's work, but they seemed pleased with themselves and our gratitude. We were visited by a few curious townsfolk and Chris and Paul chatted with them while Ellen and I crawled into our wet blankets and slept like dead people.

Next morning was warm and sunny and the boat soon looked like a gypsy caravan, with almost everything we owned dragged out to dry in the sun. Paul and I headed off to the town hospital – he for a possible broken finger, suffered when somebody closed a hatch cover on it, and me for a very sore left elbow, apparently bruised during our scramble to recover the rescue line.

Paul got a splint and I got a cortisone injection and we straggled back to the boat. Next day we got a clipping of the story from Russell Lynch, a power boat owner who recognized us in a local cafe. The front page of the Oct. 12 issue of *The Whale* featured a small picture of TURTLE DOVE tied up at the city dock, bedraggled with drying sheets and bedding, with this story on an inside page by Joe Clancy:

> *Although resting comfortably in Lewes Harbor Monday afternoon, the TURTLE DOVE had survived the worst of a fierce northeast storm just days before.*

> *The 36-foot wooden sailboat was caught off the coast in ferocious weather late Friday night with no engine power and nowhere to go, but quick action by Coast Guard personnel from Indian River Inlet rescued the boat and its crew of four from Rhode Island.*

> *Indian River Coast Guard commanding officer Lt. Rob Wilkins said the unit received a distress call about 11:25 p.m. Friday from the Turtle Dove, which listed the position as 15 miles northeast of the inlet.*

> *Boat owner Jack Thompson of Warwick, R.I. was battling against 8-10 foot seas and 25-knot winds solely with the boat's auxiliary engine, which stopped operating shortly before the distress call was made. The radio call also reported that the boat could not turn into Delaware Bay due to the strong Northeast winds and high seas.*

Wilkins dispatched a 44-foot motor lifeboat and a crew of four from Indian River, which used radio direction finder equipment and made an intercept allowing for drift to find Thompson's boat. Coast Guard personnel arrived at the scene at 2:05 a.m. Saturday and began rescue operations.

The TURTLE DOVE's mast is too high to fit under the inlet bridge, which is 35 feet high at high tide. Saturday's high tide mark at the bridge came at 7:33 a.m. The boat's height forced the rescuers to tow it against the wind and waves to Roosevelt Inlet at Lewes, where they arrived at 9:12 a.m. after a six-hour tow.

Wilkins reported no injuries other than seasickness and an injured finger on the part of a crew member, whose hand was slammed in a hatch during the nearly 10-hour ordeal. Thompson and the crew were set to make a few repairs in Lewes before heading back to Rhode Island, most likely with a long glance at the weather report.

Except for the last bit, we thought the story was reasonably accurate, though we questioned the "25-knot winds." We were convinced it had blown at least twice that hard.

Chris and Paul departed for home via Greyhound bus, lugging the rented liferaft, and Ellen and I settled in at the Lewes town dock for about a week. We had an oil leak in the engine repaired and became friendly with Russell Lynch, who helped us pump out our fuel tanks and refill them with what we hoped was fresh clean diesel. Both of us were feeling gun-shy about venturing out into the Big Briny again. We decided to head up Delaware Bay, cross through the canal into the head of Chesapeake Bay, and cruise down the Chesapeake to Norfolk.

In Chesapeake Bay we headed for the home of Russ Lynch's brother Don on Dividing Creek, one of the hundreds of tributaries that feed the big bay. This was beautiful fall cruising – cold nights, sunny days and a plethora of lovely anchorages. The only trouble was the left elbow that I had banged up during the rescue operation. Despite the cortisone injection, it was steadily swelling and getting more painful.

Don Lynch's home was beautiful: surrounded by hardwood trees in a blaze of fall colors, with a sturdy dock sheltering his 40-foot cruising sailboat. We crept in alongside and were greeted warmly by Don and his wife Hank.

When they learned of my problem they bundled us off to hospital. The doctor, himself a sailor, said my elbow was seriously infected. On learning that I had an artificial hip, he insisted that I be admitted for intravenous antibiotics. So here I was in a private room in a strange hospital, with Ellen living on our boat at the home of strangers. We worried about overstaying our welcome, but Don Lynch insisted that we stay as long as necessary. And he offered the use of a car so Ellen could visit me. We felt overwhelmed by kindness.

We stayed 10 days, five with me in the hospital and another five parked at the dock. A Home Health nurse visited us there and instructed Ellen on maintaining the IV drip into my arm. When we left at last, we overlooked Smokey the cat, who had gotten accustomed to prowling around ashore. About ten miles out we discovered we were catless. We swung into the Rappahannock River, motored to a marina, rented a car and drove back to the Lynches at Dividing Creek. There was Smokey, moping around the dock and evidently wondering what had happened to his home. We gathered him up, said goodbye all over again, and drove back to TURTLE DOVE. It would be our last car travel for some time.

Entering Hampton Roads approaching Norfolk, we motored past endless rows of Navy destroyers, submarines, and aircraft carriers. We passed under our first bridge, a fixed structure with 65-foot clearance, according to the chart. Nevertheless, we gaped nervously up at the top of our mast, approximately 55 feet above the water. We cleared easily, of course, and then worked our way through a succession of bridges. Most were lift bridges, and we soon learned that the bridge operators would respond readily to our call on the VHF radio. But invariably they would want us to get a lot closer before they put the machinery in motion.

"Move up, Captain," they would drawl over the static. "Don't worry – I see you and I'll be open for you-all in plenty'a time."

And, hearts in mouths, we would continue motoring toward a huge immoveable steel bridge with cars steadily moving across it. Then, at last, we would hear a warning bell start to ring, the traffic gates would swing slowly down across the road, the line of cars would halt, and the bridge would slowly open for us. I felt a vague guilt that all those drivers had to wait for us, plus a fear that the good old Westerbeke would stop just as we were halfway through the opening. But it never did. We easily negotiated the one and only lock on the waterway, where attendants cheerfully assisted with docking lines.

Our first marina stop was at Coinjock, just over the North Carolina line. We tied up at a rickety dock at the head of a long line of boats and met the crew of GREEN DOLPHIN, a 32-foot gaff-rigged Quoddy Pilot sailboat. We had waved to them as we passed in Norfolk Harbor, but this was our first chance to talk. Aboard were Chris and Virginia, a young couple heading for Florida. We liked their spirit – they told us that they often danced in the cockpit while sailing. And we met another couple who were celebrating their 40th wedding anniversary that day, while making their seventh trip on the Inland Waterway.

Then we walked to a public fishing area nearby, where a man proudly displayed a big "channel cat" – a catfish. It was swimming gloomily in the shallows, tethered to a line while he tried to catch another. That night we ate catfish and crab cakes and hush-puppies in the marina restaurant. We were in the South now – a transformation that seemed to happen suddenly. Talk was slower, people more friendly.

Next day we traversed Albemarle Sound, which has a reputation of getting rough. Small-craft warnings had been posted, the radio told us, but we took off bravely, motor-sailing with jib and mizzen and followed by Chris and Virginia in GREEN DOLPHIN. Halfway across the sound we passed PATIENCE B, a pretty Canadian gaff-rigger we had encountered in the upper Chesapeake. When the wind started to blow hard she fell off, apparently trying to find a lee. Both boats had small engines, and we worried about them.

We were taking a beating as we tried to motor directly into the fierce headwind. Far ahead was the Alligator River Bridge across the south end of the sound. We radioed ahead and the operator told us to keep on truckin'. The bridge would be open for us, she said. She must have misread our speed, for she opened well ahead of time and the line of waiting cars and trucks grew steadily longer as we crept through the flying spray, engine churning madly. I felt even more guilty this time, but there was nothing to be done about it. We had another half-mile of struggle and finally found a small bay that offered a lee. We got the anchor down and tottered below for a slug of brandy. It was great to stop at last.

The next few days were typical – negotiating narrow creeks and canals, navigating buoy-to-buoy across open bays and sounds, winding along beautiful dark rivers, deeps and shallows, much of it rimmed with vast marshy stretches.

In Beaufort, N.C., we met the crew on PATIENCE B.: Harry, a boatbuilder from New Brunswick, Canada, his wife Martha and their two kids, a boy and a girl. We watched election returns on their tiny television set. Bush won, Dukakis lost.

They told us they were heading for Florida, then the Bahamas, and finally on to visit friends in Australia. He had built their beautiful boat himself and they would be away from home for three years. They had arranged for correspondence courses to keep the kids up in their schoolwork, and she had canned vast quantities of food for the voyage. It was evident that they had been planning this adventure for a long time. We were impressed.

We spent several days in Beaufort, dining out and paying bills. We were dismayed to learn that mail, addressed to us care of General Delivery, had been held only two weeks and then sent back to Rhode Island. It was one of the very few occasions when the mail went wrong.

There are a great many channel markers on the ICW, and they certainly helped, particularly where we encountered what I called "the invisible channel." This was when we faced a stretch of water that might be miles wide but with navigable water only in a narrow trench dredged through it. Stay within the markers and you'd have at least 10 feet of water; outside, a whole lot less. That usually meant instant grounding if we strayed outside the markers, so we had to pay close attention. We marveled at the way the husky tugboats, pushing as many as 10 big barges lined up ahead of them, could negotiate these channels, particularly where there were major curves. But we never saw a tug or barge aground.

For 10 miles the waterway carried us through Camp Lejeune, the Marine Corps training camp where the chartbook said we might find the passage "temporarily closed for gunnery practice." But all was serene as we chugged through. Later we had to anchor and wait for the Onslow Beach Bridge to open. The bridge tender reported on radio that contractors working on the bridge had "lost something." Whatever it was, they apparently found it because the bridge finally swung open an hour later. That night we tied up to the rickety Carolina Beach town dock and hiked to a shopping center for groceries and a Laundromat. We lugged $66 worth of food back to the boat, returned for our clothes, and dragged the bag with us into a nearby movie. It felt strange to sit there in a darkened movie house, as if we were ordinary civilians again. We were seafarers now, we thought.

A strong northeast wind came up during the night and I woke with something thumping gently against our bow. I clambered out into the wind and found a big fishing boat nuzzling us. It had been tied up with a single stern line and nothing more. I climbed aboard, found another line and tied off the bow in the darkness. In the morning we decided to leave, despite the wind. I recruited a bashful fisherman to help hold us off the dock as we moved out and revved the motor in reverse, only to discover that we were still attached by our bow line. Embarrassing. We moved out backwards with our helper pushing vigorously. But the wind still swung our bow into the end of the dock, and our long bowsprit scraped heavily past the lone piling there. No harm done, apparently.

Difficulties increased once we were out in the narrow channel. The wind immediately pushed our bow down the wrong way, directly toward a string of big charter boats tied up along both sides and at the end of the channel, only a short distance away. I tried to rev up enough forward momentum to swing us around against the wind but failed. There was nothing to do but put her in reverse and try to back out, stern heading into the wind.

So we churned down the long channel backward, trying to look nonchalant as we passed outdoor diners enjoying leisurely breakfasts at waterside restaurants. Nobody seemed to find it strange. Finally we found a basin wide enough to make a big turn and we were under way, bow first again.

The ICW route markers led us down the Waccamaw River: fresh water, lined with brooding cypress trees, coffee-colored and 40 feet deep in places. Following Russ Lynch's recommendation, we turned off into Prince Creek, a little jug-handle that meandered through a beautiful wilderness. We anchored here in the slow current and explored in the dinghy with Smokey the cat as an uneasy passenger.

We saw only one other sailboat in Prince Creek as we returned to the main stream of the Waccamaw. We passed a little one-car ferry running across the river, passed silent stands of grey cypress trees, their trunks hanging in air and supported by ungainly knees leading down into the dark water. Pale grey skeins of Spanish moss drooped from their branches, silhouetted against the dark green of pines and firs. We saw an eagle perched in a tree, a number of great blue herons which persisted in taking off in alarm, flying far ahead of us to land in the stream, then repeating the process as we approached. We saw a raccoon strolling slowly along a mudbank, apparently searching for shellfish.

We were watching closely for alligators because we had a bet – first to spot one would be treated to a fine dinner ashore. So far no saurians.

We anchored in a deep arm of the Harbor River, surrounded by a sea of grass. I rowed into the marsh to scoop up some small oysters that lay in heaps along a muddy bank. They were tough to open but they tasted great. Oyster-catcher birds, natty with their long bright orange bills and black and white tuxedo jackets, patrolled the shoreline and a pair of porpoises cruised lazily by. We had two other anchored sailboats for company in this peaceful spot.

Next day we moved through long stretches of marsh with low sandbars on each side, part of the Cape Romain National Wildlife Refuge. Still no alligators but a plethora of birds – cormorants, gulls, terns, oyster-catchers and pelicans. Almost every one of the big channel markers – stout posts with signs and solar panels on top – was festooned with an ungainly osprey nest, often occupied by a fierce-looking osprey staring at us as we moved by.

We made our way across big Charleston Harbor, where there seemed to be almost a total absence of commercial shipping, gawked at historic Fort Sumter, and headed up the Ashley River to the municipal marina. Russ Lynch was right – he had said the place looked like a prison and it did, walled in by great grey concrete slabs. We tied up next to a handsome young couple, Cathy and Bill Williamson. They too were heading to Florida. Next night we stopped in Church Creek for an early anchorage, motoring past one anchored sailboat and dropping the hook in what appeared to be a comfortable 12 feet of water. But a strong current pushed us aside and at 8 p.m. we noticed a listing of our quarters. By 9 we were hard aground and trying to live at a 45-degree angle. The current had swung us out of a hole and into shallow ground. Our cat seemed genuinely puzzled at this development. We took a photo of him perched on the table at 45 degrees, seemingly defying gravity and looking perturbed. By midnight we were upright again as the tide rose.

We talked that morning with the couple who had celebrated their 40th anniversary in Coinjock. They said they also had anchored in Church Creek, to take their German shepherd ashore, "but it was too late." We were learning that dog-owners had to get their animals ashore twice a day to crap, come hell or high water. Apparently most dogs, unlike cats, could not learn to do their business in a pan aboard ship.

A small rather beat-up little power boat had been following us and I was dismayed to find him anchoring much too close in Beaufort Harbor. I asked him to move and he declined, saying "I'll keep an eye on you." But when he started swinging close to us again I had more words with him. The exchange provided great amusement for Bill and Cathy Williamson, who had anchored near us and were visiting aboard. *"You got the whole haaba to anchor in!"* I heard her chanting later, mimicking me and my New England accent.

They told us of an earlier episode, when Bill had hurled an orange at a big powerboat charging past so close that its wake almost overturned them. The missile splattered against its windshield and the captain turned his boat around and came up alongside, infuriated. Cathy said a tremendous shouting match erupted between Bill and the people in the other boat "complete with crotch-grabbing, fingers in the air and every dirty name you could think of." It probably would have led to violence if the participants had been able to get at each other ashore, she said. It was a fact that many powerboats in the waterway overtook us and charged past with little regard for the huge wake they caused. TURTLE DOVE was heavy enough to handle it, but a little boat like the Williamson's could get an unmerciful tossing around.

We stayed five days in Beaufort, hobnobbing with Bill and Cathy and two new friends, Joe and Marilyn Harvey of the trawler yacht VAGABOND SHOES. We liked the name.

This was a friendly town. We were chatting with the two other boats on the VHF radio, making plans for a joint Thanksgiving dinner, when a new voice interrupted. It was the owner of a nearby marina, who invited us all to a Thanksgiving feast at his place – no charge and all visiting boaters welcome. It was a tradition, he said. Later we learned of another free meal, this one offered at the local Episcopal church. We went to both. The church dinner was traditional and good; the second, at the funky Lady's Island Marina, excellent and unusual. After the turkey and all the fixin's we had taken on at the church, we now were regaled with roast pig, duck, turkey and venison, with collard greens and side dishes galore. We staggered back into our dinghies completely stuffed.

We had four big sounds to cross – St. Catherine's, Sapelo, Doboy and Buttermilk, with creeks and rivers in between. In Sapelo Sound we watched a crabber in an outboard-powered skiff working a string of crab traps, his pet bulldog standing balanced in the bow of the boat. He would race up to a float marking a sunken trap, shift into slow speed and turn sharply, grab the float with a boathook while the skiff performed a circle on its own, haul up the trap from the bottom, shake out the captured crabs into the skiff, throw fresh bait into the trap, shift into fast-forward again and heave the trap and its attached float over the side, all the while charging down on the next float as the bulldog calmly stood in the bow, apparently on lookout duty.

Lows in the 30s were forecast for the next night, and we piled on extra blankets. It was still cold as we crossed St. Simons Sound and headed down narrow Jekyll Creek, past a number of luxury homes. Approaching the Jekyll Island lift bridge we made the usual radio call to the bridge tender: "Jekyll Island bridge, Jekyll Island bridge, this is yacht TURTLE DOVE approaching from the north. Can you tell us when you will be opening?"

The answer came swiftly, in a woman's southern drawl: "TURTLE DOVE, I see you. And I think you're goin' to run aground." Before I could answer we came to a slow grinding halt. The lady was right – we weren't moving any more. We managed to back off and we gave her the a special wave as we passed. It was our first grounding, but not the last.

At the Cumberland Island National Seashore we anchored near the park dock and rowed ashore. The place is covered with palmettos and big live oak trees guarding narrow dirt roads deep in shade. We walked to the ruins of Dungeness, a huge mansion built by Andrew Carnegie, where a meandering armadillo posed for our camera. Then we hiked to an immense Atlantic beach where we saw our first wild horses grazing in the cold sunlight. Next morning we crossed Cumberland Sound and entered Florida – at last. We anchored that night about 10 miles north of St. Augustine. The trip next day was short and peaceful – under an old-fashioned little lift bridge, then through the handsome Bridge of Lions, decorated with stern statues of the same, and into the St. Augustine municipal marina.

After one night in the marina we moved out into the anchorage nearby. We toured the old section of the city and decided to stay awhile to see the annual Grand Illumination, a fireworks display that ushers in the Christmas season. It was Dec. 2. That night we watched a space shuttle lifting off from Cape Canaveral.

Underway again, the route led us down long rivers and cuts near the ocean, past a picturesque old fort at Matanzas Inlet. By early afternoon we could see high – rise buildings in Daytona Beach. We anchored between two bridges at the north end of town. Next day we settled in at English Jim's Marina, which was recommended as a good spot with reasonable prices. This turned out to be a three-month stay, and both our situations would be considerably different by the end of it.

CHAPTER 3

Ringers

Horseshoes in Florida, nude volleys in Bahamas, trip to Japan.

1988-89

Daytona Beach is the home of a world-famous beach and an auto speedway (you can hear those high-powered engines howling from miles away); it's host to thousands of tourists, including – simultaneously – the annual Bike Week, which attracts thousands of huge drunken bikers, and the annual celebration of spring break, which attracts thousands of smaller drunken sophomores.

There were a number of live-aboards at English Jim's and most were reasonably friendly, especially one cruising couple. She was friendly, a compulsive clothes-washer who had quit her job when her husband stopped working as a civil engineer. He was soft-spoken and heavily bearded, considerably smaller than she. He wore tattered old clothes and looked as if he had emerged from a homeless shelter. They seemed to like being with each other. But one morning she turned up bruised and bloody-faced; we finally figured out that he had beaten her, and not for the first time. Ellen tried to persuade her to leave him but she wouldn't. Trying to remain civil to him after that definitely cooled our friendship. We finally stopped suggesting outings together.

Russ Lynch and his wife Buddy, our helpful friends from back in Lewes, Delaware, had made their annual run south in their power boat and were settled in at a nearby marina. We visited them frequently. We also began traveling by bus across Florida to Treasure Island, St. Petersburg, to see my parents. My mother was in a hospital with Alzheimer's disease. She looked so shrunken, so disheveled and distraught that I failed to recognize her on our first visit. I walked right past her in her wheelchair. It was an agonizing and unforgettable moment.

My father came to see us in Daytona one day, chauffeured by the obnoxious housekeeper who had been engaged by my brother Bob. We drove back with them to Treasure Island, where I found a confusing ménage of attendants who had been hired by my brother. These people seemed to be operating on their own, and it was painfully clear that somebody had better take charge. Ellen offered to stay on. I was to remain in Daytona, ostensibly to work on the boat but partly because I found the Treasure Island situation too disturbing. I had to take Dad's car keys away from him. It seemed clear that he couldn't stay in the house much longer.

I continued commuting to Treasure Island. Ellen started looking for a part-time job in the St. Pete area and eventually found one, teaching English as a Second Language at a community college. She was taking the first steps of breaking away. Both of us knew it, I think, but we seemed unable to do anything about it.

By February my father had joined my mother in the nursing home. They were on separate floors, but occasionally the staff would find them in bed together; why not? They had been married more than 50 years. Ellen was busy teaching and getting the Treasure Island house ready to be sold. I provided some help, but at the same time I was getting ready to head farther south. Once again, I recruited Paul Harrigan and my son Chris, who signed on a friend, Jack Baker. I hardly knew Baker, and I fretted about whether he would work out. He did.

Ellen did not stay to watch us leave. We hugged tearfully in the parking lot of English Jim's Marina, and she started back to Treasure Island in my parents' car. It was the end of a large chapter in our lives.

Our departure from English Jim's was not impressive. A strong south wind was blowing as we backed out of our slip and it immediately swung us sideways. Accompanied by a good deal of frenzied bellowing by various bystanders, our bowsprit scraped across the deck of a big power boat. No apparent damage, but the owner did not look happy as we waved goodbye and headed south. It was the 5th of March, 1989.

"I don't know anything about sailing but I like to cook," Jack Baker told me. "Can I cook?" I discovered that he had an extensive library of cookbooks at home. He produced some of the best meals I had ever eaten.

We anchored in a little inlet just north of the Canaveral Barge Canal, surrounded by posh private homes and yacht clubs. Chris and Jack rowed ashore in the dinghy and returned hours later, somewhat the worse for beer and ants. Chris had seated himself on a nest of fire ants while contemplating the beauties of the night. That night our new chef aroused us all at 3 a.m., shouting out warnings in his sleep when the wake of a passing boat rocked us.

We motored out into the Atlantic next day at noon. We had spilled diesel oil in the bilge and I tried to bail it out as we churned through a heavy chop in the inlet.

The combination of oil, close quarters and chop soon had me retching. I did not feel much like the intrepid sea dog and was conscious of the gaze of rookie Baker, who seemed cheerful and healthy. After a while my stomach quieted and I felt more like coping. I was to find this a familiar pattern – the first day or two of ocean sailing after a long layover was likely to produce some queasy feelings.

I noted in the log:

> *Finally passed Miami at 1:45 p.m. and continued on to Key Biscayne, charging through bright blue water and nervously watching out for coral. Didn't hit any, but for some unaccountable reason we missed our turning point about 10 miles down the line. Went way beyond the point and had to turn back, bucking the strong wind w. engine. Took the channel toward Key Biscayne & were almost through when a black "Cigarette" boat marked POLICE sped by, turned and came up from astern. Had three engines and three people in it – two men and a woman, all carrying automatic weapons. One guy (wearing a suit and tie!) stood balanced on the bow of the thrashing boat and hollered to us through a bullhorn:*
>
> *"U.S. Customs! Where are you coming from?*
> *"When did you leave?*
> *"How far offshore were you?*
> *"Anybody else on board?* (Chris was down below.)
> *"Do you have any weapons?"*

It was rainy and rough, and we in our foul-weather gear were marveling at this lunatic acrobat in his suit and tie balanced on the wet deck of a bucking speedboat, no doubt confiscated from some convicted drug lord. I tried to shout honest answers, except when asked how far we had been offshore. I had a definite feeling that we should not say we had been miles out, possibly off-loading contraband from some drug-ship. Finally the three enforcers exchanged nods and roared off. Somewhat shaken, we rounded a big coral patch and turned into Hurricane Harbor, another beautiful basin almost landlocked and surrounded by opulent homes. Dinner that night was another marvelous meal prepared by our resident chef, this time a six-pound mackerel we had caught during the day.

We reached Key Largo next afternoon, crept over a 5-foot depth into a narrow entrance channel and finally into a slip at the marina, after much backing and filling with advice from a gent named Captain Blackbeard, according to the sign advertising his towing service.

Log entries for the next two days:

> *Today it's windy but sunny. Many fish visible in the clear water under the boat, pelicans swimming around when they think there's a handout, and this afternoon a big scarred manatee drinking hugely from a hose off the main dock!*

Said goodbye to the crew at noon today – a sad moment, and somewhat scary since I know nobody here, but I guess I'll survive. Last nite we all attended the Friday Nite Fish-Fry & Video Sing-a-Long at the marina restaurant. The four of us, after several beers, sang "Mack the Knife," "Help Me, Rachel," and "Hound Dog". A mixed reception, at best. (One lady in the audience announced loudly, "YOU GUYS STINK!")

A lot of activity around here – dive boats & sightseeing boats in the channel, people fishing off the docks, pelicans marching around. The original AFRICAN QUEEN wheezes by under steam power, packed with tourists and tooting triumphantly. Glass-bottom boat doing a big business, too.

For the next six weeks I was a resident of Key Largo, baking in the hot spring sunshine of Florida. A huge metal building next to the docks made it life in a reflector oven. I sweated so much I had to put a towel under my arm in order to write a letter. I did a lot of bike-riding and a lot of waiting for mail and phone calls from Ellen, who was still in Treasure Island, selling the house. Then there came a call when she said she had been offered a job teaching English as a Second Language in Japan, was accepting it, and would like me to come along.

I didn't think this proposition would work, and I think she probably felt relieved when I turned it down. This would be her first real chance to practice the profession she had trained for, and I saw myself as a distraction if I joined her to languish nearby in a tiny apartment in a foreign country where I couldn't even speak the language.

We promised each other eternal fealty and agreed that I would come to Treasure Island before it was time for her to leave.

I became a compulsive bicyclist and on one trip I discovered a bar where people were pitching horseshoes. A sign read "HOME OF THE KEY LARGO RINGERS, STATE CHAMPIONS." I had pitched a lot of horseshoes during my two years in the Army, and finally I summoned the nerve to go to the bar and get in a game. I did rather well and returned to play every week. A log entry for April 12 reads:

Let the log show that tonight, with "Tomato Bob" (white hair, craggy face, deeply tanned, cigarette perpetually drooping from mouth) as partner, we won the doubles horseshoe tournament at the Eagles Lodge in Key Largo, pitching with state champion Key Largo Ringers. Among opponents were "D.C." (skinny, deeply tanned, has throat cancer & can't speak above a whisper, receiving radiation but continues to smoke cigarettes) and "Old Fart" (rather like Clem Kadiddlehopper), wears straw fedora, threw seven consecutive ringers but still lost due to Tomato Bob's topping his ringers). A big night. Won $12.

I liked being with the Ringers, though it was hard to stomach the casual racism that permeated their conversation. And they seemed to like me. When one of them asked me to become an official team member, I tried to explain my transient status. "Really, I'm just passing through," I said.

He smiled. "That's what we're all doin', Bro," he said.

Back at the sweltering marina, I hung a "CREW WANTED" sign from the bowsprit, where people on passing boats could see it. I typed out notices and posted them in several places, including a check-cashing shop up on the main highway. I waited a few days and then went to the check-casher to see if there had been any response. He said, "Well, your man was here talking to a couple people who were interested."

"*What* man?" I asked. "I don't have any man."

It turned out that some total stranger had come in, looked at my ad and arranged to interview several candidates for crew. I never saw any of them, I never met the interviewer, and to this day I don't know what it was all about. My advertising produced only a handful of applicants, and only one seemed to be a possibility. Eventually he dropped out and I was back to Square One. Then I remembered that Bill and Cathy Williamson had talked about sailing to the Bahamas but thought their boat was inadequate. Would they be interested?

It turned out that they were, and the three of us left April 29, bound for our first foreign port of call – Cat Cay(pronounced "Key"), in the Bahamas. We motored out the Key Largo entrance channel to tie up to a dive-boat buoy at Molasses Reef, a popular spot for diving and viewing from the glass-bottom boat. This was a tough spot after weeks ashore – TURTLE DOVE rolled and pitched unmercifully. After a while a little sailboat took a mooring near us and its occupants, two giant young men, swam over for a visit.

They were young brothers heading for the Bahamas and proposed that we sail there together. They were known as the Young Redwoods, they told us, and their boat had no name at all. It seemed to me that they were incredibly casual about working their way across the Gulf Stream in their tiny boat. But even they had to give it up when their forestay snapped from the pitching and rolling during the night. They decided to make temporary repairs and creep back to Key Largo in the morning.

The log reads:

> *We ate (sparingly – everybody queasy) & tried to sleep a little, without much success. Up again at 1 a.m. Cast off mooring and started off for Cat Cay. Wind light but on the nose, unfortunately. Motored all night, with time out for two filter changes when motor faltered, just like in Delaware. Changing small oil filter seemed to solve the problem, though.*

> *Around 4 p.m. we hit the Bahama Banks – but at Orange Key, 36 miles south of Cat Cay! So we sailed north, past Riding Rocks with its one flashing light, past Ocean Cay with cranes and gear, arriving at the lighthouse at the channel*

between Gun Cay and Cat Cay at 1 a.m. Then had a miserable night – the boat tossed, pitched and rolled wildly all night long and nobody got any sleep. It was so rough that I wanted to up-anchor in the dark and brave the channel. (We didn't, though – we wisely decided to wait for daylight.)

When I reached the Customs office at the Cat Cay Club I was given a hard time by the two guys there because I wasn't at their door at 7 a.m.! They threatened to charge me overtime. I had a feeling there was a little "Let's make honky sweat" going on here.

Prices at this place seemed outrageous – $1.60 per foot for dock space, showers $3 each, and water 48 cents a gallon! I had never yet paid for water at a dock. We motored to a fine anchorage just inside the dreaded point of land, outside of which we had spent such a bad night. Here all was calm and serene. One of the boats there was a big craft, maybe 60 feet long, with six people aboard. They told us that a few days earlier their anchor fell out of its fitting on the bow, dragging all 500 feet of half-inch chain out of the locker. This left them with an enormous weight hanging straight down in very deep water. Their electric windlass lacked the power to lift it, and it took all six to haul it up by hand. They couldn't lift it at all with the boat moving, so they spent most of a day drifting while they slowly dragged in the chain and the big anchor at the end of it.

(I couldn't foresee it then, but much later I was to find myself wrestling with a similar problem.)

We left early next morning, aiming across the shallow Bahama Bank to Russell Light Buoy, a marker 48 miles away. From there we were to make a turn to avoid an even shallower area and continue on to Chub Point on Frazers Hog Cay. We were charging smoothly along with a 10-knot following breeze over a bottom of smooth white sand never more than 15 feet below the surface, and sometimes as close as 6 feet. The water was a bright turquoise. Looking straight down was a dizzying experience: the snow-white sand, rippled evenly in tiny waves and dotted now and then with a spray of dark seaweed, rushed past underneath us so close that it looked as if any second we would come to a grinding halt. But we never did.

Around the 40-mile mile mark I discovered that a steel wrench had slid across the bridge deck until it was almost touching the compass. When I removed the wrench I saw, to my horror, that the compass suddenly swung about 20 degrees to the east. We had been sailing off course for a considerable period of time. The question was, how far off were we?

We decided to continue eastward and then, when it seemed that we should be due south of the buoy, turn north and look for it. We motored east until almost dark, then anchored out in the middle of nowhere. It was a calm, quiet night with a bright moon. We rocked gently in 12 feet of crystal-clear water, as if suspended in air. In the distance we saw several vessels crossing westward. There was no sight of land.

Next morning we set out northward again, hearts in mouths and eyes straining for the elusive Russell Light Buoy.

I wrote in the log:

> *Motored about one mile and spotted it – but Russell Light Buoy is neither lighted nor a buoy! It's a wooden & concrete tower without a mark on it. Sooner or later I guess somebody will paint "Russell" on it. At 9 a.m. hoisted sail and started off for Northwest Light and Northwest Channel marker.*

Two hours later we passed the light, headed out a channel leading through a big reef, and suddenly slid into indigo water thousands of feet deep, heading for Chub Cay. We reached it by mid-afternoon and anchored off the island in seven feet of crystal-clear water. "It's like swimming in glass," I noted in the log. Signs on the beach forbade dinghy landings, so we had to row down a long channel to the marina. There we found a small commissary, a bar-restaurant and a telephone.

Next day I noted:

> *Left Chub Cay about 8 a.m. with 2 misadventures – first, dropped the Danforth (our smaller anchor) while leaving harbor and fouled another boat's anchor chain. (We had to swim to untangle it.)*

> *Then lost Cathy's swimsuit top and couldn't find it. Topless from here on in, I hope. We did well keeping track of the cays as we passed them – Chub, Frazers Hog, Bird, Whale, Little Whale, Bond's, Alder and Frozen. We anchored in a little bight about 1/4 mile off Frozen Cay – beautiful white sand underneath, white sand beach, black coral and coconut palms nodding on the shore.*

> *Walked around on the shore for a while, feeling very like Robinson Crusoe. Snorkeled all the way in to shore and then into the tiny harbor. Read numerous messages stuck on a post referring to feeding and watering an abandoned dog. Never saw the dog, though.*

We spent two days anchored among tiny cays, snorkeling and diving for conch, which we ate after prying out the meat with enormous difficulty. We watched natives casually opening them with one deft twist of what looked like an unsharpened butter knife. One night we had a driftwood bonfire on the beach, sitting in the moonlight and watching TURTLE DOVE lying quietly at anchor.

Huge piles of empty conch shells, gleaming with unearthly pinks and purples, probably worth several dollars each at a Nassau tourist stand, stood in small silent mountains on these little islands. They were testament to the eating habits of generations of islanders. Some of these piles were 40 feet high. Our cruising guide said that one of these tiny cays was the home of the Darvilles, light-skinned survivors of what once was a settlement of people working in the now-defunct sponge-collecting industry. Reportedly these people were hospitable, but somehow I couldn't face the idea of trooping in to stare at them as if they were animals in a zoo.

Heading for Nassau next day we saw *five* waterspouts lined up across the horizon, their ominous skinny fingers twisting down into the sea. It was a sight both scary and impressive, but the spouts dissipated long before we came near them. (Later I was to see a waterspout a lot closer.)

I had read that the main harbor of Nassau would be closed in the event of a "rage" – an apt term meaning heavy seas at the harbor entrance brought by a high wind – and wondered if we would have difficulty getting in. But we didn't. The town was noisy, dirty, crowded with natives and tourists, busy with hustlers and sellers and buyers under a sweltering sun. I wrote later:

> *Impressions after a 5-mile hike through Nassau town: E. end much less sophisticated – big contrast with shopping center near cruise boat piers (tried to get on one cruise ship but couldn't; lacked a green ticket). A lot of contrasts here – last night saw a barefoot black man carrying a dead dog over his shoulder. Watched crew of a fishing boat divvying up their catch, then dined in a relatively modest restaurant where my drink cost $4.50.*

> *A lot of old men hanging around – the dogs generally are uncollared, thin and looking half-wild. Flowers, palm trees, some beautiful residences. Government seems omni-present (it is the capital, of course), but still there seems to be an amazing number of govt. buildings and govt. functionaries.*

> *A lot of big young black guys & a lot of free-swinging basketball and soccer games being played. Old horse trough with brass water tap next to a park nearby. Water tasted fine. At the Palm Restaurant, where I had lunch, all the help was black except for the white maitre d'/cashier – a woman.*

We visited the opulent casino on Paradise Island, where I was told natives were allowed only as employees, not as customers. Last of the big spenders, I lost $7 at the slots and quit. We walked to the Produce Exchange and bought a big crate of mixed vegetables for $10. Nearby were mail boats tied up at a pier. You can travel cheap from island to island on these boats, which meander around carrying almost everything. As we were to learn later, some of the islands get mail only once a week.

We visited the old watering trough and lugged 12 full jerry cans back to the boat to fill up our water tanks. The next stop was Allens Cay, about 35 miles away, and we anchored there with a welcoming committee of iguanas staring balefully at us from the beach. This was one of a very few Bahamian islands with native iguanas, and we had fun trying to stare them down. We hadn't been there long when a small sailboat swept in, leaning hard on the turns with a diaper-clad baby standing jauntily at the bow, clutching the netting attached to a lifeline and grinning at us. He was the youngest Old Salt I had ever seen.

These sailors were 9-month-old Falcon Riley and his parents, Mike and Karen. Mike had started out from California five years earlier alone in TOLA, his engineless 24-foot sailboat. On his way around the world he met and married Karen, who subsequently produced young Falcon. The baby had spent very little time ashore, as was evident from the way he rambled around the little boat. Now they were heading home by way of the Panama Canal.

I asked Mike if the lack of an engine had been a problem on his circumnavigation. After some thought he said he could recall only two occasions when it proved difficult. But aside from those moments, he said, he was glad not to bother with it. When I asked whether such a small boat meant traveling slower, Mike surprised me again. "Most of the time the problem is not going slow enough," he said. "I have to try to slow down to keep from tearing things apart."

At Staniel Cay we anchored near the cave featured in the James Bond movie *Thunderball.* In the movie the cave was the secret haven for a full-sized submarine and crew. The reality was a little different – any submarine would have to be a pretty small model to fit inside this cave. Still, it was a great sight – narrow entrances through the coral rock to swim through (one entirely underwater), thousands of solemn almost-tame fish, sunlight streaming through holes in the arched ceiling high above.

We headed next for Little Farmer's Cay, where I hoped to get mail. The entrance to the anchorage was tricky, with a number of unexpected turns to avoid coral patches. But we managed it successfully and settled into a narrow waterway opposite the little settlement. A little later we watched another sailboat get into difficulty on the passage in. They went aground on a coral patch, were stuck for some time but finally got off safely with the help of a rising tide.

The mailboat had arrived, but with no mail for us. I wanted to wait six days for its next visit. Cathy and Bill were somewhat disgruntled at this development, but agreed to it in fairly good humor.

It turned out to be an interesting visit. I wrote about it later:

> Community of about 50 people – primitive, but some surprises, most notable Terry Bain, 42-year-old operator of Ocean Cabin Restaurant & apparently the Big Man on the Island. Angry, bitter, humorous, wry, highly intelligent, handsome, provocative, combative, arrogant, sensitive. Now living here alone, planning to divorce his 2d wife who has returned to England.

I could see that Bain might be difficult to live with. He claimed to have visited Libya on several occasions, hinting that he had been involved in some kind of terrorist training there. He obviously hated the United States, though he seemed quite willing to talk with me. He insisted that I could not just be cruising for pleasure – most likely I was a CIA operative, he suggested. He seemed to take some kind of pleasure in this idea. We had several lengthy seminars over $3.50 pina coladas – the last one joined by his friend "Bluefish," also handsome, intelligent and articulate.

I noted:

> *Houses small & brightly colored. Predominant sound is chickens clucking and roosters crowing, at all hours. Only 5-6 vehicles on the whole island. Store seems never to be open. Post Office open only once a week when the mailboat comes.*

The next mailboat brought the long-awaited letter from Ellen in Japan. With it safely in hand, we worked our way out through the opening and headed for George Town, which looked almost like a city. The guidebook said it had a real post office, a proper grocery, even a library. We dropped anchor after the usual reconnoitering (On arrival, you always try to find somebody who can tell you where to take trash, where to find water and where to park the dinghy) and almost immediately, it seemed, Cathy and Bill started packing. Next day I went with them to the little airport and saw them off.

Leave-taking is always hard. The log notes:

> *Said goodbye, went to library, visited Post Office (no mail), returned to boat, moped around, read book, moped, read some more, cleaned house a little, made bread, moped some more, tried to get head straight. Not successful.*

Stocking Island was the place to anchor, I was told, so next day I rowed the dinghy across the big shallow harbor to check it out. The island is a long narrow sandy reef with green mangroves and grasses on the George Town Harbour side and pristine white sand beaches facing the deep blue Atlantic on the other. There were three deep little harbors (called "basins") to anchor in, I found, each one offering almost perfect shelter.

The entrance harbor, Basin One, had 15-20 yachts in it. It opened on the left into Basin Two, containing several boats, one of them a piratical-looking steel vessel named MYSTERY which wore a weathered "For Sale" sign. At the right side of the main harbor a narrow winding creek led to a third anchor hole, Basin Zero. The creek looked much too tiny for TURTLE DOVE, I thought, so I didn't check out this anchorage. I rowed back to George Town, deciding I'd anchor with the majority in Basin One. (There is a pack mentality that goes with anchoring; almost invariably you tend to go where the other boats are. You think they might know something you don't – and sometimes you're right.)

Next day I motored across the big bay to take up my new residence. The one-mile crossing took about four hours, due to an embarrassing series of misadventures. First, I dropped the boathook just as I wrestled the anchor on board. The heavy bronze boathook disappeared instantly. I dropped anchor again, but the wind had carried the boat down some distance and I spent considerable time snorkeling before I located the boathook on the bottom.

I had just hauled up the anchor for the second time when a heavy bronze block on the bowsprit parted its lashings and dropped in the drink. Another re-anchoring and another swim to retrieve it – all this in full view of the lounging vacationers at the Peace & Plenty hotel, about 100 yards to starboard.

I stayed in Basin One almost five weeks, working my way out of the loneliness of losing my crew and gradually getting to know the denizens of Stocking Island. They included the professional artist Donnie Wood, owner of MYSTERY, and his exuberant dachshund Rusty Pipes; a Colorado man and his wife, who said she was a witch; an Israeli man and his girlfriend, a thin young woman with enormous breasts; a guitar-playing retired fire department captain whose boat was named FIRE ESCAPE; a gentleman privately known as Sid the Sinner, who reputedly was having simultaneous affairs with other people's Significant Others on two other boats; a Florida couple with four kids who conducted an enthusiastic nude volleyball game on the beach every afternoon, and an ever-changing list of other "yachties", most of them busily eavesdropping and gossiping about each other on their VHF radios. As a late arrival, still uncommitted, I found myself becoming the recipient of all the scandal, intrigue and Rabelaisian grotesqueries that went with the place. It kept life interesting.

I became particularly friendly with Donnie the artist and his dog Rusty Pipes. Donnie constantly wore a battered felt hat and carved beautiful fish and turtles out of driftwood. He was highly talented, original and eccentric. Each morning he and Rusty would motor ashore in his big aluminum skiff to walk the ocean beach on the far side of the dunes. In a frenzy, Rusty would charge from one sand-crab hole to the next, rooting frantically until his eyebrows disappeared and his head was covered with sand. Donnie said he actually uncovered a live crab sometimes, but I didn't see it happen. He never lost his enthusiasm, though.

Donnie seemed quite content to live alone. When I asked him about it he said, "I'm not alone – I've got Pipes." His studio was a big engineless power cruiser anchored in Basin Zero. The boat was littered with pieces of driftwood, woodworking tools and carvings in progress. He wanted to make a permanent mooring for it there, and he agreed that we could each make one. I could leave TURTLE DOVE there while I spent two months with Ellen in Japan. Donnie said we could get my boat in through the little creek on a high tide.

With little more than a week to spare, the project began. We visited an old shipwreck on another island and salvaged a lot of twisted iron and heavy metal scrap. We collected a skiff-load of scrap planks and plywood from another wreck, bought sacks of cement from the lumber store in George Town, and started in at hard labor. We built wooden molds on the beach and moved them to the edge of the water at dead low tide. Then we shoveled them full of sand and cement mixed with seawater, scrap iron and rocks. Each mooring had a hole through the middle for a heavy chain.

We had to work fast in the hot sun, timing the operation so the molds would be full and the cement starting to harden before they were covered by the rising tide.

These were to be big concrete blocks, each weighing between 500 and 700 pounds. We figured we could lift them on a rising tide, suspended from a heavy pole lashed across our two dinghies to make a kind of crude catamaran.

It worked, at least at first. We lifted Donnie's new mooring without a hitch, paddled it slowly out into the middle of the basin, cut the rope and dropped it in place. But we didn't do so well with mine. I had foolishly used a piece of old rope as a lashing to the cross beam. The big block lifted with the rising tide, but we had hardly started paddling when the rope broke and the block went to the bottom in about six feet of water, far too shallow for a decent mooring.

By now it was high tide and there was no way to lift the block off the bottom again. We would have to wait six hours for low tide to re-tie it, then wait more hours for the new rising tide to float it once more. Low tide was due at 11 p.m. but Donnie, muttering darkly about the feeding habits of Bahamian sharks, wanted no part of messing around in shallow water in the middle of the night. If I wanted to get it done I would have to do it myself. So with grave misgivings I set the alarm for 10, woke up in the dark, rowed the two dinghies to the beach and maneuvered them and the cross-beam over the mooring, now only a foot below the surface.

I thought very seriously about Donnie's sharks as I stood there in the dark water, fumbling underwater to get the rope lashing tight. I was ready to make a mad dash to shore if I felt anything come even close to a precious body part. Nothing happened, though, and I swam nervously in the dark back to my anchored boat, leaving the two dinghies lashed to the sunken mooring. I would have to swim in again at high tide next morning, hoping the whole lashup was now afloat.

It worked. At dawn I awoke to see the two dinghies low in the water but afloat, the big concrete block suspended beneath them. I swam in and found I could swim the whole rig out to the right spot, where I cut the rope and planted the mooring. Next I had to attach the mooring chain to the block underwater, since I had thought it would be easier to launch the block without the chain. This took a number of dives but at last the job was done, and TURTLE DOVE was firmly hooked up to a good permanent mooring. I even autographed it – "J.T. '89" scratched in the top of the still-hardening concrete.

Donnie had moved MYSTERY into the basin to be tied up at his new mooring next to his floating studio, so he would be living next door. I was ready to head for Japan and a long-awaited reunion with my wife.

Leaving this little island with its tiny collection of cruising boats, and landing just hours later in teeming Tokyo, was an exercise in culture shock. I spent almost two months in Japan and learned to like it. And I learned to like my wife all over again, though there were clear signs that our lives had taken different paths. It was difficult to leave, particularly since I wasn't sure that I would still have a boat waiting for me in the Exumas. A major hurricane was reported, heading straight for the Bahamas.

CHAPTER 4

Bahamas

Finding crew, Rum Cay, Puerto Plata and denizens, Ellen.

1989

Hurricane Hugo swept through the Caribbean, leaving death and destruction in the Virgin Islands. The big storm was headed directly for the Exumas, but at the last minute it swerved north and moved out to sea. When the plane swung over Stocking Island before landing in George Town, I caught a quick glimpse of TURTLE DOVE resting quietly in its Basin Zero hideaway, and felt enormously relieved. She looked safe and sound.

But Donnie and Rusty Pipes and MYSTERY were gone. In TURTLE DOVE I found a note: he had decided to move to another island.

Before leaving for Japan I had placed an ad for crew in *Cruising World* magazine. I picked two applicants: Gunter Schuller, an English professor in New York who was on sabbatical leave, and Hank Lowry, a retired college administrator who lived in Florida.

While waiting for them to arrive I met A. O. Halsey, a delightful dwarf-like man on POLARIS JACK, a beautiful dark green Bristol Channel Cutter only 24 feet long. Halsey, a descendant of a famous seafaring family, was on leave from his job as a dispatcher for pilot boats in Charleston Harbor, South Carolina. He was born misshapen and crippled, with a host of physical problems, but nothing seemed to dampen his spirit. He was sailing alone for a year while his wife continued her teaching job in Charleston, and he and I hit it off immediately.

Halsey sang and played the guitar and introduced me to the songs of Jimmy Buffet. I had invested in two new harmonicas during my stop in the States and we had many music sessions, sometimes joined by Jack Olson, the retired fire captain, another lone sailor. Saturdays we went to a big catamaran which hosted a weekly bring-your-own party. And there were the nude volleyball games, another diversion.

The volleyball beach offered several homemade tables and chairs, kids' tree houses and forts, and a "weather station." This was a big tree branch with a rope suspended from it. Tied to the end of the rope was a rock weighing maybe 20 pounds hanging a foot off the sand. A sign tacked to the tree branch read: WHEN THIS ROCK STANDS STRAIGHT OUT IT'S A HURRICANE! I was glad I hadn't seen it in operation.

A.O. and I did a little local cruising in POLARIS JACK. We went to San Salvador, supposed to be Columbus's first landfall in the New World, but couldn't get ashore because the seas were too rough. Then we spent two nights at tiny Rum Cay, and got stuck on a coral reef there while attempting an early-morning departure: A.O. was so busy singing at the top of his lungs that he wasn't paying attention. We got ourselves off without excessive embarrassment and returned to Stocking Island after a long day's sail. It was a blustery day and A.O. insisted on storming into the anchorage and anchoring under full sail, which attracted much attention.

Gunter arrived in mid-November and our differences grew quickly. He was an experienced sailor and an excellent athlete who clearly considered himself far more competent than I. A favorite expression was, "I'm so excited my nipples are getting hard!" – a comment that left me distinctly uneasy. After a few days he announced that he had changed his mind about sailing on TURTLE DOVE, and I was relieved. But I wondered if Hank would bail out too, when he arrived and heard the news. Gunter found a new berth with Sid the Sinner and they left shortly before Hank arrived. He said he was quite willing to make the trip with just me and we started making final preparations, including a brief warm-up sail. Hank had told me earlier that his eyesight was bad, but it was a lot worse than I had imagined. During our warmup sail at night I pointed out to him a huge cruise ship a couple miles away, in plain view and blazing with enough lights to illuminate Manhattan. He was steering.

"Keep an eye on the cruise ship," I said. He looked all the way around. "What cruise ship?" he asked. Not a good sign. But he said he had sailed before, and I didn't have anybody else.

We left Stocking Island Nov. 21, heading for Conception Island, about 40 miles away. It's a national land and sea park with waters marvelously transparent: I could see objects on the bottom more than 100 feet down. For two days we snorkeled and hiked on the beaches, all alone. The second day was Thanksgiving, and I had neglected to pack anything festive. We made do with canned hotdogs.

Next day we motored off to Rum Cay and rowed ashore to place a dinner order at Kay's Bar, the only restaurant on the tiny island. That night we joined what appeared to be the entire population of the island, including a number of children and dogs, to view a Rambo movie brought in from another visiting yacht. The villagers loved it, roaring with laughter at every Rambo exploit.

Although fewer than 100 people lived on Rum Cay, the island had telephone service. I hiked up a long dusty trail to a tiny wooden shack at the base of a tall tower, where the only sign of life was a pair of bare feet sticking out the window. The sleepy young telephone operator assured me there would be no difficulty in calling Japan. He punched in a few numbers and here, to my amazement, was Ellen talking to me from 10,000 miles away

Aside from the telephone office and Kay's Bar there seemed to be almost no activity on Rum Cay. I was told that the island had once had an industry – collecting salt from sea water evaporated in huge man-made salt pans. These could be opened to the ocean tides, then closed to allow the water to evaporate in the tropical sun. But a hurricane wrecked the salt pans and killed the industry. It is possible that the operation might be rebuilt some day, I was told. This sounded hopeful, until I learned that the hurricane had hit the island 63 years ago.

We found an old cemetery and a number of ruined and abandoned houses. Aside from the occasional mail boat, it looked as if the only visitors were cruising boats like ours. The villagers still lit a lantern every night on a wooden tower that looked like a lifeguard station at Scarborough Beach: from our anchorage we could see the little yellow light flickering in the darkness on shore. An old lady told me that a man named Strahan maintained the light, but we never saw him.

We stayed a week, waiting for the southeast winds to blow themselves out. As we finally sailed away in a calm light rain we could see a U.S. Coast Guard ship in the distance. It was lowering a boat and we soon learned why. A big inflatable carrying eight armed men overtook us and told us to turn on our radio. When we did, the ship asked a number of identifying questions, then politely asked if they could board us.

I had been told earlier that you could refuse such a request, but that you would then be towed, unboarded, to the nearest port for examination – a Hobson's choice indeed. So we said OK, and seven young men clambered aboard, all wearing guns, foul-weather gear and life jackets. We had the hatches closed because of the rain – Hank was stark naked and I wore only a pair of shorts. But our visitors, soon pouring sweat, kept everything on during a two-hour search of the boat.

The search, ostensibly conducted in the name of boating safety, produced no contraband but two minor warnings: (1), I must post the proper placard listing penalties for oil pollution, and (2), My signal flares, still in their original wrappings, were three months out of date.

I was annoyed at the intrusion, since we weren't even in U.S. waters, but I couldn't help liking our visitors. They all seemed fascinated with the boat. One offered to steer, and he held the tiller happily during the entire encounter. I asked if they had stopped us just because they wanted to look at a wooden boat and they said no, they searched all vessels. But when I asked if this included the big ships that passed occasionally, they said no, that would be done when the ship reached port. (Apparently it would be OK if the ship offloaded its contraband before docking.)

After they left with good wishes, I had a radio call from the Coast Guard captain asking about my family. An hour later the inflatable returned with a five-page computer printout – a few paragraphs of weather forecast and the rest entitled *"Thompson Family Notes."* Turned out the ship captain was a genealogy freak whose name was Thompson also. Altogether a rather peculiar encounter, I thought.

We planned to pass close by Samana Cay, a long narrow island surrounded by coral reefs. By 5 a.m. it was light enough to show us the island close by. We motored the length of the island and rounded the eastern end, passing a wrecked ship well offshore. (Wrecked ships are a clear indicator of where the reefs are, and we gave this one a wide berth. Our guidebook warned:

> *(. . . its rusting hulk a dangerous booby trap; do not venture aboard it.)*

Approaching West Plana Cay we caught two fish – payoff for continued efforts by Hank, an ardent angler. He was already at the frying pan while we scouted out an anchorage on clear sand between large patches of coral. A small cruise ship anchored near us as dusk fell and we looked at bright lights and listened to dinner music that night, feeling rather forlorn. Shortly after dark a helicopter made repeated noisy passes over our heads. Later we learned that an EPIRB (Emergency Position Indicating Radio Beacon) had been overturned aboard the cruise ship, sending out emergency signals. We imagined the hot water some unhappy crewman must have found himself in after that episode.

When we left next morning I discovered that my almost-new 3/4-inch anchor line had two of its three nylon strands completely chewed through – the result of the line's dragging over a coral patch during the night. I had avoided using an all-chain anchor rode up to now. It was time to switch to chain.

I tested our luck with chain that night when we anchored at Mayaguena Island. We had enjoyed a grand run of almost 30 miles under full sail. Looking for shelter from the strong south wind, we swept north along the island's western shore and rounded its Northwest Point, where the guidebook tells you:

> *The entrance through the reef lies close under the point, where a draft of about 7 feet can be taken in, but the water shoals gradually and if you draw over 5 feet you may touch occasionally.*

We headed for the entrance and immediately found ourselves in very shallow water surrounded by coral heads. There seemed to be no way through, so we anchored in what appeared to be the only clear spot available, using all chain for the first time. With dusk the wind shifted and now we found ourselves in rising wind on a lee shore. As the waves built we occasionally thumped down hard on a coral patch. I let out chain and I took in chain, trying to get clear of the coral, but to no avail. Every few minutes we would hit bottom. This was mightily distressing.

By now it was dark and there seemed little we could do – no way could we work our way out of there without daylight. I spent most of the night gritting my teeth and picturing the keel pounding on those rocks. We also slammed horribly each time the chain jerked taut. Finally Hank recalled that he had seen a nylon snubber line rigged with the anchor chain on another boat to take up some of the shock. With great difficulty we rigged the snubber in the dark. During this I dropped a flashlight off the plunging bowsprit and watched it bravely shining on the rocky bottom a few feet (far too few!) below us. We didn't try to retrieve it.

At first light we hauled up the anchor and got the hell out of there, somehow maneuvering through the coral heads without mishap: except that Hank lost his favorite OLD FATHER FART baseball cap in the wind and I refused to try to turn around and retrieve it. (That night I discovered that our 40-pound fisherman anchor had one fluke severely bent, apparently the result of our slamming against the tautened chain before we rigged the snubber.)

With the north wind pushing us hard we swept back around the west end of the island and crept past more reefs into Abraham Bay. There we found the elegant Block Island 40 sailboat SEAL, first met at George Town with Jerry and Marcia Packer aboard. We made plans to sail together to the Turks & Caicos Islands, and our little convoy left shortly after midnight on an all-night sail to Sapodilla Bay in West Caicos. There we found a number of yachts, including FIRE ESCAPE, our fire captain friend from George Town, as well as two native sloops, fully rigged but sunken in the harbor. We were told they had been seized for drug-smuggling.

Next day a group of us yachties hitched a ride down a long dusty road into town, which seemed a curious mixture of frontier and sophistication. Caicos was entering a boom of foreign investment and tourism, but construction had not entirely caught up. The town was dusty and treeless – a wide main street with half-built structures everywhere, sprinkled with handsome buildings already doing business.

We tried to leave early the next day but had to turn back when we ran into a strong headwind and a vicious chop that sent waves across the deck and down the forward hatch, which I had neglected to close. My berth was soaked. We crept back, tail 'twixt legs, and re-anchored. Since we had already cleared out with Customs and Immigration the day before, we wondered if we'd have to hide out aboard the boat. But eventually we went ashore and nobody questioned us. (It's always awkward when you say goodbye to people and then turn up again, long after they think you've gone. I usually try to limit the goodbyes as much as possible, but it doesn't seem right to just sneak away without telling anybody). Next day we tried again, this time tacking under both sail and power and heading for Big Ambergris Island. The name intrigued me.

As the breeze died to a perfect calm, we saw a lone sailboat anchored in the distance near two little islands. One island was Big Ambergris, and the boat was MISTY, another George Town friend with Marge and Dave Comersan aboard. They fed us macaroni and wine and we watched the sun set at the end of a very good day. Dave and Marge said they had been horrified to see us motoring directly toward them, seemingly unaware of the coral heads lurking along the way. We hadn't seen anything menacing as we approached. Next morning we let them lead the way through the reefs as we started off for Big Sand Cay, about 25 miles away.

We got there so easily we decided to press on to Puerta Plata in the Dominican Republic. We were motor-sailing in light air, but the engine choked with clogged filters and we shut it down, sailing slowly through the night. With new filters installed and the first light of dawn, we saw great grey fog-shrouded mountains miles ahead – our first view of Hispaniola. It was spectacular. It took hours to get near that mountainous coast, and when we did we were nonplussed – which way to turn? We saw a ruined tower on the shore but could find nothing to indicate it on our chart. We took a chance and turned east. Finally we passed a little oval-shaped fishing harbor that did show up on the chart, about five miles west of Puerto Plata. Then a huge cruise ship steamed past and turned in a few miles down the coast. We followed it gratefully. If they could get in there, we could too.

We entered Puerto Plata Harbor in a sudden torrent of rain and found it a cesspool. It looked as if all the garbage on the land, including dead animals, was being washed in around us. Among the trash was MISTY, which had pulled away from us as we dawdled in the dark.

A tough-looking guy with a sawed-off shotgun met us at the dock and told us (through a young interpreter, who sold me a D.R. courtesy flag for $7) to wait on our boat for the Customs people to clear us. We waited about two hours and finally a small skiff arrived with an interpreter and three swarthy guys in uniform. They checked our papers and asked for a "tip". We gave them two U.S. dollars and they departed.

The place looked beautiful at a distance – mountainous, wooded and green with cultivated fields and hillsides. Ashore we found it wasn't so pretty, but it certainly was interesting. Burros and mules shared the streets with cars and trucks. The place was littered with trash and crowded with people. Uniformed boys, armed with wicked-looking guns and looking about 15 years old, were everywhere, guarding places as innocuous as grocery stores and barbershops. Competing with cars, trucks, donkeys and horses pulling rickety carts were hundreds of motorcycles and scooters. These were the poor man's taxis – you could rent the back seat of a motorcycle for about 25 cents and go almost anywhere.

We visited a huge open-air market where fruit of every description was piled high along the sidewalks, gutters were heaped with rotting vegetables, 10 different record players blared music all at once, and vendors shouted and laughed and waved their wares in our faces. After the aridity of the Bahamas this exuberance was staggering.

The log:

With Dave and Marge, walked up Isabel de Torres Mountain, about 2,400 feet high. Cable car not working. Walked thru jungle along cow & donkey paths – saw and ate oranges, lemons, grapefruit, olives, coffee beans, avocados hanging from huge trees. Our 15-year-old guide, Jose, led us back down an almost sheer drop from the top of the cable car stop. Turned out he'd never gone that way before. We walked down past isolated little jungle farms with pigs, turkeys, chickens and ducks. Many cows grazing in the green sections. Through one little village where radios blared, people giving each other haircuts, women walking with huge buckets of water on their heads, patient little donkeys with straw saddles on their backs carrying sacks of coffee beans. Everybody very friendly . . . Then to the Queens Head Pub for beer, where the English prop. offered us the use of his shower.

I spent three weeks in Puerto Plata, waiting for Ellen to arrive for a week's visit. I fell in with a bunch of yachties and expatriates who hung out in Captain Dick's American Bar. Among them was Cedric, a young Englishman who sailed alone in an old racing sloop once owned by the British Prime Minister, Edward Heath; George, a diffident Canadian gent of about my age, who said he had been proprietor of a whorehouse in town for a number of years and was now married to one of his girls; Marie, a pretty Canadian woman with bad teeth who liked to hang out with young Dominican men and was on an extended vacation from her job as a cook in camps on the Canadian Dew Line, plus several Americans who seemed to have lots of money but no visible means of support.

While I visited Captain Dick's, Hank worked the discos and nightclubs frequented by female tourists. He showed up one day with two vacationing American schoolteachers, both of them entranced at the thought of visiting a real cruising yacht in a foreign port. Hank managed to grope both of them as he boosted them out of the dinghy and into TURTLE DOVE They didn't stay long, pleading seasickness, and he had another good grab on the return trip. Next day he turned up with Dagmar, a beautiful German who carried her own condoms. According to Hugh, the two of them made heavy inroads on her supply.

I discovered that Hugh was dickering with a cruise line for a job as a dance partner on a ship. There would be no pay, but he'd get free passage and food and drink (with lots of chances for more groping, I figured). I thought of it privately as The Gigolo Job. One afternoon when a big cruise ship pulled in we wandered over to check out the lady passengers. We watched a long string of them tottering down the gangplank, heading for a tour bus, and Hugh muttered, "Jeez, they look old as hell!"

"You were expecting Marilyn Monroe?" I replied.

The brief reunion with Ellen was bittersweet. We knew we were living very separate lives, but we agonized over the parting as it drew steadily closer. When the day finally arrived, we hired an ancient taxi with holes in its floor to haul us out to the airport. The terminal was huge, crowded, and haphazard. We stood in a checkout line marked MIAMI for half an hour and then somebody changed the sign to NEW YORK at the last minute, throwing the entire crowd into confusion. There was another hubbub when one of the windows marked DEPARTURE TAX suddenly closed and everybody in that line tried to jam into the middle of the other. It seemed that Dominicans didn't really like waiting in line.

The plane flight was delayed and we sat for an hour holding hands, saying little. It was dark when Ellen finally boarded and I walked gloomily around the airport for a while, feeling terrible. Finally I contracted with a kid on a motorcycle and we hurtled back to the harbor, 20 miles in the dark with my arms wrapped around his stomach. I really didn't much care whether we crashed or not.

CHAPTER 5

Crash

Hitting a reef, Boca de Yuma, Mona Passage, Boqueron, Dad's death.

1990

Hank and I left early next day for Samana, at the east end of the Dominican Republic. It was my birthday. I was trying to reconcile anticipation about seeing a new place, much touted by fellow yachties, with a growing leaden sense that Ellen was gone from my life for good.

The log:

> *Thursday at 6 a.m. I was awakened by the horrible sound of the keel crashing across coral. By the time I got out on deck we had hit another reef and were stuck fast. Much yelling in the dark. Boat finally swung off and we started sailing out, only to hit a third reef. Again we slid off, got the engine started and finally worked our way out into deep water. No apparent damage (except to my nerves), but I haven't yet checked the keel. I'm sure it's gouged.*

There's nothing like running onto a reef in the dark for a quick wakeup call. Hank, so contrite he could hardly speak, told me he saw lights and started steering for them. Since the lights were pretty obviously on shore this didn't make much sense, but it was the best he could do. We were off the rocks, but I had a new worry: what if we had punched a hole in the bottom? I kept checking the bilges, but there was only the usual pailful of oily water sloshing around. I gave fervent thanks to that big lead keel down there. Apparently its mass had absorbed the shock without serious damage.

Later that day the engine turned mean, first balking with clogged fuel filters and then developing a pinhole leak in a fuel line which sprayed diesel oil over everything. We managed to seal the pinhole with a short length of rubber hose fastened with hose clamps cranked up tight. Then the knotlog quit registering, making navigation much more difficult. When we reached what appeared to be Samana Bay we were much relieved. The place was spectacular: rocky cliffs rising straight out of gnarled coral banks with spray spouting up from the surging waves. We headed in with a strong following wind, close beside a tiny fishing boat propelled by a sail that had more holes than cloth. It easily kept pace with us.

Somehow, this huge bay didn't look as I had pictured it from the chart. We kept pointing ahead and yelling "Samana?" to the young fishermen alongside. Each time they would nod and wave us on.

The log:

> *We crept into a tiny little harbor and then into a river, so narrow that I had to stop and back out when we couldn't fit under a wire strung across. Sheer rock walls festooned with Spanish moss and big cacti with big white pelicans roosting in them – most exotic.*

> *Tried to anchor in outer harbor and then were approached by a skiff full of men who said we should go back into the river. A real Chinese fire drill, with ropes being tied to rocks along the river and everybody talking at once. One rope too short and we were treated to the sight of a human bridge – one guy holding the end of the rope at his end of the skiff, the other guy hanging on to a rock with only his feet in the skiff at the other end. Finally we got tied up and everybody trooped below, where we learned that this was not Samana at all. The Commandante finally agreed to let us stay till tomorrow when, Gawd help us, we probably will tackle the Mona Passage.*

> *No diesel and no telephone here, anywhere.*

We were in Boca de Yuma, miles south of Samana, a tiny fishing village that saw tourists only once a year during an annual fishing derby. We went ashore to find clean-swept dirt streets, thatched roofs and nothing but lantern light. Nobody spoke English, but we located a little bar/restaurant and had a chicken dinner. The place had a large population of chickens – they seemed to be everywhere. We saw no cars.

Next day's log:

> *Preparing for the Mona Passage – hope to leave this evening. With Hank & the dinghy ashore, anchor started dragging. I hollered for help & some netcasters rowed*

over & we secured to a big eyebolt in the rock wall of the river. We now have a tree branch hanging on the forestay at the top of the mast, & Spanish moss streaming off from the radar reflector. Looks rather jaunty.

Have patched fuel line, now broken clean through, with more rubber tubing & hose clamps. Trouble is that one end has only about a 1/4-inch tit to attach to. Hope it holds. Hugh has brought water & diesel – now he's grocery shopping. The 100-foot rock walls of this little river are festooned with drooping vines & cacti & big old pelicans are sailing in & out. What a great place – I'd like to stay a while.

Following the advice of our guidebook, *The Gentleman's Guide to Passages South*, we planned to make the dreaded crossing from the Dominican Republic to Puerto Rico in two nights and one day. The guide said:

Should you leave Samana in the morning, trying to cross the Mona Passage in one day, there will be no margin for error or problems enroute, and you probably will have the stuffing kicked out of you on both sides of the passage.

We motored slowly out of the dark silent river at 9 p.m. I was at the bow with our super-bright spotlight. As I swung it to the right, the beam caught a small crowd of villagers on the rocks watching us leave. Somebody lifted an arm as we passed. Nobody said anything.

The passage turned out to be bumpy but not as tough as advertised. Our makeshift repairs held together, and we actually had to wait for several hours until we had enough light to make sure we were looking at Boqueron Bay. And then, tacking in, we managed to get too close to the mangroves on the north side of the bay (with me steering this time), and got stuck in the shallows. A passing runabout pulled us off. All this within view of a whole crowd of anchored cruisers, including our friends on MISTY.

MISTY gave us a warm welcome, along with considerable ribbing for running aground again: everybody agreed that it took real ingenuity to get stuck in this big bay. Somebody suggested we should change our name to CRAB-CRUSHER.

Boqueron lived up to expectations. It offered a big beautiful harbor, a wide sandy beach on the south side, a reasonably substantial dinghy dock, and Schamar's Bar about five steps away: home of a perpetual pool game and a motley squad of natives and expatriates who had settled in for the long haul. The place pretty much belonged to the yachties on weekdays. On weekends it was jammed with holiday-makers who sampled the native clams and oysters in the little stands that lined the streets. Loud music blared for long hours on weekend nights, but we anchored far enough out to keep it tolerable.

Hank left almost immediately, heading off to his gigolo job, but I stayed almost a month, including 10 days with the boat hauled out in Puerto Real, a nearby fishing village. I slept on the boat in the boatyard, made friends with the local dogs and cats, listened to the yard workers singing in the early morning, watched the fishing boats move in and out, and worked alone for long hours. I repaired many minor gouges in the keel, souvenirs of our encounter with the reefs, sanded and applied two coats of paint to the entire boat, and returned to Boqueron Harbor with a craft that looked brand new. The gang at Schamar's was impressed.

Paul Harrigan arrived for another stint as crew, laden with motor parts and a SatNav for electronic-aided navigation. I had decided that we must avoid another "Whatever-happened-to-Samana?" experience. Harrigan liked Boqueron as much as I did. One high point was the open-air wedding of two yachties who had decided to settle down and open a sail repair business in town. They were wed under the trees in the little town square, with everybody bringing food for a pot-luck meal. It was a happy ceremony.

Underway our first stop was Guanica, passing through an imposing entrance between steep hills with power lines strung high above us. We anchored in a small shallow harbor lined with mangroves, a regiment of roosters on one shore crowing lustily: no waiting 'till dawn for them. When they ran out of steam, another flock took over on the other side. The competition continued without letup most of the night. Next day, heading for Salinas, at least 100 porpoises rushed to join us right under our bowsprit, crisscrossing and leaping so close we could almost touch them. One did full twists and flips in mid-air, apparently out of sheer exuberance.

Salinas was our guidebook author's favorite anchorage. We liked it, especially the marina's outdoor bar built right into the mangroves, but it seemed to lack some of the friendly raunchiness of Boqueron. Maybe it was just that they didn't have a pool table. We stayed three days, delayed by strong winds that made it difficult even to row out to the boat in the sheltered anchorage. We stocked food, water, and fuel and hung out in the outdoor bar. There were worse places to spend time.

We left Salinas at dusk, hoping to get calmer conditions en route to our next stop, the little harbor of Palmas del Mar. But it turned out to be a long night. Once, when we were both down below, our 15-ton boat was lifted and actually flung through the air, crashing down on its side. Neither of us was hurt, but crockery and loose gear flew in all directions. The two of us stared at each other, mouths agape. Finally we both started to laugh: there was nothing else to do.

Palmas del Mar was a tiny man-made harbor, enclosed on three sides by huge rocks. Boats were allowed to anchor inside and we did so, never going ashore. Later I was to encounter many little harbors like this in the Mediterranean, but this was a first for me. The contrast between the big rollers smashing across the narrow entrance and the calm water just a few feet inside was startling. Next day we worked our way up the Vieques Passage, motor-tacking interminably against the wind. By the middle of the night we were down to double reefs in both main and mizzen. Harrigan woke me up, announcing calmly: "You might want to take a look at this." I climbed out and found myself staring at a small freighter, heading straight at us and apparently oblivious. We swerved out of the way and I asked Harrigan to indicate a little more urgency next time.

We reached St. Thomas after 24 hours and 106 miles of tacking. Harrigan had to leave the next day.

I spent almost two months in and around the Virgin Islands, taking short cruises with daughter Mary and son Ange in separate visits, then again with Ellen for a trip through the string of Leeward and Windward Islands which make up the Lesser Antilles. She had finished a year in Japan and was due next to go to Guatemala on a Fulbright scholarship.

We spent a few days in St. Thomas and then took off for Coral Harbor in St. John and my third stop at Redbeard's Saloon, a funky tavern where you could sit at the bar and watch sci-fi videos while herds of wild donkeys scampered past the window. From there we did an overnighter involving much tacking to Anguilla, where we crept into the harbor at dusk and left next morning, never going ashore. (I was never sure whether you are legally required to clear Customs if you don't go ashore – fortunately, the question was not put to the test.)

Leaving Anguilla we tacked south toward the mysterious island of Saba. I'd never heard of the place until I saw it pictured on a spectacular poster at Captain Dick's in Puerto Plata. Seeing this marvelous cone-shaped mountain rising straight out of the sea made us eager to visit. But I'd heard that anchoring there was extremely difficult.

(That problem was resolved when we anchored for a week in Simpson Bay, St. Martin. We flew to Saba in a small plane, landing on a tiny field shorter than the flight deck of an aircraft carrier. The island was fascinating – all hills and meadows, steep concrete roadways, goats, flowers and friendly people. True to its Dutch heritage, the place was scrupulously clean. Leaving next day was even more harrowing than arriving. Racing along with the plane's engine roaring at full throttle we could see the end of the runway approaching all too rapidly, with a sheer drop off to the sea. We made it.)

Next stop was St. Eustatius (Statia), a little island with a small town built on two levels. At sea level were restaurants, a hotel and dive shops. A steep hike up the cobbled Old Slave Road led to stores, a handsome old fort, an even older church and a museum. Everything was Dutch clean.

The log:

> *Shoreline lined with stone ruins of warehouses – once Statia was a hub of world commerce, dealing in slaves, arms, food & stolen pirate booty. Snorkeling in the harbor we spotted an old anchor – maybe 10 feet long & weighing a ton or more. Big thing here is finding blue 'slave beads' – a kind of scrip discarded when the slaves were freed 100 years ago. We didn't find any.*

Then on to Nevis:

Left Statia at 10:15 & motor-tacked (almost a single tack) to Nevis. A beautiful sail – wind strong but steady; chugged right past St. Kitts, which looked agricultural & pretty with a cloud-capped old volcano. Checked the harbor of Nevis & then anchored off beautiful Pinney's Beach. Swam, checked anchors & emerged in time for a fresh – water shower from a brief rain squall. Decided to deal with Customs in the morning. A good day.

Cleared Customs easily next day & toured Charlestown on foot – next day took a bus (van) out to a pottery & a former plantation, very posh. Hitched back to boat w. a friendly lady.

Nevis is the greatest so far!!

Next was Montserrat. The main harbor looked rough and unprotected, so we anchored in Old Road Bay. We had just set two anchors when a police boat showed up and ordered us back to Customs in the main harbor. We protested in vain, re-anchored and cleared in at a surly Customs office, then adjourned for drinks. At the bar we arranged to buy a quarter of a goat and take a taxi tour next day, then returned to the boat and spent a bad night in a heavy roll. Next morning we decided to get out, rowed ashore to clear out and returned to the boat, sans goat and tour, and getting swamped in the dinghy both ways. Montserrat was not a big hit.

(Years later, heading north, I saw what was left of Montserrat from Antigua, a safe distance away. A huge plume of grey smoke and ash was still churning up from the volcano after a series of powerful eruptions. Television news showed not a roof left standing in the town, and almost everybody on Montserrat had fled.)

About 35 miles away was Guadeloupe and the tiny fishing village of Deshaies, where we cleared in by rowing ashore, filling out a form and leaving it in a box – our kind of Customs! The town had another nice feature: a row of free laundry tubs on a back street. We lugged in our dirty clothes and washed them with the townsfolk. We were learning that most foreign ports don't offer Laundromats. That night we fell asleep happily listening to a saxophonist playing jazz tunes in a nearby boat.

After a rough choppy passage to Prince Rupert Bay in Dominica, we were immediately beset by "boat boys" with names like *Capt. Spice, Pinky, Alexander the Great* and *Lawrence of Arabia*. Lawrence and Alexander had the only outboard-powered boat and we selected them to buy veggies and take us on a rowboat trip up the Indian River. The two were vastly entertaining as they rowed us through the turns, kidding each other constantly. We became good friends, and I gave them a broken-down British Seagull outboard motor when we finally said goodbye.

Dominica is lush, mountainous, beautiful, friendly and poor. There were three big wrecked boats on the beach in front of the police station, still left from the last hurricane. We waited almost two hours for the Customs officer, and when he finally appeared he didn't have the keys to his office and told us to return next day. We did, and then moved the boat down to the Coconut Beach Hotel, which offered a free mooring. We stayed six days.

The hotel had a telephone and I learned that my father was seriously ill in the Florida nursing home. My brother Jim had flown there from California and a little later, on Monday, June 18, 1990, Jim called to tell me that Dad had died. He was 91. I was half expecting it, and had agonized over whether I should try to get back in time to see him. I decided not to, and immediately began berating myself. I told myself that I couldn't have reached him in time (probably true), but it was small comfort. This was one of those times when I realized the price I was paying for the carefree cruising life. I had two grandchildren that I barely knew, and now I was a thousand miles away while my father died.

Ellen was to leave for Guatemala from here. We stood in the hot dusty main street of the town and I tearfully pleaded with her to stay a little longer. She agreed – mostly, I think, because I was so upset about my father. She stayed wth me until we reached St. Lucia, where we toured the island and met the Binders, an English father, mother, son and two daughters, all squeezed together into a 24-foot catamaran named, appropriately, BINDERS. After two weeks Ellen finally flew out for Guatemala. She was overdue and had to leave.

CHAPTER 6

Colombia

Grenada and The Recovering Adults, Venezuela, Cartagena.

1990

I had trouble finding someone to sail with me after Ellen left. Finally I asked the Binders if their 16-year-old son J.J. could go with me to Grenada, where he could rejoin the family yacht. Given the crowded conditions on their tiny catamaran, I wasn't surprised when they agreed.

J.J. was the youngest crew member I'd had, but he was a veteran sailor. He was quiet and shy, an ardent fisherman who was constantly trailing a line off the stern. He seemed able to snag fish at will. I figured he would suit me very well.

When we hauled up anchor and started the engine to leave, the propeller refused to move. The propeller shaft had worked itself out of the coupling on the engine. We hired a mechanic from the marina and spent most of the day messing with it, in and out of the foul water of the marina lagoon. Finally the job was done and we moved to the clear water of the outer bay, where we had a peaceful night. Next day we started off for Blue Lagoon on St. Vincent, a day behind BINDERS.

We didn't quite make it and had to turn into Kingstown Harbor, one bay short, as darkness fell. The only available anchorage was in deep water close to the cliff side, near a small freighter with no other anchored yachts around.

Early next day, we proceeded cautiously into the next bay and through a stake-marked passage into Blue Lagoon. There was BINDERS and we woke them up: it was still before 7 a.m. We took one of the little Caribbean taxi-vans into town to clear Customs, and I treated J.J. to a celebratory breakfast. When his scrambled eggs arrived he doused them with the local hot sauce, apparently thinking it was ketchup. Too shy to make a fuss, the poor kid downed the red-hot stuff and shortly afterward began showing signs of acute distress. He didn't eat much for the next few days and I knew he was hurting, but he said little about it. He was a very shy kid.

Arrived Admiralty Bay, Bequia, shortly before noon – anchored off a beautiful sand beach about a mile south of town.

2 pleasant nights & 2 visits to town – one along a pretty foot path all along the shoreline, the other by dinghy. A nice little town & good anchorage. Then about 25 miles to Union, rolling along on a beautiful broad reach. Later hit by three heavy thundersqualls – blinding sheets of rain and strong winds. Finally ended up taking down all sail & powering into Clifton Harbor, Union. Crowded anchorage. Rained some more & finally calmed down.

Aug. 4:

Heading for Grenada in light wind. Talked to Ellen in Guatemala last night. Apparently she's doing well. Has house & cleaning lady & may get a car.

Reached north end of Grenada around noon – a fine reach across. Shortly afterward we caught a tuna about 6 lbs. – first fish in a hell of a long time! A good day so far.

Wind went light & finally reached Spice Island Marina in Prickly Bay. A pretty place. Next day hitched over to the lagoon & returned J.J. to his family aboard BINDERS.

I told the parents about J.J. and the hot sauce, fearing that they might hold me responsible. But they took the news calmly, especially when I told them that J.J. was eating properly again. I'm sure he would never have mentioned the incident.

Aug. 4 was my last log entry for almost four months. I went home for a while, but mostly I visited Grenada and a lot of old and new friends. I spent most of my time in Prickly Bay, home of the Spice Island Boatyard and a young one-armed Englishman who made a modest living catering to yachties. (He looked after TURTLE DOVE while I was home and even sent me a letter confessing that he had over-watered one of my house plants on the boat.) Every morning I'd see him racing down the steps from his house to his little dock followed by several madly-careening dogs, with everybody flying off the end into the water. This guy had a zest for life.

I made lots of friends in Grenada: Ian and Diane of CYRENA, a New Zealand couple with a lovely wooden racing yacht, now two-thirds of the way on their trip around the world; Lou and Nancy of BARRY DUCKWORTH, he working on a novel and she a professional navigator on cruise ships; Frank and Jo An of LADY JO AN, two Texans; Chris and Johan, two young Danes who built a plywood dinghy on the dock and then forgot it briefly when they sailed away (they seemed to subsist entirely on canned sausage – they had left Denmark equipped with several hundred glass bottles of the stuff, didn't break one and were still eating it on shore), and Winston and Kurt of New Orleans, aboard their big ketch FINISTERRE.

I became particularly friendly with Kurt and with Lou, who lived alone on his boat while his wife earned the bread on a cruise ship. The three of us formed a musical group called *The Recovering Adults* (name suggested by Winston): Lou and Kurt (a professional musician) on guitars and me on harmonica. We practiced regularly at the marina on Thursday nights when the bar was closed. Now and then we even had an audience. Winston was a lawyer. Kurt had once played guitar and told jokes on a New Orleans radio station where he was known as The Tabasco Trucker. He and Winston had sailed from New Orleans, suffering an endless list of difficulties with their opulent boat.

I loved Prickly Bay. One morning I rowed in early to the club and encountered an elderly worker leisurely raking the lawn. When I wished him good morning he smiled and returned the greeting:

"Oh mon, that sun come up so sweet this mornin'!" he said.

Marge and Dave of MISTY were there too, and they helped me scrape and sand when I had TURTLE DOVE hauled out for bottom-painting. While she was on the hard we organized a pot-luck supper one night in the boatyard. When we surveyed the party we counted 25 different countries represented.

I joined another group of yachties anchored at nearby Hog Island for a while. This was a more isolated spot, perhaps even more beautiful than Prickly Bay. The only store within rowing distance was a little shack at the upper end of an adjoining bay. The proprietor, an amiable black man, showed me his guest book. It contained many names, some well known in sailing circles. He had me sign and then announced that it was time for my "initiation." This involved two glasses of clear liquid from a bottle labeled "STRONG RUM" – one for him and one for me. He said we were to down the liquor in one gulp, which he promptly did. I tried to follow suit and got half my glassful down before the stuff exploded in my throat. After that I could proceed only in tiny sips, and each one felt devastating. My host watched this with great delight. I finally managed it, but my throat remained numb throughout the long row back to the boat.

My son Ange arrived once again toward the end of my stay and he soon fell into the easygoing atmosphere of the place. We spent a week together there before our leave-taking, complete with a major sendoff from our friends. As we started out of Prickly Bay, Kurt and Winston churned up alongside in their outboard-powered dinghy and tossed fake money into the cockpit.

"Lucky coins!" they shouted above the roar of the outboard. I still have a few of them.

Just out of the harbor I remarked to Ange that for once it seemed that we had done everything possible to get the boat ready for the next leg. We were in top shape, I announced. I regretted that comment a few days later.

The log:

> *9 a.m. Thurs. 11/22 (Thanksgiving Day) – Approaching Testigos, part of Venezuela – A new continent!*

> *Around noon we anchored at Playa Real, off a pristine white sand beach w. a pleasant breeze filling the wind scoop. A most beautiful spot. We cleaned the anchor chain again (still horribly stinky from almost four months in the Grenada mud), & I snorkeled ashore to the inlet. A few fishermen's shacks on the beach & a few fishing boats plus one catamaran – that's all. We caught a small tuna & will have it for Thanksgiving dinner tonight.*

Next day:

> *Up early & away for Margarita (big island off the coast of mainland Venezuela) after a quiet night. Got there around 4 after a good sail but some indecision as to which point sheltered Pampatar (point of entry). Finally found it & anchored right next to Pete & Barb on MISTY (another one). Went ashore & left papers w. Shore Base Yacht Services, which will handle 4-stop clearance for $11 U.S. Had some beers, bought bread & steak, returned to boat & pigged out on beef – 2.2 pounds for about $4.50 U.S.* (The log does not record that almost immediately ashore, while goggling at the huge old gas-guzzler Buicks and Chevvies plowing by on the crowded streets, I got my foot under the wheel of a passing taxi. It scared me but didn't do much harm.)

Four days later the log continues:

> *Nearing Isla Coche when we discovered that the prop shaft had once again parted from the engine coupling – this time leaving a 1½" gap. Tacked in to Isla Cache & attempted repairs – Ange overboard, trying to force shaft back into coupling, I trying to lock it in place w. wire & hose clamps. We'll try to sail on to Mochima (on the mainland) tomorrow, assuming that the shaft doesn't slip back out again the minute we start sailing, which it may very well do. Lost my straw hat, too – not a very good day, really. Blowing pretty hard right now.*

Next day's log:

Had a grand sail down, covering 50 miles in all. Decided to skip Mochima & visit Ensenada Tigrillo – but SatNav rang up a string of no-fixes & despite much work w. hand-bearing compass we missed the turn, confused by the plethora of islands. Tried to tack our way up the bay without engine, but wind died so reached up to a VERY deep (50') anchorage off a fishing camp. Fishermen much amused at our Chinese fire drill at anchoring – dumped jib in water, much yelling, etc. Finally settled in w. 2 big anchors out, real close to shore. Will be mucho work in the a.m. But it was a good day's sail, & cockamamie prop shaft is still holding on.

Next day:

Up at 7 after many trips on deck to make sure our deep anchors were holding. Hauled them up w. much labor, turned rather precariously in our little harbor & drifted out in a fading breeze. No laughing audience this time – the fishermen had already gone. Got out in the big bay & wind died altogether – have been drifting slack for some time.

Last night after anchoring, SatNav finally told us where we were – Caracas del Oeste, several islands farther east than we had thought. Islands & peninsulas are so irregular & scattered here that it's hard to tell one from the other.

We drifted a long time & finally rigged the outboard on the dinghy as a push boat. With this & a 2-knot breeze we worked our way into what was supposed to be Chris Robinson's boatyard, according to our cruising guide, at I. de Plata. But it looked like a fishing camp, nobody answered the radio, & it was 84' deep about 100 yards off the beach. Can't anchor that deep.

As breeze came up we hoisted sail again & took off; under full sail we tacked out of the bay around a succession of points to Puerto La Cruz. Found lots of sailboats here – shortened down to reefed main & jib & stormed through the anchorage, checking depths. Jibed around, tacked & stormed back again, rounded up, furled jib & anchored successfully without engine. Put out the other anchor & had a peaceful night, despite strong N.E. wind.

Today I tackle the prop shaft.

Three days later:

Spent much of the last 2 days in the engine room, made a new key for the shaft & drilled two 1/4-inch holes in it for new set screws. Had to drill out the broken set *screw, took coupling to a machine shop for re-threading ($1 U.S.). Sounds fairly simple but it was a lot of work.*

We liked Puerto LaCruz – a lively city w. many modern buildings & friendly people. Wandered around town several times – had a great meal (Paella Valenciana) at La Parador (waiters in posh evening clothes, but still cheap by our standards) last night. Much Latino music from shore until about 3 a.m., but it's so cheerful-sounding I don't mind it. Great gray islands like sleeping herds of elephants huddled offshore. Unfortunately a lot of oil (tanker spill?) washed up on shore yesterday.

Fixed engine shaft seems OK. Found us approaching Cabo Codera around 11 p.m. – rounded it at 11:30. (Through some miscalculation, plus unexpected strong westerly current, I'd figured it would take us till dawn!) Sailed west down extremely rugged coastline w. a full moon shining. Reached Puerto Azul around 9 a.m. & gratefully anchored after 130 miles in about 10 1/2 hours (a truly remarkable run). Took a nap.

Went ashore @ Puerto Azul last nite & were told, politely, that we couldn't. Returned disgruntled to boat, dined on pea soup & went to bed. Left early, heading for Carabelleda Yacht Club 5 miles west, hoping it would be more hospitable. (A 9-year-old guidebook presents some problems.) Approaching Carabelleda in heavy swell & strong wind, the towed dinghy suddenly lost its oars, which I stupidly had left in the oarlocks. Luckily, Ange saw them go & we retrieved them w. the boathook & much difficulty. Found half a doz. cruisers anchored in the tiny harbor.

We bussed in to Caracas, a huge and surprisingly modern city with a magnificent subway. We did a lot of walking, trying to locate a cable car attached to a mountain that seemed to promise a great view. A number of people gave us directions, but nobody mentioned that the ride had been closed for some time. During our hike we gawked at the acres of dismal tin-roofed and cardboard slum shacks surrounding the city, almost touching many modern buildings.

I had thought when I went sailing that it would take me away from bureaucrats and their little fiefdoms. Hardly. After much colloquy in pidgin Spanish we learned that to sign out of Venezuela we must trek back and forth between two buildings approximately a half-mile apart, presenting papers to a number of office-holders. And the papers had to be signed in sequence – if Bureaucrat No. 2 was out to lunch, it would do no good to proceed to No. 3.

We would walk to No. 1, then back a half-mile to No. 2, then return the half-mile to No. 3, and so on. The icing on the cake came when we were told sternly that we could not enter one office because I was wearing shorts! I had to hike back to the boat in the 90-degree heat to struggle into long pants, the first I'd worn in some time.

Eventually, we gave up and sought help from one of the many "agents" who importuned us. These guys, apparently self-appointed, obviously had the inside track with officialdom. By day's end we had shelled out nearly $100 U.S. to our "agent", for various "fees." But we were, at last, free to leave Venezuela.

I had been vacillating about visiting Colombia for some time, not wanting to pass up an entire country. But I worried about the reputation of the place as a nest of kidnappers, murderers and drug fiends. When I had inquired at the U.S. Embassy in Grenada, I was advised to give it a miss. But in Carabelleda we met Floyd and Davey of the yacht TOREM, who urged us to go there, and I decided to follow their advice.

First to come would be the Netherland Antilles – Curacao, Bonaire and Aruba. We left Venezuela Dec. 7 and had a fast sail to Bonaire. We crept along its lee shore and waited for enough daylight to anchor amidst a half-dozen other sailboats on a narrow sand ledge near a big concrete breakwater. After a two-hour nap who should dinghy over but Chrissie & Andrea of BINDERS! They told us that Andy (the father) was crewing on a 75-footer and was stuck in Panama with blown-out sails. On their advice, we hauled up both anchors and motored over to a big pier so Customs could search. We had a struggle getting tied up side-to against a strong wind. Once tied, the authorities were a snap – they didn't visit the boat and didn't even glance at the Venezuelan papers we worked so hard (and paid so much) for.

The town looked like a doll's village – immaculately clean, all stone and brick and paving, buildings yellow, orange & gray. We anchored near a nice beach bar and dinghy dock with good Amstel beer, which tasted great.

Bonaire's clear waters are renowned among divers. Stretched across the white sand bottom we could see enormous old chains, apparently laid there to hold anchored vessels safely. But they hadn't done the job a few weeks earlier – a sudden freak storm had reversed the usual east wind and put a number of anchored yachts in peril. Two damaged sailboats were still careened up on the big concrete seawall.

Clearing Customs here was a snap. When our official heard that our next stop would be Aruba he grinned and said, "They like stamps over there," and stamped our clearance paper in about a dozen different spots, all with the same stamp.

I noted in the log:

> *Have finally seen the famous Green Flash – and twice! Had a fairly positive sighting last night from shore in Bonaire, & tonight Ange & I saw it clearly while sailing toward Curacao. Another dream realized.*

(The Green Flash, thought by some to be only a sailor's myth, may be visible on the horizon just as the setting sun dips below. I had been watching for it for years.)

We wanted to get to Aruba in plenty of time to meet a new crewman – Bill Callanan, a friend of all my offspring. After a comfortably slow 25-hour sail we anchored there with three other boats in shallow water, at the west end of Aruba International airport, with big jets flying over us almost constantly. We figured we could walk to the terminal, but the runway stretched for miles and hitch-hiking failed. We had to hoof the distance.

Callanan, recovered from troubles with both booze and drugs, was a physical fitness fanatic who arrived at the airport with rollerblades at the ready. He competed regularly in triathlons and insisted on swimming ashore from every anchorage, no matter how far offshore we were. He would put his clothes, passport and money in a plastic bag, then hold the bag aloft with one arm while churning through the water. He could swim faster than we could row. We used him as a courier in Aruba, sending him zooming out on the rollerblades to find gas stations where we could buy diesel fuel. Apparently his were the first blades to be seen in Aruba and he attracted a lot of attention, particularly in heavy traffic.

Our cruising guide had warned us of the evil reputation of much of Colombia, particularly along the big Guajera Peninsula, which extends northwest out into the Caribbean. Reportedly it was the refuge of the worst pirates, drug lords and other bad guys. We planned to stay several hundred miles offshore, with 440 miles to reach Cartagena.

As we left Aruba the wind was strong and almost dead astern, producing big breaking waves. TURTLE DOVE, as usual, rode them like a duck, but they were fearsome to look at. I was extremely glad we weren't trying to head into them. I took photos of Callanan clinging grimly to the tiller with big mountains of white-capped blue churning up behind him. He wouldn't turn around to look. "I'm scared enough already," he announced. (I had read that sometimes on the old sailing ships in the Southern Ocean they'd hang a big canvas, or build a temporary wall behind the helmsman, so he couldn't see the huge following seas.)

Dec. 18:

> *Now preparing for our third night offshore since leaving Aruba – hope to reach Cartagena tomorrow. Currently suffering through heavy prolonged squalls, then brief calms. Following seas are getting BIG. Magnificent snow-capped peaks to the south. Destroyed one block of mainsheet tackle in an accidental jibe. Boat doing 8 knots occasionally under very short rig. Time to douse the staysail, I think.*

> *I have two good crew members here. (Just told them that, too.)*

> *So far have lost two fish – apparently big – and two lures.*

Later:

> *Well, we're heading toward the city (what we see looks pretty modern) after a hard night's sail, most of it under just the little staysail, & still averaging better than 5 knots. BIG following seas. But we're making it.*

Cartagena is an old walled city full of history. To reach the harbor we had to sail beyond the city and past a false passage, jammed with huge rocks many years ago as a trap for marauders. Those early Cartagenians were a cautious lot. When we reached the real entrance several miles away, we had to pass directly between two menacing forts. Beyond them, the Old City was entirely circled by an enormous stone wall.

We motored up to the Club Nautico and were waved in to the dock, where we were immediately given three cold beers – one of our nicest receptions. We met several other cruisers, then a Customs agent, and later still more officials to sign papers and stamp documents. Cleared at last, we took a taxi through a darkened city (power was off) to Paco's Restaurant and had tapas for dinner. The Old City looked mysterious but friendly, even in the dark.

We had a grand time in Cartagena, lunching at the little portable juice bars that lined the old harbor, wandering through the cobbled streets at all hours, and hanging out in the Club Nautico bar. We attended a festive cruisers' Christmas dinner there, with everybody contributing part of the meal and a comic gift. (Mine was a used engine alternator, rather rusty.) And the prices were amazingly low. When we finally left after an eight – day stay (much longer than we'd intended), the total marina bill, including a bar tab, was about $48 U.S.

We headed for the San Blas Islands off Panama, occupied by Kuna Indians who reportedly were still living a Stone-Age existence.

CHAPTER 7

San Blas

Kuna Indians singing "Jingle Bells", mola peddlers.

1991

As always, everybody felt queasy after a long stay ashore. It didn't help that we had to wrestle the tiller against big following seas that kept slewing the stern around. We rushed through the black water at seven knots or more – fast traveling for TURTLE DOVE. The following afternoon we cranked up the engine, looking for our first San Blas island before darkness. We found it.

This was Holander Cays, a group of palm-covered islets, each with its own little circle of clean white sand and palm trees, the whole collection protected by coral reefs in deep blue water. Three boats were anchored there – one French, one German and the Austrian aluminum cutter we had met in Aruba.

Next day cleaned ship, scrubbed bottom & snorkeled nearby reefs. Were visited by Kuna Indians in dugout canoes – they sold us molas (colorful hand – made tapestries decorated with fine – sewn birds and fish). Later the Austrian sailor told us he'd seen a hammerhead shark – "at least two meters" – here. We're still swimming, though.

Left Holander Cays after a spear-fishing trip with Lars of SAVANNA, heading for Rio Diablo, 15 miles away, to deliver Bill Callanan to plane. He's been feeling ill for days & wants to leave. Worked our way between reefs & islands & anchored off the town, a strange collection of palm-thatched shacks & more solid buildings. Went ashore at police station; friendly greetings. Streets all dirt, but clean, lined w. palm dwellings. Stopped at beer house & greeted by "Sammy" & friends – he an Oklahoma-educated retired jr. hi school principal. He took us to his house, where his wife was entertaining many Kuna kids with music and Pinata. Dined at a little restaurant. Later I went ashore to observe a dance & New Year church service.

(At the church I listened to little kids singing "Jingle Bells" in Kuna Indian. I wondered what the line "dashing through the snow" meant to them. This was the first time I'd had kids sidle up and take my hand, uninvited. At times all three of us were at the center of a long line of little kids, all holding hands and grinning at everybody. These people offered an innocence and trust that was almost heart-breaking.)

Up early to put Bill on crowded little plane for Panama City – commuted to the only airstrip (on a nearby island) via big outboard-powered dugout with many passengers. Then we left for Soledad and its molas. Some tricky navigating past reefs but no real trouble – a good sail.

Soledad was a tiny island completely covered w. thatched huts, all the way down to the water. What followed was right out of 'South Pacific' – as we anchored, about 20 dugouts came out to meet us & soon the boat held about 40 women and kids and 40,000 molas. I got rid of $70 in short order. Much harder to get rid of the visitors – finally we rowed ashore for beer, escorted by kids in dugouts, laughing & splashing & swimming like fish – great uproar of gayety & fun. Ashore, we toured the village w. 10 kids as guides. Bought cold beer (cooled by generator), talked w. people, declined countless offers of molas. The village is jammed w. huts, separated by little aisles about 2 feet wide.

Everything neat & clean – almost spotless. Chickens & a few dogs running loose, pigs in pens, coconuts at the store, smell of wood smoke, a few TV aerials, no outboards but beautiful sailing dugouts pulled up on shore, muted grays & browns but women wearing gold nose ornaments & colorful dresses & leg wrappings. We felt like the whalers must have felt 150 years ago on first arriving in the South Seas. And no film for the camera!

That night the entire village was stone dark and dead quiet. From our anchorage near shore we couldn't see even a lantern light. It looked as if everybody had gone to sleep as soon as darkness fell. But the tranquility ended when a dugout bumped alongside: Not women with molas this time, but two men offering plastic bags packed with white powder. Looked like cocaine, all right. We declined, as politely as possible.

(In the Bahamas the locals liked to talk about finding "square grouper" – a bale of marijuana, neatly wrapped in plastic, dropped from a plane or ship to be picked up by a small boat. We wondered what we'd do if we found one, out of sight of land. We agreed, reluctantly, that we'd probably leave it alone. This didn't come from any great surge of good citizenship – it was the thought that the U.S. government could seize your boat if they found even one shred of the stuff aboard. Guess you can legislate morality, after all.)

These San Blas folks really did look primitive. They were small and wiry (although all the men were about five feet tall at most, there were basketball courts in every open spot), with straight black hair and glossy brown skin the color of a horse chestnut. They smiled a lot, and they either had no teeth or a full set of beautiful big white choppers. Dr. Cunanan, my Filipino dentist back in Rhode Island, would have been fascinated.

We saw almost no outboard motors – everybody either paddled or sailed the narrow little dugout canoes. The sails seemed to be mostly rags and patches, but the little boats skimmed along in the wind at twice our speed. Apparently everybody lived mostly on fish and coconuts, which were plentiful. We did visit a few tiny stores, but they offered little beyond onions, rice and a few dusty cans of corned beef. The omnipresent Coca Cola was available, plus beer in cans. The only local industry seemed to be making molas (and peddling the occasional plastic bag of white powder.)

The log:

> *Farewell to Soledad & on to new mola-sellers. Motor-tacked past Porvenir the 10 miles to Chichine Cays, reportedly a great diving place. It's entirely surrounded by reefs except for one deep entry spot, 2 jewel – like islands with white sand beaches & coconut palms. People living in thatched huts on both islands. And there were Hans & Karin, our Austrian friends from Aruba & Holander Cays. Spent 2 days here in idyllic surroundings, snorkeling & trying unsuccessfully to spear lobsters & fish. Tried to swap old cans of corn & beans from Dominican Republic for a mola – any mola. No soap. Indians smarter than I, apparently.*

Next day we had a 43-mile run to Isla Grande, where Columbus had spent 10 days, on our way to the Panama Canal. We were heading for an anchorage near the north end of the island. This meant a trip down a narrow channel between island and mainland, and it looked rough. Hearts in mouths, we swung in, aimed directly at big waves crashing through the entrance. It was a roller-coaster ride, much more exciting than I wanted. Once into the channel we had only a little chop from the following wind, but looking back through the entrance was a sobering experience.

"We came through *that?*" Ange asked.

This anchorage was at the other end of the channel, with a crowded parking lot on the mainland side and a bathing beach on the other. I used the binoculars for a few peeks at topless beauties sunning themselves. Our only company there was a loud

Norwegian who joined us toward nightfall and left early in the morning. I immediately disliked the guy when I saw him casually toss an empty beer can over the side.

On Jan. 8, my birthday, we rolled down along the coastline with wind and waves dead astern, heading for Colon at the eastern end of the Panama Canal.

> *Reached Colon around 1 p.m. after a fast sail; rolled in between the breakwaters & motored over to anchorage in stiff NE wind. Got both anchors down in 37 feet of water, then chugged with dinghy into yacht club & agonized through 2 sets of immigration people & one fumbling Customs guy – nobody seemed to know what they were doing. Dined at yacht club & got back to boat just at dark. What we've seen of Colon so far looks bad – tenants of housing devts. burning garbage in their yards, drunks lying on the sidewalk, garbage & trash everywhere. Fenced-in yacht club looks rather like a small fortified factory, but facilities seem OK.*

CHAPTER 8

Canal

Beseiged in Panama, Mary and Homer mugged, Kelly P.

1991

We spent 34 days in Colon, a most aptly-named community. The place was rife with crime – even the police warned us not to walk through certain sections downtown. Much of it looked like London after the Blitz, with buildings collapsing in the city center, rubble and trash everywhere. The police station, now closed, was shot full of holes from the U.S. invasion to kidnap Noriega.

At least half the sailors in the yacht club, which was sealed off with high wire fences and armed guards, had personal crime stories to tell. Three Finnish yachties, rather large gents, had been held up at gunpoint, in a crowded restaurant, by the party dining at the next table. Ian Rowan, an American sailor anchored with his family near me, had the strap of his wristwatch slashed through and the watch stolen as he walked into town. Bleeding and in his flip-flops, he chased the thief into a housing project but made an abrupt retreat when he found a number of the inmates staring balefully at him.

There was Steve, a bashful young city planner from Chicago who had sailed his 12-foot double-ender SQUEAK down the Mississippi and was trying to hitch a ride through the canal with his tiny boat as deck cargo on a bigger yacht. He was recovering from being robbed at knifepoint in Colon, but was still planning to sail down the west coast of South America.

I was fortunate. I had a bodyguard – Ange, who was planning to head home from here but was supposed to help with the trip through the canal to the Pacific side. With his dark shaggy beard and that *I-don't-give-a-fuck* stare in his piercing blue eyes, he seemed to be all shoulders. People tended to keep out of his way and I was glad to have him walking shotgun on our forays downtown.

My daughter Mary and her friend Homer Fishman were to join us: that would give us the necessary four for the canal transit. Kelly Pokorney, a Florida woman who had answered a "Crew Wanted" ad I'd run in *Cruising World* magazine, was to come aboard in Panama City at the other end of the canal. We had exchanged letters and had one brief meeting in Florida when I was visiting my folks. She seemed congenial and said she had some sailing experience.

But everybody was delayed in arriving, and Ange and I spent the time shooting pool in the yacht club bar and sneaking an occasional nervous probe into downtown Colon. I also labored with arrangements to buy a life raft (insisted upon by my daughter) and have it shipped from Rhode Island. After a long struggle with the Panamanian bureaucracy it finally arrived, shortly before we planned to leave.

Another diversion was the Canal itself. Since the regulations required four people on board a yacht during transit, it was easy to sign on another boat as a volunteer deckhand. I went through the canal aboard the 42-foot ketch HARLEQUIN with an Austrian couple, Wolf and Antonia. Fellow deckhands were Ian and Josh Rowan, sons of the American sailor whose watch was stolen. These kids were making a career out of transiting the canal on other people's boats. They loved it.

The canal itself was a marvel of efficiency and purpose with its six 1,000-foot locks and the powerful little "locomotives" that move huge ships in and out. Every vessel must have a canal pilot, with yachts likely to get the young apprentice pilots. Ours on HARLEQUIN was Raoul, a lanky young guy who was half-German, half-Panamanian and slightly daft. He guzzled Austrian beer throughout the trip, let us do all the navigating and steering, and erupted in occasional loud monkey-howls as we traversed sections of jungle. I hoped we'd have him aboard when TURTLE DOVE went through.

Slow-moving yachts anchor overnight in the big freshwater lake halfway through the canal. It offers excellent fishing and swimming, and Raoul left us here. He was replaced next day by Ron, an older American who insisted on steering the whole way and kept demanding that we go faster because "I want to get through early." Everybody agreed that he was a total asshole.

There was much talk about the takeover of the canal by Panama, a process already underway and due to be completed by the end of 1999. Americans seemed to agree that the takeover would be a disaster. Nobody gave much credence to my argument that similar predictions of doom, which didn't materialize, were made when Egypt took over operation of the Suez Canal.

By now Ange had departed after the inevitable squabble – this one brought on when I said I was tired of having to pay for everything, even a stamp for his postcard, as well as the postcard itself. I felt quite alone as I saw him stalking off toward the airport ticket counter.

Mary and Homer finally arrived in Panama City and we bused the 40 miles back to the boat in Colon, arriving there about 2 a.m. My new crew gaped nervously out the grimy bus windows as we trundled through the dim streets, past ruined buildings and occasional slumbering bystanders who looked just as ruined. We climbed off into the darkness and hurriedly loaded everything into a taxi piloted by an elderly gent who seemed equally apprehensive. It was a relief to get inside the yacht club fences. We loaded everything into the little dinghy and motored carefully out to TURTLE DOVE with very little freeboard showing.

My new crew were appalled at the misery of Colon. They agreed with me that we should move out quickly, and I dispatched them next day to load up with fruit and vegetables at the market downtown.

We started through the canal early on Feb. 21, 1991, rafting together in the locks with Mike of California and Pru of New Zealand on their boat, RAINBOW. For line handlers we had all five of the Rowan family, distributed between the two boats. We anchored and swam in the enormous man-made freshwater lake in the center of the isthmus. I noted in the log:

> *A nice day & an exciting trip. Our pilot, the Yugoslav Lugo, is a friendly chap, but wish we had Raoul. 8-year-old Ian caught the only fish – his first. Much excitement. He was awarded a 25-cent prize. A quiet, still night & next day a beauteous morning w. much swimming.*

Next day we worked our way through the last three locks and settled in on a mooring off the Balboa Yacht Club to wait for Kelly Pokorney to arrive. We were in a new ocean, and we had celebratory drinks at the club and listened to much Friday-night revelry till the small hours. This yacht club on the Pacific side seemed a little more agreeable, though the 20-foot Pacific tides made things awkward. At low tide the main dock was perched ridiculously high above the water on long thin legs, and it was a steep descent to the club launch. All the yachts were on moorings, and nobody used their dinghies because of the strong tidal current.

Next day Mary and Homer walked through a nearby park to attend Sunday church services and were mugged as they returned. The two young robbers menaced them with homemade knives, pulled two rings off Mary's fingers, stole their backpacks and took off on foot. Mary and Mike ran after them as a truckload of soldiers passed by. When the thieves heard them yell for help to the soldiers they dropped the backpacks and escaped. It was a frightening experience but it could have been worse – they only lost the rings and their pride – particularly Homer's, who berated himself for not battling the robbers. He is a big strong outdoor guy, but I tried to convince him that no resistance was the right thing against two men with knives.

I spent a day in Panama City, shopping and waiting for Kelly, whose plane was due in that night. She had asked me to book a room for two at a particular hotel and I did so, wondering whether there might be a little romance involved. It was not to be. Kelly arrived and we settled into our hotel room in a businesslike and all-too-chaste manner. Next morning we took a cab to the yacht club to join Mary and Homer and complete our stowage for the Pacific. We were still sorting gear when our taxi returned. The driver had discovered my newly-purchased roll of charts, forgotten in the back seat, and had returned with them. I was impressed by his honesty – it did a lot toward improving my impressions of Panama. I gave him a handsome tip and heartfelt thanks. We were going to need those charts.

CHAPTER 9

Pacific

Balboa, Crossing the Line, Galapagos, 3,000 miles to Marquesas.

1991

Feb. 27:

We're off into the Pacific!

Motored in almost no wind till it came up a little around 2 p.m. Shortly after turning off the engine & putting it into reverse we found the new bolt through the propeller shaft broken clean off! Sailed through the night w. following breeze, making pretty good speed. Changed to 255 degrees, heading for Cocos I. & trending away from coast of Panama.

Wind got lighter as dark progressed. Caught a fine Spanish mackerel (maybe 7 pounds) and had her for dinner, then lunch next day. Mike put a new bolt in prop shaft, but we kept engine off and didn't try it out. A frustrating night of almost no wind – made little progress. Trying to head west toward Cocos.

March 2:

A rainy, uncomfortable night slatting around w. almost no wind at all . . . Checked out again by a U.S. Navy plane, Mare was seasick last night – poor kid. Lost our good new fishing lure – something hit it and broke the leader. A lot of lightning last night – fortunately, nothing very close.

March 3:

Yesterday we lost the entire fishing pole – what a bummer! Apparently the sheet for the mizzen staysail tweaked it out of its holder. Now fishing w. a handline.

March 4:

Another day of calms, w. maddening little wind shifts that call for sail changes, then die. Were able to actually move the boat maybe half the night. The Doldrums are truly living up to their name. Motored for awhile yesterday – broke the new bolt Mike had installed. AGAIN! Mary baked bread – excellent. Another spectacular sunrise this morning, followed by a brief rain squall. With the seas so flat & calm, this ocean looks enormous. You can see half a dozen rainstorms under way at almost any time, yet we've had very little rain – just enough this morning for me to wash off with a rag.

(I was depressed about the prop shaft – it was beginning to seem impossible to keep it bolted securely to the engine. We decided to skip Cocos Island and head directly for the Galapagos. This was disappointing, since we had heard good things about Cocos: that it was almost completely unspoiled, looked after by a single caretaker, and overrun with wild pigs and other animals. I hated missing it, but we didn't dare use the engine for anything except a real emergency. So goodby Cocos, hello, we hoped, Galapagos.)

March 6:

The Doldrums struck back last night – three times, three of us were struggling in wind & lashing rain. Finally took down all sail, but we rolled so bad we put up staysail & double-reefed main, our heavy-weather rig. Sometime during this the wind turned to SSE & has stayed that way. Still sailing w. heavy rig but added storm jib as a steering sail. Works pretty well but not perfectly. Fun to fool w., though. Rolling caused wet floor – a real pain in the ass. Reminded me of Cape May debacle. Visited by big porpoises & pilot whales!

March 7:

> *A booby made repeated passes at the bowsprit & finally landed on the pulpit. Went to sleep & was still there this morning, resting comfortably & allowing us to get close to it.*

March 8:

> *Rained almost all day yesterday & we collected lots of water – will probably arrive w. more than when we started out. Alternator belt (only 6 months old!) broke while charging batteries – SatNav quit in middle of night, of low voltage. Charged batteries w. little portable generator and started it up again, but still went 12 hours or more without a (position) fix. Everything rather wet down below. Not a pleasant night.*

March 9 (estimated 125 miles to go):

> *This morning Kelly told me she'd be leaving in the Galapagos – said she didn't feel safe in TURTLE DOVE. Apparently the engine problems & wet floorboards have done her in. Disappointing news.*

> *Homer & I replaced the broken belt & then (using the little portable generator) drilled a 3/8" hole in prop shaft for a bigger bolt. Then the so-called 3/8" stainless bolt refused to fit (apparently it was metric measurement). Tried to drill hole 1/64" bigger, broke drill. Rigged grinding wheel on little drill & re-ground drill point. It broke again, but not before Homer had managed to drill it. Finally fitted the new bolt in. Hope it works!*

> *Three of us swam overboard in amazingly clear water – then wind came up, but fitfully. Now sailing 220 degrees for Academy Bay on Santa Cruz Island.*

Early next morning:

> *A long & totally uneventful night. Went through at least three 2-hour shifts w. absolutely no wind – much of the time just drifted, w. an anchor light showing & nobody topside.*

(During these periods of dead calm, I realized that Kelly was working hard at attempting to keep the boat pointed in the right direction. I tried to persuade her that the way we were pointed made little difference, since we weren't moving, but she never seemed really convinced.

(I was not hugely surprised when she told me she intended to bail out. It had become apparent that we had large philosophical differences: her late husband had been an Air Force jet pilot who disappeared over Laos in the Viet Nam war, and she was a devout supporter of the U.S. position. I felt quite the opposite, and after a few verbal skirmishes we tried to avoid the subject.)

I was "only interested in pussy," she told me when we talked about her decision to leave. True, "pussy" was fairly high on my list of interests, but I thought I had made this clear in our early exchange of letters, and I also thought I had been careful not to make her feel she was being forced into anything. I didn't like her concluding that I was some sex-crazed demon roaming the seas. Not much I could do about it, apparently.

Kelly was a somewhat reluctant participant in shipboard ceremonies when we crossed the Equator. This was a first for us all, but somebody had to play King Neptune, and I had elected myself. My costume was a mop for a wig, swim goggles, snorkel and flippers; my scepter was the toilet plunger.

My speech:

> *At 10:15 a.m. this Sunday, March 10, 1991, I, King Neptune, by virtue of my authority as Lord of the Deep, do hereby declare that you, lowly personages, have officially Crossed the Line into the Southern Hemisphere.*
>
> *No longer are you pollywogs, also known as Mangy Swabs or Incompetent Bunglers. You have graduated into the ranks of seasoned salts and fellow travelers – you are now true, Grade-A, 100% Shellbacks.*
>
> *You will repeat this oath after me, as I confer your new status upon you with my royal scepter:*
>
> *I, (your name), hereby swear to uphold all the duties and responsibilities of an official Shellback, with all the rights and privileges appertaining thereto, and swear furthermore to participate fully in future ceremonies initiating other lowly pollywogs into our exalted ranks.*

I then declared, waving the plunger furiously:

> "I now pronounce you *SHELLBACKS!*"

The program notes read (*Brief Rabelaisian Grotesqueries To Follow*), but in fact everybody went back to work or sleep. Still, I thought it was a satisfactory ceremony.

March 10:

> *Sighted I. San Cristobal during the afternoon but couldn't see Santa Cruz, our destination. Had a big debate over whether we were headed for the right island – finally decided we did. As night fell, switched to jib only & sailed slowly downwind.*

> *Sighted lights of Academy Bay around 4 a.m. By daybreak we were off the island. Raised main & tacked downwind without engine into harbor, rounded up smartly & dropped anchor among several other yachts & a number of power boats. Yacht SAVANNAH w. Terry & Judy (met in Colon) was here – arrived yesterday.*

Not surprisingly, the Galapagos differed considerably from expectations. I had envisioned barren black lava islets a-crawl with iguanas, the waters a-swarm with seals and fish. We did see some iguanas and seals, but they were hanging around on the doorstep of a thriving small town with grocery stores, restaurants, and even a disco. There were some peculiarities – Mary noted that it was the first place she'd seen where the post office didn't sell stamps (you got them at the drugstore) and the bank didn't change money (you did that at the hotel).

Kelly promptly moved ashore and we didn't see much of her, though she did let us use her hotel room for long-awaited baths. She planned to travel on one of the charter boats to see some of the islands that are off-limits to private yachts.

We threaded our way through the formalities: the port captain asked to see our Visitor's Permit, which everybody knew could be obtained (if at all) only in Ecuador. Since we had no permit, we had to pay a "fine" of about $150 U.S. Then we had to negotiate the length of time we'd be allowed to stay. When we pleaded engine trouble (in this case the truth), we were reluctantly granted five days. Later we learned that almost everybody got five days, and some yachties even longer. We liked the little town of Santa Cruz. We replenished supplies in a small grocery and discovered that food was cheap, apparently subsidized by mainland Ecuador. We hiked out to a beautiful white sand beach, walking down a lane of rough-barked cactus plants as big as full-grown trees. The enormous beach was populated by a lone black iguana which emerged from the sea and stalked slowly along the water's edge, ignoring us altogether.

Back at the boat, Homer and I worked on the propeller shaft and its benighted coupling. After a full day of drilling, fitting and cursing, we thought we had a hookup that should last for some time. We drank beer with Terry and Judy of SAVANNAH, who also were heading for the Marquesas, and decided we'd leave together. We all were a little apprehensive, I think. The run from the Galapagos to the Marquesas is the longest uninterrupted voyage you can make on earth – at midpoint the nearest land is 1,500 miles away (if you don't count the distance straight down to the bottom, which is about three miles below in some places).

March 16:

Up fairly early & away (under engine power!) at 8 a.m. – 3,000 miles to go!

March 17:

A night of calms & slatting around – Mare seasick again, despite patch. Saw Terry's light ahead & in the morning he was still there, way off to the north. Crew & capt. still a bit woozy, but improving after a big spaghetti dinner.

Next day:

Sailing beautifully after a good night, with steady close-reaching wind; heading for what will be for us a record-breaking day's sail. (Already we're at 118 miles with 3 hours to go!) Mike was hit on the chest by a flying squid during the night – this morning I found two more little ones on the deck.

Noon measurement shows 132 miles!

March 20:

A great day so far, navigation-wise. First hit the "Auto-Locate" button & apparently re-programmed the SatNav so it started providing fixes. Second, I managed to work out a star fix (using celestial navigation) where I had used the Starfinder to identify three stars – Altair, Antares & Arcturus. Fix seemed to confirm the SatNav – a proud moment. And beyond that, we're about 100 miles farther along than I'd figured by dead-reckoning! Apparently a considerable favorable current here – great!

March 22:

A new record day's run – 146 miles & under reduced rig to facilitate self-steering (which still isn't working right). Seas somewhat choppy but a pretty good night. Caught a small dolphin-fish (my first) on the handline – a beautiful golden fish which should give us a nice dinner tonight. Another sunny day w. a lot of flying fish zooming by.

March 24, under reefed main and staysail only:

A rather rough night – squally rainy weather moved in about 2 a.m. during Mare's shift. Homer & I out wrestling in big jib, reefing main, removing storm (steering) sail & hoisting staysail. After an hour or so everything subsided to a flat calm – ran engine for awhile (first time, I think, since leaving Galapagos).

Intermittent rain ever since then – everybody's clothes pretty soaked. Boat rolling horribly at the moment, since we really don't have enough sail up.

Next day:

Rained & blew heavily during the afternoon – Mare & I collected about 30 gals. of water, which was pouring off the reefed main like a faucet. Filled the tank. Calm last night & a lot of rolling around – pretty uncomfortable. Today bright & sunny; a hint of the SE Trades has returned. A good day for drying out wet stuff, which we accumulated in large measure yesterday. The sudden calm has broken our great sailing record – only did 51 miles to noon.

March 26 (Jib, staysail, reefed main):

A beautiful moonlit night last night. Today looks good – seems as if we're back in the Trades now. Some kind of small bird flies around the masts at night, crying plaintively. We think we hear porpoises alongside but don't see them. SatNav worked fine yesterday. I think the long-awaited shipboard routine is finally settling in. We think we may hit the halfway point – 1,500 miles – this evening & we plan a party. Everybody invited.

(After a while on a small boat in the ocean it does seem as if your whole world is with you. You find yourself wondering if there will be anybody there when you finally reach shore. And if you're lucky you like the company you've got. I was lucky.

(Homer was an interesting study – big, apparently indestructible, quiet, an agonizingly slow reader, remarkably sensitive and intuitive. He loved outdoor life – thought nothing of paddling a kayak among huge icebergs in his native Alaska. He told me he owned an incontinent dog named Snappy with only two working legs which maneuvered itself around on a little homemade trolley.

(My daughter Mary was bright, sensitive, humorous, cheerful, earnest, absorbed in nature. I liked to watch her in the dark preparing for her watch, shuffling around down below making tea, wearing her baseball hat backward, whistling softly, collecting her regular "nest" of blankets for a three-hour watch. She was a great shipmate.)

March 27:

A ship passing to port! Our second sighting only since leaving the Galapagos. Looks like a big fishing vessel – maybe Japanese? Tried to call on VHF; no response. We're almost exactly at the halfway spot – will have a celebratory drink. Weather unsettled last night & this morning – calms, rain, then gusty shifting winds. Homer thought he saw lights to the south. He also visited by porpoises. Had our "Halfway to Marquesas" dinner – canned ham, sauerkraut, peas, boiled potatoes w.

fresh – baked bread. Very good. Big fish swimming ahead of us this morning – did not hit at our lure.

March 28: (Reefed main, jib, steering sail):

Yesterday we saw four ships – all, apparently, part of a Korean fishing fleet. Talked briefly w. one guy, whose English was understandable (he kept apologizing for it.) He gave us a radar bearing & distance, so apparently we do show up on radar. Also heard one yacht, DOLPHIN, talking to the same ship, but we couldn't reach them on our set. We think they're behind us. Self-steering rig working better now, though still not great.

March 29:

Rained briefly in afternoon & we had a sail drill that proved to be unnecessary: squall did not materialize. Spotted more Korean fishing boats & tried to talk w. one but he had little English. He, or his brother, passed us during the night. A spectacular full moon was almost dazzling – we easily could see the horizon to take star sights at 9 p.m. Trolled all day; caught nada.

April 1 (Full main & jib):

Another beauty day. Wind shifted to NE & jibed onto other tack – first time mainsail has been on the port side in about two weeks. Took more star sights @ 8 p.m. last night – came out well. Feeling good about celestial nav – Mare is catching me out in mistakes now. (Prof. gets his comeuppance.)

April 3:

Wind went light today. For first time, added water (15 gals.) from jerrycans to main tank.

April 6 (Big jib only):

Caught a weird snakelike fish w. big sharp ugly teeth during the night – threw it back; looked too mean. Hot this morning. We seem to be back in the Doldrums.

April 7 (Full main, jib w. pole):

Wind returned but almost from east – we're attempting to run wing & wing. Big fish followed lure but refused to strike. Mike baked a casserole – smells excellent. Everybody doing a lot of sleeping.

April 9 (Noon):

Strong E wind all night. Today we left the big chart & went to the more detailed Marquesas chart – at 12:30 p.m. we altered course to 235 degrees, to take us 10 miles south of Ua Huka during the night (we hope) and get us to Nuku Hiva some time around mid-day tomorrow. First person to sight land is to be bought a fine dinner by the others. Today a long-tailed kind of gull made two passes at our trailing lure. Fortunately he didn't get it on either try. Feeling excited as we approach landfall.

5:30 p.m.:

LAND HO! Looks like Ua Huka off the starboard bow, maybe 40 miles off. Homer wins the dinner!

April 10 (Noon – Full main only):

A morning of contrasts – trade wind all night w. full main & jib, then two strong squalls this morning that had us down to double-reefed main & jib – roughest weather we've had on the entire trip! Now sunny & back to trades. Nuku Hiva about five miles to starboard – craggy & green & steep w. a jagged skyline – spectacular. Even more so is Ua Pu, to the south, with huge tall volcanic plugs rearing above its skyline – Bali Hai for sure. It will be exciting to walk on land again – it's been 25 days and 2,750 miles!

CHAPTER 10

South Pacific

Nuku Hiva, Fatu Hiva, Tahiti, "Mad Czech", Suvarov out.

1991

April 10, (4 p.m. Anchored in Baie de Taiohae, Nuku Hiva):

Of course the engine refused to start – batteries too low. We ran the Honda generator for an hour while slowly tacking toward the harbor entrance; once inside we got the motor started and we chugged up and anchored with about 10 other yachts. We were immediately visited by three of them – CACIQUE, a 27-footer skippered by Rhona, an Englishwoman, and NAGADA II, both last seen in Colon, and then in came ELVIKA, the unpleasant Norwegian vessel last seen in San Blas.

Suddenly we had that "OK, what do we do now?" feeling that sometimes hits you in a secure anchorage after a long passage. The shore looked inviting, but it seemed too difficult to muster the strength to reach it. We chatted with our visitors, who stayed in their bobbing dinghies because we hadn't cleared Customs and Immigration yet, and we collected the usual data – where to find water, groceries, telephones, Authorities, where to dump the trash we'd accumulated, etc. But we decided to stay on board awhile.

Next morning we swam around and under the boat and scraped off thousands of big ugly gooseneck barnacles, two-inch appendages that somehow had attached themselves en route. The bottom was covered with them. Also two large sucker fish had suctioned themselves onto the hull near the keel. They were reluctant to leave but finally wriggled away when I prodded them with a scrub brush. Apparently they had traveled a long way.

Our planked deck needed salt-water soaking. We had been sailing under a hot sun in relatively calm water so long that the planks were dried out and shrunken. The deck had leaked copiously when we started taking heavy spray approaching Nuku Hiva.

This was Taiohae, port of entry for the French-controlled Marquesas Islands. The little town stretched along the harbor's inner curve, where gentle rollers washed a clean white sand beach rimmed with palms. In a far corner of the harbor where there was a modest cluster of buildings we could see a big boat that turned out to be the ferry connecting other spots on the island – the interior was so steep there were few roads. Beyond the ferry dock a narrow paved road wound past a pretty little park, a post office and the gendarme's station. There were flowers everywhere. The authorities seemed easy-going: on learning we were headed for Tahiti they said we could wait until we arrived there to post the required bonds. (To discourage penniless sailors from settling in, the French require arriving yachties to deposit the price of one-way plane fare to their nearest home port – in our case about $500.)

On our first morning ashore we saw horses, spurred on by boys riding bareback, madly galloping through shallow waves along the beach, – a memorable scene with the deep green mountains rearing up behind them. We bought big pampelmousse (sounds so much better than grapefruit) and other fresh stuff at a little market on the waterfront. Homer set off on foot to explore native villages in the mountains and Mary and I had some welcome time to ourselves. But she stayed only three days and then took the ferry to the island airport. From there she flew to Tahiti, then on to Alaska and home. It was a real wrench to say goodbye to her.

Three days later, Homer and I motored to Baia Taioa, locally known as Daniel's Bay. We had been told it was a perfectly – protected little anchorage with good water, and so it was – so well hidden that we almost missed it. A sharp right turn between steep black rock walls, another right, and we were in a lovely quiet little harbor with a grassy meadow, a rushing river and a little house next to a sandy beach – Daniel's place.

Already at anchor here were NAGADA II, which had moved down from the main harbor, AFRODITE, and AMATEUR, a small steel sloop painted red and manned by a friendly German single-hander.

Daniel was a stocky smiling man with white teeth, bushy black hair and skin the color of milk chocolate. He helped us fill our water jugs at his well. Next day we set off to see a 2,000-foot waterfall, climbing a twisting path in a narrow valley through coconut palms. The rocky trail was marked at each turn by little monuments of rocks carefully piled in stacks. From a distance they looked like small figures silently standing there – an eerie sight in the half-light filtering between the trees. The waterfall was a thin veil of misty water drifting down a sheer black rock face that disappeared above the tree tops. The falling water formed a shallow black pool surrounded by the rock cairns standing silently in the gloom. We weren't sorry to return to the harbor. That scene was a little spooky.

The little river near Daniel's house flowed through coconut groves and over rounded rocks into the harbor. We washed clothes in it, stripped naked and splashed around in waist-deep pools. The water was cool and clear. It felt wonderful. We stayed there two days and then left for the island of Hiva Oa, planning to continue on to Fatu Hiva, where the Norwegian anthropologist Thor Heyerdahl had once hoped to found an island paradise.

April 19:

At 2:30 p.m. passing the spectacular skyline of Ua Pu, with its steep jagged pinnacles hidden in the clouds. Tacked all night and in a.m. were about 20 m. west of Hiva Oa. But that 20 mi. turned out to be tough – first not enough wind, then too much. Finally motor-tacked through stiff NE wind & a hellish chop to Havia Menu Bay, a little bay at NW corner of the island. Put 2 anchors down as wind turned north & blew right down the bay.

We spent a nervous night at anchor, conscious of the menacing rocks along both sides of the funnel-shaped harbor. Not a promising spot, with a north wind blowing down it. But the wind eased at nightfall and in the morning we rowed the dinghy ashore. It was worth it for what was on shore – a beautiful little ranch with nobody there but wild horses, thatched-roof huts and a waterfall pouring into a crystal-clear pool surrounded by rocks & trees with flowers. The pool emptied into a little stream running down through the beach. Lots of coconuts, limes, oranges & grapefruit. We picked a few. Homer climbed the hill & said the waterfall came from a spring up top. The stream was almost too cold. A lovely lovely spot.

(Some hours later I discovered that the lovely spot had been home to hordes of biting midges or no-see-ums. My legs and arms blossomed into bright-red itching welts that took weeks to subside.)

We left at sunup April 23 and sailed all day to get to Fatu Hiva. It was almost dark when we reached the harbor, and we had some anxious moments trying to find our way. We were greatly relieved when one of the anchored yachts inside the harbor turned on its masthead lights to guide us in.

April 24:

> *TURTLE DOVE had a quiet third birthday yesterday – seemed fitting that she'd be in a place as spectacularly different as Fatu Hiva. The rock formations are so incredible they look almost fake, Disney-ish. Went ashore twice during the day – first to explore, then for water. Filled up everything, about 50 gals. worth. Boys were flailing big octopuses on the jetty, apparently to soften them up for eating. Invited to join some young delinquents in pot-smoking; declined.*

> *Apparently most commerce here is by barter. Yesterday traded fishing sinkers for fish, a cheap sewing kit (left by the departed Kelly) for five tangerines. May do some more swapping today. With the possible exception of the San Blas Indian village, this is the most foreign-looking place I've seen yet.*

(Fatu Hiva seemed to be just beginning to move into the 20th Century. The island's first public telephone booth was under construction. Many of the native huts displayed tapa, a kind of primitive heavy paper made from tree bark pounded flat, then decorated with intricate designs. At the same time, along the same trail in several of the same huts, I saw television sets showing reruns of *I Love Lucy*).

April 25:

> *Leisurely upped anchors, said goodbye to Ulrich & Marge, the folks on SPIRIT OF SYDNEY who had guided us in with their masthead light, & departed for the Tuomotus. A thunderstorm to the south appears to be dissipating.*

> *Saw a spectacular 'hole in the wall' – a rectangular slot cut by Nature completely through a mountain ridge running into the sea, which we hadn't noticed on entering in the dark. Took pix. A professional photog would have a field day here . . . Escorted out by a herd of porpoises, maybe 100, as we leave the island's wind shadow. They criss-cross smoothly in front of our bowsprit, snorting & twisting & jumping without apparent effort. Beautiful friendly wild animals.*

The Tuomotous, our next destination, were known to earlier mariners as the Dangerous Archipelago. Completely unlike the jagged volcanic peaks of the Marquesas, these islands are coral atolls, so low in the water that they are below the horizon and invisible from only a few miles away. Even in clear weather they were difficult to spot before the development of electronic navigation, and in bad conditions a mariner might sight them too late to steer safely away. It took us five days to cover the 500 miles to Manihi, the nearest island with a navigable pass into a sheltering lagoon.

April 30, 7 a.m.:

> *Landfall on Manihi atoll – low-lying & palm-fringed. Motored through the pass against a hellish outgoing tidal current – sailing directions said 7 knots max, & it seemed at least that. Threaded between big coral heads & anchored in lee of a motu (one of a ring of islands forming the atoll). Water a million shades of blue, like the Bahamas. Our first atoll.*

We might well have come to grief in that pass if a local outboard-powered skiff hadn't come out to pilot us through. The two young guys aboard stayed just ahead, beckoning us to follow as we churned away in the middle of the stream, making almost no headway and praying that the engine wouldn't quit. Our guides led us over to one side, where the current wasn't so fierce, and we slowly worked our way through. Once into the lagoon all was peaceful and serene.

We anchored near MERCATOR, a big wooden ketch sailed by a Canadian and his Kiwi girl friend. The water was so clear we could see the big coral heads below. We carefully dropped anchor to keep clear of them, but later learned that some sailors deliberately wrap their anchor chain around the coral to give them secure holding. This usually meant diving to unwrap when it was time to leave, so it was well to pick a coral head that wasn't too deep.

We quickly fell into the island life, watching schools of fish all around us, exploring the enormous barrier reef connecting the ring of islands (called "motus"), and observing what seemed to be the only local business: the production of cultured pearls in captive oysters. The oysters were big and flat, gray to black on the outside but cream-colored and iridescent inside the shell. If a foreign object like a grain of sand gets inside an oyster the creature slowly covers it with a translucent coating. The sand eventually becomes a natural pearl. But natural pearls are hard to come by, so men (in this case, Japanese technicians) insert a tiny plastic ball into an oyster, then wait while the shellfish turns it into a pearl.

Native divers bring up the wild oysters, the technicians perform their delicate surgery, and the little living pearl factories are then suspended on strings from floating rafts while they do their thing. It's a profitable enterprise.

The weather was almost perfect: a good thing, because we were anchored on one side of a big salt-water lagoon studded with coral heads that reached the surface at low tide. In the lee of the nearby motus we were fine, but it looked as if a major wind shift could put us in serious trouble. This didn't happen and we spent five happy days there, entertained royally by the locals who worked in the pearl business. We were sorry to leave.

May 4, 1:30 p.m.:

> *Chugged through the pass, with the current this time, after a party-filled 5 days.*
> *I felt really sorry to leave the natives – particularly Ellis, the town drunk, who*
> *entertained, wined & dined us. (We stayed over at his place one night after an*
> *all-male beer-music blast.) Amazingly generous, warm & hospitable people, and*
> *the most musical bunch I've ever seen. They all play everything, including spoons*
> *& armpits. One guy was belching in tune – any minute I expected him to start*
> *farting in rhythm.*

(At one point during the all-nighter at Ellis's place, when the armpit instruments were tuning up, Homer whispered to me, *"Is this where it gets bizarre?"* We learned later that Ellis became so taken with the folks on MERCATOR, who left just after we did, that he offered to guide them out through the pass and then refused to leave the boat. They had to stop at the town dock and literally drag him off. I wondered what would happen to him. Maybe he would attach himself to another boat, rather like the suckerfish we found on our keel in Nuku Hiva.)

I wrote in the log:

> *The reef next to our anchorage was so beautiful, loaded with fish, like swimming*
> *in a tropical aquarium. A lovely lovely experience – I feel sad to be leaving. Next*
> *stop Rangiroa – maybe more of the same?*

May 6, 10:30 a.m.:

> *Came through the big wide deep pass (a light current w. us, this time) to anchor*
> *off the village of Avatorn in Rangiroa after a second night of trying to sail w. no*
> *wind. Turned on engine at 5 a.m. & motored the remaining 22 miles. The lagoon*
> *here is beautiful – magnificent white sand & coral & clear clean water, teeming*
> *with fish. Tomorrow we will swim/drift the pass, in company with MERCATOR's*
> *gang, who were here when we arrived.*

May 8, 11 a.m.:

> *Departed Rangiroa, reluctantly – not so much for leaving the natives, who were*
> *rather stand-offish, but for leaving the crystal-clear water, beautiful coral & more*
> *fish than I've ever seen before. Caught four of the little zebra-striped guys in the*
> *landing net last evening & ate them. Tasted good (but I felt guilty – they're so*
> *trusting.)*

We reached Papeete, (pronounced 'Pap-ay-*ay*-tay", capital of Tahiti, in two days, following old landing-craft ferryboats through a wide pass with enormous rollers. We joined the line of boats anchored pointing out into the harbor, attached with long stern lines to big old iron bollards set along the shore. Traffic rushed by continually, just a few feet away. We were almost in the center of a busy, exciting (and expensive) city. I stayed there almost a month, during which:

- Homer finally left and I acquired two new crew: Sid, "the mad Czech," and Gilles, "the French boy."
- I unsuccessfully tried to recruit as crew a pretty American lady who visited TURTLE DOVE and said, declining my invitation, "I had expected something more *exquisite.*"
- Mike and I attended Sunday services in the big church just opposite our mooring place, reluctantly accepted seats of honor in the very front, and were bowled over by the many-part hymn-singing of the lady parishioners, large dark women wearing wide-brimmed white hats and colorful long gowns. Their music absolutely overwhelmed the church.
- I was given 2,000 French Polynesian francs, instead of the 200 I wanted, when I used my credit card at a local bank, thereby wiping out my entire bank balance.
- I paid many visits to the food and drink vans that set up every night around the harbor rim, offering everything from crepes to octopuses to ice cream.
- Homer spent a day out on one of the small native fishing boats tied up along the harbor wall, returning without a fish but with a beautiful hand-made tuna lure.

Papeete was a bustling, sophisticated, very French city. Prices were high, food was excellent, tourists were all over the place. Beautiful native women were everywhere also, as well as burly workmen with flowers tucked behind their ears, wearing hard hats and grinning at me as they rode by in the back of big trucks.

Again I was looking for crew. I mounted a large sign saying CREW WANTED on the boat's stern facing the shore and its busy traffic, and was rewarded one night by a knocking on the hull and somebody calling, "Skipper! Skipper!"

Peering over the side, I found a young fellow treading water, wearing only boxer shorts and an earnest expression. It was Sid, later to be thought of as "The Mad Czech". His real name was Zdenek Hanzlik. He was rawboned with reddish hair and looked to be in his late 20s. He spoke English well but with a heavy accent. (Later I found that English was just one of his seven languages.) He was on a kind of personal world tour, though he would insist that he was not a tourist. He carried one bag containing spare clothes and travel gear, including a large and beloved leather David-and-Goliath sling he had acquired in Peru.

He was a trained Diesel mechanic who had fled Czechoslovakia, had worked on a Russian ship, had lived in England for some time and then decided to leave to look for better job opportunities. He had had a tough childhood – he told me once that for him it was a very special Christmas if he received a single orange as a present. He had never seen peanut butter. He was a mechanical genius but he tried to open cans from the side rather than the top.

He loved machinery, especially if it wasn't working. He didn't like people very much. At our first meeting I asked him if he had a girl friend and he said he had been married "for a while." Asked how long, he said, "17 days." As time progressed, I felt surprised it had lasted that long.

Sid seemed a little strange from the beginning, but I was impressed by his credentials. He carried several official certificates attesting to his mechanical training, particularly on diesel engines. I liked that.

Gilles, "the French boy", came aboard as a kind of afterthought. He was around 20 years old, good-looking. I thought of him as a kind of seagoing playboy. He said he'd sailed on racing sailboats. He joined us near the end of our stay in Tahiti and didn't stay long.

From the anchorage in Papeete I had an excellent view of Moorea to the west, its jagged mountains silhouetted in every sunset. One of the best photos I ever took showed a racing canoe with a dozen paddlers at sunset, with those big Moorea mountains looming behind. The paddlers were in the harbor almost every night, practicing for the big Bastille Day races coming up soon.

I had read that Moorea was the most beautiful island in the world. Now I was about to see for myself. We left Tahiti with five on board – we were giving a free ride to Mark and Polly, a honeymooning couple who wanted to visit Moorea. They slept on deck that night and left us extra beer and lunch goodies when they took off next morning.

June 7 (Moorea):

> *Motored all through Cook Bay, Moorea, taking pix – a truly beautiful place. Then motor-sailed out west for two miles into Oponohue Bay, the one shown in most photos, including the cover of Charlie's Charts. Anchored in famous Robinson's Cove – two anchors at bow with stern tied to palm tree, just like in the movies. Sat around all evening marveling at the great brooding peaks all around us . . . . Gilles plans to return to Tahiti tomorrow to get a camera being sent to him. In outer Cook Bay we saw FINBACK & ROAMA, in inner harbor KILO (Phil Kennedy). In Oponohue Bay saw MOPENO (last seen in San Blas) and one other yacht. In this entire beautiful bay there are just 3 sailboats anchored, including us!*

Sid and I hiked up a steep paved road past blooming flowers and greenery to a mountain lookout. Later we hitch-hiked along the far side of the bay and caught a ride with a man who stopped his car to show us "the pig hotel" – a little wooded peninsula occupied by half a dozen enormous black hogs, rooting away contentedly or dozing in the sun.

Four days later I noted:

> *. . . Stayed an extra day yesterday waiting for Gilles, on his second (!) trip back to Tahiti for the long-awaited camera. He got it this time, but didn't return until 3:30 p.m. Meantime, SPIRIT OF SYDNEY (Julia, Rob & George) came in, anchored near us & invited us for chicken dinner. Had a fine meal w. them.*

> *Moorea comes as close to paradise as anything I've seen – lush, spectacular scenery, much of it looking like Europe or Scandinavia. Fat sheep & cows grazing in green meadows (soon to be a golf course, thanks to the ubiquitous Japanese) – signs posted along a beautiful road, saying,* A NATURAL PARK FOR ALL TO ENJOY, *and* OUR MOTHER ISLAND IS NOT FOR RENT. *Hard to leave this place – I'd like to come back.*

But we did leave, and made stops at a series of Society Islands – Huahine, Raiatea, Tahaa. At Tahaa we put out two anchors in deep water close to shore, trying to keep out of a blustery wind, and in the morning we found both anchors well and truly fouled, much too deep for free diving.

It looked as if we might have to cut the chains and leave both anchors below. Then an athletic-looking couple motored past in a skiff and we appealed to them. They were Miriam and Jean-Marie, an Italian pair who lived nearby. To our enormous relief, they said they would return with Scuba gear. Half an hour later Jean-Marie was diving on the anchors. He managed to unhook one (he said it was about 80 feet down), and this allowed us enough maneuvering room to get the other anchor free.

We thanked them profusely (they wouldn't even let us pay to refill their air tanks) and then motored to the head of the bay, where fierce gusts continued to batter us but the water was shallow. Gilles found us there, and then announced that he was leaving. I wasn't surprised. All this dithering over a camera had seemed odd to me. But he'd been with us less than two weeks, and I was puzzled over what had gone wrong. I never found out for sure. Sid told me later that Gilles had said something about language problems. I wondered whether Sid had been unkind to him. It was quite possible, I thought.

We left June 18, the first anniversary of my father's death, for Bora Bora (last of the Societies, and James Michener's favorite in the South Pacific.). Bora Bora had a good harbor with moorings and a yacht club with a hospitable bar. Sid and I walked over much of the island, noting the excitement and extensive preparations under way to celebrate Bastille Day in three weeks. (I had been told that the Society Islands make more of this day than the French in Paris.)

I liked Bora Bora, but it didn't seem to live up to Michener's rhapsodies. I thought Moorea was far more beautiful and less built up. And it had the pig hotel, too.

We left June 25, heading for Maupiti, 25 miles away. But our progress was so slow that I decided to skip this one and aim straight for Suvarov, about 700 miles along our route to American Samoa. It was not comfortable sailing. The wind was strong and dead astern and we rolled nastily. I discovered that Sid was a projectile vomiter – he could be engrossed in a conversation, suddenly turn his head to spew violently over the side, then resume talking where he had left off. At least he remembered to turn his head.

The log entry at noon June 29:

> *106 miles. Still another difficult night, with heavy rolling – scuppers under now & then. Uncomfortable sleeping. Caught a fish at last – a 10-lb. tuna or bonito after a bigger one busted my homemade fishing rod all to hell, broke the line & made off with my new heavy-duty lure & leader.*
>
> *Sid asked me this morning if the ship could capsize (!). Apparently he was worried about it. Practiced sail-handling w. him. Now preparing to jibe – Suvarov now lies about 145 miles to the west.*

July 1, Noon:

> *135 miles – a record for this trip. Sailed fairly hard last night, trying to reach Suvarov in good daylight. At 1 p.m. we're maybe 10 miles off, but haven't yet seen it due to a succession of rain squalls which reduce visibility. Going to be pretty unsettling if we miss it altogether – but even more if we run into it in the rain. So I am, hopefully, aiming for the NE corner so we can veer off safely if it suddenly looms ahead. Here comes more rain. Argh.*

3 p.m.:

> *Now passing Suvarov – big bummer! A half-gale blew up w. big seas as we approached, and I decided not to attempt the somewhat tricky pass into the lagoon. Big disappointment. So it's on to Samoa – another 500 miles or so.*

(It took some time for me to recover from watching Suvarov fade behind us in the rain. I'd read about Tom Neale, the semi-hermit who lived there alone for almost five years, (he wrote a book called *An Island to Oneself*), and I really wanted to see the place and rest awhile. I was still chagrined when we reached American Samoa, but then I learned that Suvarov had had a serious outbreak of dengue fever, and the few yachts which stopped there were being held under strict quarantine when they arrived in Pago Pago. Some consolation, at least.

July 5, 3 p.m.:

90 miles. Arrived Pago Pago (pronounced "Pango Pango") after a few misadventures – heavy rain squalls during the night, then engine broke a belt when we started it & without charging the batteries ran down, then Honda generator wouldn't run. Sid had to repair both while I jogged away from island under reefed main in a blinding squall. Finally fixed generator, used it to start the engine, and made it in, tied up w. difficulty at Customs dock & waited for officials, all weekend long. But everybody very friendly. And I got packages & mail Sat. morning.

A total of 1,141 miles (plus a few more when knotlog not running) in 11 days – not shabby at all.

CHAPTER II

Tonga

Pago Pago poor, W. Samoa better, "New Potatoes", Vava'u.

1991

American Samoa:

We spent more than a month here, with my first favorable impression slowly diminishing. The place seemed to embody the worst of both worlds in its name: arrogance in America, indolence in Samoa.

The harbor was a magnificent deep sheltered anchorage, excellent for vessels of any size, but it was enveloped in an awful stink from two big tuna fish canneries. And yacht anchors frequently failed to take hold because the beautiful harbor was fouled on the bottom with plastic bags, apparently washed in from freshwater streams where they had been discarded. Walking back from the yacht club one night I was solicited by a middle-aged prostitute who got up close and personal while a big car with an unseen driver hovered nearby. On Friday nights Samoan women spread blankets on the sidewalk around the outdoor market to play 10 Bingo cards at once. Much of the local population was on welfare, I was told.

The U.S. bureaucracy was clearly working, which had its benefits. Since I had turned 62, I applied for and started receiving Social Security payments, which certainly helped. A big military hospital nearby reportedly had excellent service. Mail delivery

(Poste Restante) was efficient and reliable. I ordered a new fishing rod and received it with no Customs charge.

In town there were several good pizzerias, a number of dark barrooms festooned with signs warning about gangs and fighting, a place with great ice cream cones. I tried to have an outboard motor mount repaired at a local welding shop and finally, after several weeks of waiting, persuaded the owner to let Sid finish the job.

Once again, here were Rhona and Gene on CACIQUE, and Norbert on AMATEUR. We became friendly with David Johnson and Catie Biau, his French wife, on their big American sloop ARIEL. We went with them in a rented car on a tour of outlying villages, places where you had to stop walking or even talking when the 5 p.m. prayer bell rang. People might throw stones at you if you didn't, we were told.

David and Catie asked us for dinner aboard one night and David served a gourmet casserole lovingly made of shrimp and other delicacies, obviously his pride and joy. Sid silently surveyed his serving before tasting it and then asked, "Can I have ketchup?" David stiffly announced that there was none on board. So much for French cookery and Czech appetite.

I talked with the cook on one of the multi-million-dollar net seiners docked along the shore, each ship carrying its powerful net-spreading boat drawn up onto the stern deck and its jaunty little fish-spotting helicopter parked on top. The cook told me these ships measure the size of the tuna schools in tons, not in numbers. They freeze their catch on board and often wait, fully loaded, for several weeks to unload the frozen catch at the cannery. They make a *lot* of money.

I was glad to leave the place.

My first entry in a new log book, purchased in Pago Pago, is dated *Aug. 12, 1991*:

> *Departed after almost 5 weeks in this strange place. Engine vibrating heavily, apparently due to load of barnacles on prop – harbor too dirty to go swimming. Heading for Apia, Western Samoa.*

Aug 13, 5 p.m.:

> *Arrived in Apia after a slow 27-hour sail – almost no wind most of the night. W. Samoa looked beautiful as we sailed along the northern shore – saw a no. of waterfalls & spectacular mountain ridges, all coated w. greenery. Turned into Apia Harbor & there found MERCATOR, ARIEL, AMATEUR & Ron of MALIESH, last seen in Grenada, now heading home to Australia. So far, Apia looks very nice, especially the police marching band & parade which parades the colors every weekday at 8 a.m., the policemen all decked out in white helmets & blue lava-lavas. Quaint & impressive. The band sounded good, too.*

Western Samoa, not many miles distant from American Samoa, was rather poor, but it had a much greater feel of independence and self-sufficiency. The people seemed proud of their island. (Years later I saw pictures of thousands who turned out in the middle of the night to cheer on the Western Samoa football team competing in the World Cup, televised on a huge outdoor screen.)

With David and Catie we walked past thatched-roof houses with rolled-up straw mats for walls and all the household furnishings wide open for viewing. We visited a natural waterslide in a lovely park-like setting where a narrow stream rushed down a glade and plunged into a deep black pool. The stream bed was coated with dark fine weed, as slippery as glass. While the rest of us sat down in the chute and sedately slid over the edge, Sid managed to stand up and dive from the brink. It looked dangerous and I was startled, but he landed safely in the pool. He did it several times.

This is where Robert Louis Stevenson lived and wrote. I could see why he loved the place.

We left Aug. 24 and took four days to cover the 180 miles to Niuatoputapu Island, part of the Kingdom of Tonga though a long way from the rest of the country. Several yachties had told me this was a "must-see" island. Everybody had trouble saying its name: "*New Potatoes*" was the best most of them could do.

Wed., Aug. 28, 1 p.m.:

> *Tacked back & forth all night, making almost no headway in the chop. Finally started engine at 7 a.m. and motor-tacked to Niuatoputapu (I think I'm learning how to pronounce it.)*

> *Here were Norbert on AMATEUR and Dave on HALCYON, plus the Dutch couple on 24-foot ASEALOTH. Negotiated the well-marked pass w/out difficulty & anchored just off the town dock, which was awash with kids. Were visited by Customs, a little polite fellow wearing a lava-lava. Tomorrow we will see Quarantine & Immigration. Island looks very beautiful – about a thousand people & no electricity, says Norbert. Welcome to Tonga!*

Soon after reaching shore Sid volunteered to do repair work for any islander with balky machinery. That night there were electric lights on shore (contrary to Norbert's report), but a little later every light went out for an hour or so. Sid had shorted out the entire power supply in tackling one of his repair jobs.

Two trucks and a tractor made up the total vehicle fleet for the island. Most commerce was by horse and cart. The main highway was a beautiful one-track sandy lane running between rows of palm trees to the little settlement at the other end of the island. Here one small store offered a limited selection: it didn't even have Coca Cola. Until then, I thought Coke was the one commodity sold everywhere.

We were invited to a big luau-style native dinner staged for the yachties. It was held in a little house near the harbor and, at something less than $10 U.S. each, it was a bargain. Waited upon by native girls and gawked at by native kids peering through the windows, we all sat cross-legged around a big straw mat spread across the floor, laden with roast baby pigs, fruit, fish, vegetables, coconuts and other items we could not name. We ate with our hands – a messy business when it came to the baby pigs.

These little pigs seemed to be almost all fat and were a common sight, at least those lucky enough to escape the luau. Looking like little brown footballs, they chased each other everywhere. The isolation of the place was fascinating. Aside from the limitless blue ocean and horizon all around us, the only thing visible was the mysterious island of Tafahi, about seven miles distant. It was almost a perfect cone, rising 2,000 feet out of the sea. We were told that boats went there occasionally, but no one lived there. There were intimations that the place was in some way taboo. Otherwise, the nearest land – the rest of the kingdom of Tonga – was more than 100 miles away.

Sept. 3, 1991:

> *Departed Niuatoputapu I. after a lovely week's stay. Most peaceful, unspoiled place I've seen yet. "We want to be free here – no rapes, no robberies, no murders," a 23-year-old man told me. (He works one day a week at the airport, when the plane comes in.) There is one "prisoner" on the island – a man sentenced to serve 2 years for his second offense of stealing a pig. (I wondered if it was the same pig.) But he has to stay in the jail only at night & can walk around freely during the day. He attended the dance in Hihifo, the main village, Saturday night.*

(Another yachtie told me later that he had seen the lone prisoner sleeping peacefully under a tree one day, while his two guards were busily digging a hole nearby. There must be a lot worse places to serve a jail term.)

Once again, it came time to leave.

Sept. 4:

> *Wind light from SE – sea calm. Am trying a seasick patch for the first time. Unfortunately, have had the shits since early yesterday – cause unknown. About 150 miles to go to Neiafu (capital of Vava'u, one of three island groups comprising Tonga – once known as the Friendly Islands).*

Twenty-four hours later we had covered the grand total of 32 miles, estimated, and Niuatoputapu was still in plain sight. Floating around absolutely still in the water can get rather frustrating sometimes. My inclination is to wait it out, on the theory that we are a sailboat, after all, and the wind will come up sometime, won't it? The waiting gets more difficult, though, when you can't get away from the place you're leaving. Eventually the island did disappear and we were rewarded by the sight of three whales cruising past, the first I'd seen in a long time.

Log for Sept. 7, after two days of gradually increasing winds and a total of 210 miles covered, much of it with rather laborious tacking:

> *Were about 25 miles off the big island (Neiafu) as dusk came – spent the night slowly tacking under reefed main & staysail (and we don't tack very well under that combo unless it's blowing pretty strong). At dawn we were maybe 12 miles out & we started engine & chugged in. North end of island a magnificent sight, w. 500 to 630-foot cliffs.*
>
> *Entered mouth of harbor & were approached by fisherman in skiff, who said Customs would be closed till Monday & suggested we'd save money if we anchored away from Neiafu. We agreed & motored over to #6 Anchorage (Mala). There we found CACIQUE with Rhona & Gene, plus several other unfamiliar boats, and later were joined by PATIENCE, with Max & Maria. Rhona said I have mail waiting for me at the P.O. in Neiafu – we'll go there tomorrow.*

Next day we awoke to the sound of church bells and kids singing. But it was windy with rain, and we stayed put that day. When we moved to Neiafu for mail and Customs and Immigration, we found a dusty little town with a good outdoor market, several restaurants, a small police station, a luncheon restaurant where they carved up 6-foot dorado (dolphin-fish) for sandwiches, a small boatyard with a Travelift, the rather plush Paradise Hotel, and the friendly Neiafu Club at the edge of town: a hangout for yachties. It offered drinks, snacks, occasional dinners and a snooker table, the first I'd seen. We played 8-ball pool on its enormous surface. It was fun.

We carried a great cruising guide for the Vava'u Island Group in Tonga – one given to me by son Chris back in R.I. The guide showed a score of named and numbered anchorages among the islands, and all of them reportedly were excellent. We motored 11 miles to Anchorage #11 – Topana. Dave & Catie on ARIEL had told us this was the site of a little restaurant that featured jazz music and home-made entertainment. We anchored off a pretty little beach near AMBLER, a 65-year-old lifeboat that had been converted to sail, which we learned later had been around Cape Horn. We liked the restaurant, owned by a lively French couple who loved music and nightlife, and we did a lot of work on TURTLE DOVE. I hoisted Sid up to scrape and paint both masts while I repainted the cabin top, covering boards and bulwarks on deck.

We were preparing for haulout at Don Coleman's little boatyard in Neiafu. I was determined to get that slipping prop shaft fixed for good and all.

With the boat out of the water, we lifted off the rudder and managed to extract the propeller and its shaft after much struggling. The bronze shaft was severely chewed up where it had slipped in the coupling. The only place that could repair it was the town highway department, which had a big metal lathe. I lugged the shaft up there and arranged to have the worn part built up by brazing, then placed on a lathe to get it back to its original round shape. The job took several days. Then Sid hand-cut a new keyway in the shaft (a tedious job) and made a larger steel key to fit into it, hopefully locking the shaft to a new coupling (obtained by mail order in American Samoa.) As further insurance we drilled entirely through the new coupling and the shaft to accommodate a 3/8-inch stainless bolt.

We slid the rebuilt shaft into place and Sid realigned the engine to complete the job. This was Sid at his best, and I was grateful to have him helping – I probably would not have attempted it without him.

On Oct. 3 we motored around to Anchorage #7, Port Maurelle, a little island with a tiny half-round harbor and a sandy beach bordered with palms. There was nobody anchored there. We rowed 1½ miles to visit Swallows Cave – impressive w. stalactites, bats and birds and a stone that rings like a bell when hit with an oar. The best of Vava'u, maybe? It was a Sunday morning when we left. As we started hauling up the anchor we heard church bells beyond the palm trees and then three girls appeared on the beach with guitars. They settled themselves and began singing, so sweetly it sounded almost unreal. As we labored with the rusty chain and the heavy anchor I thought, *"Why the hell are we leaving? This is Paradise."*

But we left anyway, bound for Fiji.

CHAPTER 12

Kiwis

Tonga farewell, Fiji, more crew, "Dear Jack" letter, New Zealand.

1991-92

Oct 7:

> *122 miles noon-to-noon – a good day's run . . . hooked a big dolphin fish (dorado) on new rod & got him up to the boat after a 40-minute struggle. There, fortunately, he broke the lure & took off w. the hook. He was too big for us, really a beautiful fish. But the new rig did well.*

Oct. 8:

> *141 miles noon-to-noon, & most of that w. 2 jibs, double-reefed main & single-reefed mizzen. Have now "rounded the corner" between Vatoa & Origea Ndriki – never saw either one. About 95 miles ahead (I hope) lies 1,184-foot Totoya I., which supposedly has a light, group flash 3 visible 20 miles. Plan to pass through 15-mile opening between Matuku I. & Totoya. At 5½ knots it should take 17-18 hours to get there – that would be 5-6 a.m. tomorrow.*

Oct. 9, noon:

With dawn came sight of our milepost island, Totoya, and later, Matuku to the left. But it wasn't till just now that we crossed the line between them. Straight line to Suva is now 110 miles. Today is perfect-bright sun & moderate easterly pushing us along on a broad reach.

Oct. 10, Suva:

120 miles to complete a textbook voyage – except for the usual last-minute hassle w. engine, which refused to start. Both the switch & the alternator were giving trouble. I was grimly tacking through the channel between the reefs when Sid got it going, & we motored in to anchor & await a call from Customs to clear in at the big dock. We made the 480 miles in almost exactly four days – had steady moderate winds the whole way. A lot of boats here – Suva's supposed to be a good spot.

Fiji was a good spot indeed, though the bureaucrats were rather overwhelming. In the Customs office downtown the authorities sat around drinking kava from coconut-shell bowls and watched me struggle with a four-page questionnaire, obviously designed for captains of big cargo ships, that included such questions as: *"State date, time and place of arrival at your final destination."* (I put "Boston, Mass., 3:30 p.m. June 20, 2005.") And when it came time to leave I had to fill out the same four-page form all over again! They must have tons of those completed questionnaires stored away somewhere.

The yacht anchorage, a big one but well protected, housed the Royal Suva Yacht Club, a rather posh watering hole with very few local yachts attached to it. Most of the boats there seemed to belong to yachties like me (though many of them were better dressed). The club's dress code was much starchier than I was used to. Over the bar was a sign advising gentlemen that they would be expected to buy drinks all around if they did not doff their hats in the bar. There was a bell on a pull cord next to the sign, and the bartender rang it vigorously when he spied me wearing my usual Gilligan-type topper. I hadn't noticed the sign. (I guess they took pity on me – nobody pressed the point, and I didn't buy.)

Suva was a big city, with regular bus service, a movie house (uniformed polite women ushers with flashlights and very cheap seats), hundreds of shops and restaurants and thousands of beautiful women of all hues, wearing spectacular clothes. There was a big split here between native Fijians and immigrant Indians, I was told. Each made up almost half the total population, with the Fijians owning almost all the land and the Indians running almost all the businesses. The city seemed busy but peaceful. I particularly admired the policemen, standing imperiously on almost every corner and perfectly immaculate in their red coats and white lava-lava skirts with herringbone bottom edges, as if they had been trimmed off with giant pinking shears.

It was here, courtesy of Poste Restante mail service, that I learned that Ellen had a boyfriend in Guatemala.

"There is someone else in my life," she wrote. He was a fellow Fulbright scholar studying Central American politics. The letter hit me pretty hard. I wandered around in a semi-stupor for a while, unable to stop thinking about it. Not that it should have been such a shock – we'd been apart a long time. And although I had in fact not been unfaithful, this was due to lack of opportunity as much as honor.

Fortunately, there was enough going on in Suva to offer some distraction. There were many yachts here, some familiar from previous stops, and there was much socializing. One boat housed four guys who loved to sing and play guitars, and I joined them with my harmonica for several raucous parties. There was a boat called NEUTRON, skippered by a professional entertainer and his wife, another with a very funny German sailor traveling alone. There was Maiwenn Beadle, a 25-year-old English girl employed as a seagoing nanny on a big American catamaran. She and I became friends and did some local touring, including one trip to a beautiful big woodland park where Maiwenn signed the guestbook, under Comments: "*Loved the trees.*" I liked that.

So life in Suva was lively, which helped to ease the pain in Ellen's letter.

(Maiwenn told me that at one yachties' party the lone German sailor, who spoke perfect English, asked her if she wished to dance. When she declined he said, rather wistfully, "Well, I suppose that rules out fucking, too.")

Maiwenn, not happy with the nanny job, asked to join Sid and me on the long and difficult leg to New Zealand. There was a bureaucratic problem here – her current skipper would have to sign her off his boat and I would have to sign her onto mine simultaneously to satisfy the Fiji authorities that she wouldn't be staying on illegally. (In many countries a skipper becomes legally responsible for the transgressions of his crew.) We got the paperwork accomplished and Maiwenn signed aboard.

We left Suva Harbor Oct. 26 after a 16-day stay. Maiwenn soon dispelled any doubts. She proved to be steady, reliable, hard-working, cheerful, and a good cook. The only difficulty came with Sid, who must have sensed my approval and apparently resented it. He never referred to Maiwenn by name – she was always "THE GIRL" – and half of the time he refused to eat anything she cooked. My relationship with Sid had suffered in Western Samoa, and now I found it growing steadily worse. And we had more than 1,000 miles to go, on a tough route. Eight days out, after 720 miles, in far too much rain and suffering with a cold, I wrote in the log:

> *Another tough night, made worse by continuing difficulty with Sid. His first heavy weather in a sailboat, yet he insists on pressing the boat too hard, calling for nonsensical sail changes, and continually putting down Maiwenn. He and I had a row this morning – I told him he's dangerous. In his usual infuriating pattern,*

he pointed to ear plugs he was wearing and affected not to hear me. Yet later he insisted on standing an hour of my watch at 2 a.m. so I could get some extra sleep. A strange, almost pathetic lonely figure. I feel some sympathy for him, but I'm also heartily sick of him. He'll not come sailing with me again. Maiwenn, for all her youth, is far more sensible.

Next day's entries:
1:40 a.m.:

Wind continues unabated, though it has veered slightly north so we can sail 170 degrees. Now under reefed jib and double-reefed mizzen only, and that seems plenty. Seas big and lumpy and every now & then we really crash into one – scary in the dark. But TURTLE DOVE is bearing up well, better than we are, I suppose. We're getting there but it's a hell of a hard job.

4:30 a.m.:

Finally, a turn for the better – last night wind & sea diminished & wind turned a bit north so we could steer 180, almost on course! But it's getting steadily colder as we head south: logical (we're moving away from the equator), but it still seems strange. On top I wear a T-shirt, turtleneck, sweatshirt, two long-sleeved shirts, a light jacket, then foul-weather jacket, hat & gloves, & wrap myself in two pieces of canvas to ward off spray. And I still get cold!

Even Sid seemed more chipper today. He is the original Mr. Stiff – it's a terrible temptation to make him the goat, but I'm trying not to. Maiwenn & I will have a beer in New Zealand & we can revile him then to our hearts' content.

Crew and weather did not remain salubrious for long. Entries for Nov. 6 and 7:

Now under reefed jib only as wind clocked around into the north & picked up speed. Had to referee a big fight between Maiwenn & Sid, who had turned over the helm to her, saying as usual very little, then come down below to wake me to suggest dowsing the mizzen.

I agreed, but when Sid went to do it Maiwenn objected. In the midst of the argument I came up and decided to take everything down but the jib as the wind was now howling. Sid was right in his decision on the sail, though true to form he had waited too long to do it, but he was dead wrong in ignoring Maiwenn, on her watch at the helm while the decision was being made. My attempts to explain this to him were met, as usual, with frantic (or is it fanatic?) denial. Will try again in the morning, with the two of them.

Next morning –

Tried my meeting with the two of them – did not work out well. Sid wants to blame everything on Maiwenn; ended up announcing he would wake her 1 hour ahead of her shift (!), "to make sure she reports for her watch on time." How come we could communicate before SHE came on board?, he wants to know.

Later at noon:

114 miles – not bad, considering. Still under storm rig, jogging 180-190 degrees at a little over 2 knots. Seas are impressive – like small mountains, some with transparent blue-green peaks. T. D. rides them very nicely, though, with only the occasional burst of spray. I took my shift indoors, looking out the companionway every 5 minutes or so, but Sid has elected to be Captain Courageous – he's outside now, grimly defying the elements.

Nov. 9:

An interesting 20 hours or so – after two brief periods of dead calm, which lasted about 2 minutes each, we spotted our first bit of New Zealand – Poor Knights Island. Cruised along comfortably for a while but then wind started increasing, and kept going up to about the force of the previous night. Waves didn't get so big because we had some shelter from mainland, maybe 30 miles ahead. Reduced sail to double-reefed main & staysail and tried unsuccessfully to get engine going. Sid finally started it by using a wire to bypass glow plugs – apparently batteries were still too low, despite running Honda generator two separate days. Under engine & sail we tried to tack in around Bream Head, getting thoroughly soaked with heavy spray.

Somewhere during this the staysail blew into tatters, so we rigged the little storm sail. Finally got into some lee on the E. side of Bream Head around 2 a.m. and spent the rest of the night jogging in place under engine only.

At 4:30 a.m. started off again, rounded Bream Head under power & started chugging up the long river to Whangarei. We're about halfway there now, moving along nicely. New Zealand looks great so far – rock formations & green hilly pastures with sheep grazing. But it was a hell of a job getting here, for sure.

We tied up to floating rings around four stout posts at the Whangarei Municipal Marina, in the middle of a fine-looking little town. We had sailed 1,240 miles from Fiji, some of it soaking wet and half-freezing, in 15 days.

TURTLE DOVE spent seven months in Whangarei, waiting quietly while I went home for Christmas. It wasn't so quiet for me, back in Rhode Island. Ellen had returned from Guatemala and we got divorced. Then I had a brief romance with a lady named Lorie and persuaded her to come to New Zealand. I returned to Whangarei and she joined me there, stayed two weeks and then decided she had better try to salvage the job she had abandoned back home. "I have a problem with intimacy," she told me shortly before we said goodbye. Later I met a young backpacking Canadian couple who wanted to try crewing for a while. We agreed that they would join me on the boat in the spring.

I liked Whangarei and its citizens, who seemed incredibly British. I joined a water aerobics group that met in the municipal swimming pool near the marina. Every weekend I tried to keep up with the elderly members of a local "tramping" (hiking) club who easily out-walked me. I played pool and drank beer with several large and apparently unemployed Maoris, fierce-looking gents with heavily-tattooed faces. Another player advised me, "Try not to win too often."

I also did an auto tour of New Zealand's North Island with Phil Kennedy and Gene Dutra, a cruising couple first met in the Marquesas. One high spot was a magical swim in a rushing stream with its own bubbling waterfalls and whirlpools. What made this unusual was that the water was almost unbearably hot.

I had a new mainsail and staysail made by the Auckland office of Hood Sailmakers at an excellent price. Whangarei seemed about the right size for me – big enough to have restaurants, a movie theater and a library, but small enough to be covered easily on my rusty bicycle. I found myself readily accepted by the local swimmers and hikers. They even threw a party for me when it came time, at last, to leave.

David Robertson and Annalise Van Ham, my new crew, were an adventuresome young couple who had left their home in the Northwest Territories of Canada to travel the world. They had spotted my little ad in a cruising magazine. We left our friendly municipal marina on the river in Whangarei May 10, 1992, heading north and east to Noumea, New Caledonia, more than 1,000 miles distant. The bigger objective was Australia, but this more roundabout route was supposed to be easier than battling directly across the Tasman Sea to Australia. And I hoped to have a new lady shipmate, Suzanne Walch of Bordeaux, France, join us in New Caledonia.

CHAPTER 13

Aussies

New Caledonia, Suzanne, Australia, Paul and Linda, Great Barrier.

1992

Heading out to sea after a seven-month layover is rather like being born again. Right away we had to deal with strong winds and fierce rain squalls, and both Annalise and I were seasick. I felt poorly for two days and she for longer. Crewman David was untouched, much to my chagrin. On the fifth day I wrote:

> *71 miles, according to the semi-worthless knotlog. Morning began w. rough seas, contrary winds and rain. But everything improved – some sun broke out, I caught a fine bonito for sushi and supper, and a lively herd of porpoises crossed our path. After days of hard slogging, the world looks pretty nice.*

May 19, Noon:

> *43 miles. Another slow day . . . Dave shouted us awake around 5:45 when a humpback whale, a big one, came to call. He (or she) stuck a huge black head out of the water to regard us, up close & personal. Then disappeared. Most exciting.*

On the 12th day another sailboat slowly passed us. It was BARON ROUGE out of Opua, N.Z., also heading for Noumea. They said they wanted to get there next day and were about to start motoring. As we watched, they did so and soon faded out of sight. Stubbornly, I decided to keep sailing – a poor choice.

May 23, Noon:

> *A miserable night – and morning. Wind picked up to near – gale force and swung directly ahead. Jogged & thrashed with double-reefed main and good old (new) staysail, making little headway through fierce rain squalls. Started motoring as wind eased slightly before noon. Seas rough & very confused (as are we). This is getting OLD!*

24 hours later:

> *We're here! At last – after 14 days, many of then pretty difficult. Ran engine for about 18 straight hours, motor-sailing against a strong headwind. BIG waves, some of them hitting us hard & washing over the cabin top. No green water in the cockpit, though. A very tiring and trying trip . . . Hope we like the place.*

> *Total distance (estimated): 1,126 miles.*

Noumea offered a fairly well-protected anchorage, a good dinghy dock and a fine outdoor market with several snack bars, but not much else within easy reach. The place was very French and somehow seemed less welcoming than Whangarei. But it was good to be ashore.

Suzanne Walch arrived at the airport several days later. She was athletic and lean from years of teaching and practicing yoga, and she had that indefinable French presence that makes a colorful scarf around the neck look both carefree and elegant at the same time. She kept a notebook filled with new English words and spoke English easily, but with a delightful accent. She planned to visit friends in Noumea, with the understanding that she would join us on the trip to Australia if she felt favorably impressed. I hoped she would.

(Our meeting had come about quite by chance. During my visit home for Christmas the Providence Journal had printed a feature story about my travels and dwelt on my looking for a lady companion. Though I was glad to get the story, I felt a little uncomfortable with the publicity – especially when my newly-exed wife Ellen rather tartly referred to the story as "the world's longest personal ad." Somebody back in Rhode Island sent a clipping to Shirley Nelson, widow of Ray Nelson, my old boss in the Warwick office of the Providence Journal. Shirley showed it to a friend in Washington, jokingly suggesting that the friend apply for the job. The friend showed the piece to Suzanne, who decided that she was interested. She wrote to me in Rhode Island and the letter was sent on to me in New Zealand, and the rest, as they say, was history.)

The four of us did some touring in New Caledonia, which seemed pretty primitive beyond Noumea, but most of the time we prepared for the next leg – nearly 1,000 miles across the southern Coral Sea to Bundaberg, Australia. Suzanne had decided she'd like to come along, and we left June 14, 1992.

She was astonished to discover that seasickness struck right away. "*Immediately!*" she announced after a very brief stop below decks on her first day at sea. After that she spent most of her time in the cockpit, even when she wasn't steering. I watched her out there, vigorously slapping her own shoulders in a grim attempt to keep warm. She didn't complain, and eventually the seasickness passed.

This was a fairly uneventful trip. At least 50 miles from Australia we were noisily buzzed twice by a military-looking plane. When we radioed him he quizzed us closely, asking the kind of questions usually asked when you reach shore: Name of Vessel, Home Port, Names of Crew & Passport Numbers, Port of Call, Intended Length of Stay, etc. This was a first for me. Apparently the Aussies wanted to be ready for us well in advance.

And we were getting ready for Australia, reading the guidebook *"Cruising the Coral Coast,"* by Alan Lucas. He wrote:

> *Visitors who presume that Australia's front door swings as loosely as those of many European and American countries are in for a shock. Australian entry rules are the toughest in the world . . . Australia now ranks as one of the most suspicious nations, where foreign boats are concerned. If you compare us to a Marxist nation you could not be blamed . . .*

> *"No person shall leave the vessel until it has been boarded by customs, immigration and quarantine . . . No vessel shall go alongside until boarded . . . Animals are prohibited entries . . . Many foods will be confiscated upon arrival . . . All meat, whether tinned or not (unless tinned in Australia or New Zealand), and any food that may he considered a carrier of disease by the officer of the time will be confiscated."*

Later on, Lucas warns of Australia's wildlife:

> *When swimming, choose sand-bottomed lagoons so that sharks may be seen before entering the water. During December through March, beware of the sea wasp. Entanglement in its tentacles is almost certain death . . . wear sandshoes or plastic sandals to reduce or deny the effect of standing on stonefish. A full injection from a large stonefish's 13 spines can be fatal.*

> *Crocodiles have become a menace. Since the ban on hunting, 20-odd years ago, they have recovered in extraordinary numbers, none with any memory of man the*

armed aggressor. Fatalities are occurring in increasing numbers. Never swim in any river or in the vicinity of its mouth.

Snakes are rarely seen but must be considered. Many Australian species are so highly poisonous that one bite is capable of killing a number of people, let alone a single victim. Beware, especially, the death adder, which lies in dust and sand and strikes when trodden on.

Then he adds a note, apparently designed to calm the alarmed reader:

Because of our very special problems with venomous vipers, spiders and sea life, nearly all Australian hospitals have a good stock of antivenom.

The day after the plane encounter we had our first glimpse of Australia: Lady Elliot Island, one of the few points on the Great Barrier Reef with anything above the water. (I was surprised to learn that most of this 1,400 mile reef is visible only under water, except at low tide.) Far from us, but apparently close to the island, we saw whales leaping halfway out of the water, their huge tails unfurling high above as they sounded straight down.

June 25, 10 a.m.:

Waited, becalmed, in Hervey Bay most of the night & then chugged into the boat harbor, where Customs, Health and Immigration awaited us. A vigorous, time-consuming clearance (despite the earlier quiz by plane) but very polite and friendly.

Noumea, New Caledonia, to Bundaberg, Australia: approximately 962 miles, 11½ days.

This was where we were to say goodbye to Dave and Annalise, who wanted to explore the Australian outback. They had been faithful and congenial crew members and I was sorry to see them go, but there were new developments in store.

My best buddy, Paul Harrigan, and his girlfriend Linda were to join us for a month's sail north, between the Queensland coast and the Great Barrier Reef. That was the good news. The bad was that Suzanne had decided that ocean sailing was not her cup of tea: she planned to leave. I was distraught, particularly since I had hoped we were heading toward a real relationship. Suzanne seemed regretful about her decision and listened carefully while I argued that the next stage of our journey, with good friends Paul and Linda on hand, would be greatly different from the ocean crossing. We would be making short passages with frequent stops, I said, with interesting land travel included. To my great relief she said she'd try it.

I decided to press my luck. I didn't intend to twist her arm, I said, but I certainly would be happy to have her join me in the berth in the forward cabin if she felt like doing so at any time. Pleasure compounded: Suzanne said she had thought about that earlier, but wasn't sure I was interested. I assured her I was fully in favor, and we adjourned immediately to the captain's quarters while our crew members were off somewhere in town. Later that night, the crew was discreetly silent about the change in sleeping arrangements. I think they approved, like me.

Dave and Annalise left and shortly afterward Paul and Linda arrived, exhausted from the long plane trip. But they recovered quickly, briefly enjoyed the delights of Bundaberg (many rather dark barrooms and pubs specializing in the local rum) and the four of us took off for Lady Musgrave Island, another rare above-water spot on the Great Barrier Reef.

We had almost no wind and made little headway that night (Linda was the only one seasick) and reached the island next afternoon, 73 miles out of the Mid-Town Marina in Bundaberg. On the way out we saw porpoises, many turtles, a huge ray and a booby that bit Harrigan while he was supposed to be bow lookout. It was the 4th of July.

With its waving palm trees, clear blue water and white sand, the island was a popular tourist spot. Several small cruise ships were anchored in the lagoon, unloading people to wade ashore. While quietly observing my two lovely crew members, now topless as they lolled on the beach, I was diverted by the sight of a horde of Japanese men, all barefoot and clutching their shoes, socks and ever-present cameras. With their trousers rolled up to their knees, they were earnestly wading to shore through the gentle surf, still wearing their suit coats, hats and ties.

We stayed overnight and left next morning for Fitzroy Reef, about 30 miles away.

Our guidebook called this one *similar in concept to Lady Musgrove, but without a cay* (small island), and said low tide was the best time to enter because you could see the entrance channel and the many coral heads more easily. With all this coral, said the guide, boats must be securely anchored because it wouldn't be safe to move after dark. We didn't know the state of the tide as we approached, and we almost sailed right over the reef. Suddenly we were in 6 feet of water with coral heads everywhere. We turned tail, felt our way around the edge of the reef and finally found the proper entrance, indifferently marked with small buoys and tethered bottles. We got in, gratefully, just before sunset along with two other sailboats, both from Lady Musgrave. We were 50 miles out, but anchoring there felt like being in the middle of the ocean.

Two days later:

Still here, playing poker for matches and beset by strong winds from WSW for 30-odd hours. Wind now switched to SE but still blowing like hell. Calming by 2 p.m. but we decided to stay on, then on to Great Keppel Island.

We sailed overnight, heading for Rosslyn Bay on the mainland. There we found a man-made little harbor, nicely protected and offering room to anchor. We stayed for two days, exploring the nearby little town of Yeppoon (there are a lot of odd names in Australia), and strolling along a wide beach with almost nobody on it. On the 13th, sailing faster than expected past several inviting-looking islands, we stopped at Digby Island and found three other boats there. Later another came in but next morning they were all gone. We had the whole place to ourselves. I noted in the log:

> *An idyllic uninhabited island, part of the National Park system, with a half-circle little harbor bordered by rocks and a pristine sand beach, with islands rising out of the sea everywhere you look. We have covered 129 miles from Rosslyn Bay.*

The log continues:

> *Departed Digby I., heading for Whitsunday I., after waiting all morning for strong SE winds to subside (they did, but just a little). Sailed all night under single-reefed and then double-reefed mainsail, trying to slow down (at one point registered 7.6 knots), but it was still dark when close to Edwards I. light, which was our aiming point. Took down main & jogged along under staysail alone, hoping for daylight.*

> *As it got light we finally were fairly certain where we were & turned off w. following wind, heading for Pallion Point and a lee-shore anchorage. Waves getting bigger and bigger as we rolled down before them. Finally started engine & put in slides to close hatchway. A good thing, too, because shortly afterward we were well & truly pooped for the first time – cockpit totally full of water & Harrigan, trying to steer, pretty well awash.*

> *Struggled on around Pallion Point & there found sanctuary. Anchored & slept a few hours, then moved south a bit to anchor off Whitehaven Beach – world famous for its incredible whiteness. Lucas calls it "a glaring fine salt-like sand that romantics dare not dream of."*

The sand on this beach was so fine that our bare feet actually *squeaked* – loudly – with each step.

Our next stop was Hamilton Island Marina, a ritzy spot where we reluctantly shelled out the equivalent of $50 US for a night's berthing. Next day we watched tourists feeding dolphins (every feeder-tourist holding out a fish but staring straight at the camera, not at the porpoise dutifully chomping away), then dined in a fine restaurant and ended the evening watching thousands of big black fruit bats fly out of their roosts in the trees to begin their night's foraging.

We bought more charts and left next morning for an anchorage in Hunt Channel, a passage lined with trees and rocks that looked like the coast of Maine.

Suzanne and I rowed ashore, swam, sunbathed and indulged in a little lovemaking, all alone on a tiny little beach. Then we found that another sailboat had come in and anchored not far away. We probably provided them with a little quick entertainment, but nobody said anything. We had a big dinner on the boat, a brief poker game and an incredibly starry night. Life seemed perfect.

Five days later we arrived in Townsville and settled into a berth at the Townsville Motor Boat Club, a hospitable marina with dock space at $80 US per week – not bad at all. With fine sailing conditions and short runs of 30 to 50 miles each day we had made stops near Cape Gloucester, close to the 2,400-foot headlands of Cape Upstart (named by Captain Cook), then at Bowling Green Cape and Cape Cleveland.

In Townsville we rented a car and headed inland; I wanted a chance to use the little tent I had carried on board for many miles. We visited Innisfail, Cairns, Ravenshoe and the rain forests of Atherton Tablelands. We saw kangaroos, wallabies, one snake, and spectacular "lava tubes": huge natural tunnels melted through the rock by volcanic eruptions thousands of years ago. In Townsville we played pool, drank beer, ate out every night and admired thousands of brightly-colored wild parrots roosting in trees in the middle of the downtown shopping mall.

Sadly, we said goodbye there to Paul and Linda. We posted Crew Wanted notices on the marina billboard and recruited two young English backpackers, Maria Ottley and Zara Trimlett. Zara, blonde and lissome, said she had done a little sailing. Maria was black, originally from Jamaica, and even more beautiful than Zara. She knew nothing about boats and arrived on board with a huge box of cosmetics – not a good sign. Though she said she had a boyfriend back in England and never seemed to advertise herself, she turned out to be irresistible to every male who set eyes on her. Wherever we went on land she was followed by eager suitors. It was a little disconcerting, but Zara seemed to take it in good humor.

I now had an entire crew of lovely female neophytes. Their ignorance and my poor judgment got us into serious trouble right away.

CHAPTER 14

Danger

New crew, hitting reef, Lizard I., Thursday I., rounding Australia.

We left Townsville Aug. 8, heading for what looked like a good anchorage at Palm Island. We motored all day to get there and then the wind picked up from the north-northwest and I decided to anchor in a big bay on the east side of the island. It looked good on the chart, assuming the wind didn't shift. We had to anchor rather far out because the bay shoaled rapidly with coral. It was the first night on board for my two newest crew members.

Just at dark the wind shifted into the southeast, blowing directly into the bay and leaving us with no lee at all. Worse yet, it steadily increased. While my crew slumbered peacefully below I fretted miserably, listening to the wind blow ever harder and trying to persuade myself that we could tough it out till morning, when we'd have light enough to see what we were doing. I couldn't ask my new crew to start thrashing around weighing anchor in the dark, I told myself.

At first light we started the engine. I had rigged a trip line on our big fisherman anchor to help us recover it if it snagged on the coral. Suzanne ran the engine in forward gear while I grappled for the line with the boathook. I hooked it, but Suzanne didn't shift into neutral quickly, the boat ran past the anchor and I couldn't hold it. The boathook slipped from my hand, we drifted back and ran over the tripline, which immediately wrapped itself around the propeller. The engine stopped.

We continued to drift back in the wind, dragging the anchor with us. I felt a heavy thump as the rudder hit rocks. I grabbed a knife and jumped overboard and started hacking at the trip line wrapped around the propeller. Before I got it freed we hit bottom, hard, at least twice more. I got the line free, clambered back into the boat and, mercifully, got the engine started. I was shifting into gear when Suzanne pointed out that the rudder was no longer attached to the boat. It had been knocked out of its fittings and was floating free – the only thing keeping it with us was the mizzen sheet, a line that led through a block on the top of the rudder.

With all three girls trying to wrestle the heavy rudder upright, I got us in gear and we started moving forward – only to find that the anchor had now taken hold again and wouldn't budge.

Thoroughly rattled, I started trying to free the anchor when Suzanne showed the most sense.

"*Can't we cut it loose?*" she yelled. Good idea: this was not the time for further heroics. I hacked through the anchor line and we managed to crawl off the reef and out into deep water, trying to steer with three pairs of hands holding a huge rudder and abandoning a perfectly good anchor with 50 feet of newly-galvanized chain. We struggled about a mile and found a lee at little Falcon Island nearby. There, after much grappling with rope and winches (Zara in the water in her new white bikini, to help maneuver it), we managed to get the rudder at least most of the way back into its fittings.

I noted in the log:

> *Damage: Lost anchor & chain, stanchion support torn off, chain roller support severely bent and port whisker stay damaged – all by chain. Plus many dents & gouges from wildly-flailing rudder, plus possibly a bent pintle that prevents rudder from seating properly.*

> *Lesson: When wind shifts to trade-wind direction, putting you on a lee shore, MOVE – even if it's dark!*

> *(Could have been a hell of a lot worse, of course.)*

This was a sobering experience: we came close to losing everything. (And our two newest crew members apparently thought that was the way we usually left an overnight anchorage.)

Aug. 12:

> *Reached Johnstone River marker buoy shortly before 5 p.m. & started in. Depth sounder went to 3.0 ft(!) several times as we crossed the bar and we bumped softly at least once, but kept on truckin'. Negotiated our way all the way to Innisfail, inquired of a friendly Greek yachtie (Stamatis on ECLECTIC) as to boat anchorage, then proceeded to get ourselves firmly aground on a sand bar, heeled over slightly with*

incoming tidal current rushing past, in full view of everybody in town. Sat there awhile & then Stamatis rowed out to us in his dinghy & carried out our plow anchor. Shortly afterward we swung around & came off. Hauled in that anchor, motored a short distance & anchored again.

We had entered a section of the Queensland coastline where many little wiggly rivers enter the sea. They offer nice anchorages, but many rivers have bars: shallow banks of sand or mud at their entrances. TURTLE DOVE needed 3.2 feet showing on the depth gauge (her real draft is about 4 feet 10 inches), meaning that if the gauge showed less than 3.2 feet we were hitting bottom. But often the bottom was soft sand or mud and we could plow slowly through it without damage. Still, these shallow entrances caused a lot of anxious consulting of timetables and charts.

Aug. 13:

Spent the day in Innisfail – a pretty little town of 7,500. Entered a pool tournament that night & was roundly beaten in the first round by Henry, a pleasant aboriginal.

We stayed a night at Fitzroy, near Cairns, and then strong and steady south winds pushed us the 45 miles to Fort Douglas. We spent a week in this little town, delayed in part by warnings of strong winds. Maria, still pursued by eager suitors, landed a job in a noisy bar-restaurant and moved into town. We left Aug. 22, now with a two-woman crew.

That night we struggled into the Endeavor River (named after Capt. James Cook's ship) in the dark after a long day's sail. The river seemed to have no channel buoys whatever and finally we ran aground, on a falling tide. We managed to get off, but our much-abused rudder ground over something on the way out. We finally got anchors down fore and aft, with an extra line from the bow to the mangroves, about 20 feet away. Once settled in, it seemed to be a good spot.

Lucas writes in *Cruising the Coral Coast*:

Historically, this section of the Coral Coast has more significance than any other part of Australia, for it was here where ENDEAVOR came close to disaster. Had she been lost with all hands during her encounter with the reef, it is entirely probable that we would all be speaking French now, the British Crown being reluctant to act on recommendations based on Cook's voyage at a time when France was actively expanding her Pacific interest.

However, as we all know, ENDEAVOR did survive to sail back to England, leaving us only to conjecture on Captain Cook's extraordinary decision to sail offshore during the night when he should have come to anchor. This happened immediately north of Cape Tribulation, and leaves us in no doubt that neither he nor any of his officers had any notion of the extent of the barrier reef. Even in this day and age of accurate charts, excellent navigational aids and electronic wizardry aboard ship, one does not sail amongst coral reefs after dark.

Captain Cook's decision to sail offshore was based on his desire to get around a danger sighted ahead before dusk. This was the Hope Islets, and his actions are well documented in his journal:

"At this time (when close to the mainland), we shortened sail and hauled off east north east by east close upon the wind, for it was my design to stretch off all night, as well as avoid the danger we saw ahead." (Hope Islets).

Deepening their water, they were alarmed when it suddenly shoaled (probably passing over the tail of Pickersgill Reef), but it deepened again as the following confirms:

"But meeting at the next cast of the lead with deep water again we concluded that we had gone over the tail of the shoals which had been seen at sunset and that all danger was past; before ten we had twenty and one and twenty fathoms, and this depth continuing the gentlemen left the deck in great tranquility and went to bed."

Soon after, ENDEAVOR struck the reef that would bear her name.

Lucas writes:

Having freed his ship from Endeavor Reef, Captain Cook and his men struggled into the Endeavor River, there to spend 48 days in repair and refit as well as to rest the sick and refill the larder. While stranded there, they established a number of historical firsts, it being the first recorded place in Australia where Englishmen spent more than few days ashore; where the kangaroo was first sighted and named, and where the first true contact with the Australian Aborigine occurred, the indigenes slowly but surely trusting in the visitors' signs of peaceful intent.

I marveled that Cook, working his way through these waters with no charts or prior knowledge, avoided disaster as long as he did. We had all sorts of modern assistance and still we went aground frequently. I gave fervent thanks for TURTLE DOVE's stout full-length keel, with the massive four tons of lead underneath it, and for the big outboard rudder that protected the propeller and helped keep stray lines from getting wrapped up in it. I was convinced that more modern craft, with their fin keels, unguarded propellers and spade rudders, might well have come to grief by now.

We left Cooktown Aug. 25, my son Ange's birthday and one day after Hurricane Andrew devastated much of the Florida Keys. We had a fast sail to Lizard Island, pushed by a steady reaching wind all the way. (Lucas calls this anchorage the best on the north coast.) We stayed three days, made friends with Hans, a lone Danish sailor aboard SEAGOON, and climbed the 1,190 feet to Cook's Lookout. A rock cairn there marks the spot where Cook spotted an escape route through the Great Barrier Reef into the open sea.

From this lookout, the openings through the reef show clearly: Cormorant Pass, Half-Mile Opening, Cook's Passage, One-Mile Opening, One and a Half-Mile Opening. All of them were mined during World War II and the chart still says: *Don't Anchor.*

We snorkeled a lot around a beautiful reef in the harbor. where turtles, rays, and thousands of fish swam. It was like swimming in the world's biggest aquarium. Hans speared a beautiful coral trout which we had for dinner.

We looked at the remains of the stone cottage of the ill-fated Mrs. Watson, whose tragic story is told in Lucas's guidebook:

Mary Phillips became Mary Watson by marriage to one of two partners who worked beche-de-mer (sea slug) from their base on Lizard Island. Mr. Watson, with his partner, Fuller, sailed north to fish near Night Island, leaving Mary – now with baby – alone with her two Chinese servants.

An uneventful month passed, then one of the servants went to the garden and was never seen again. His pigtail, however, was found on the mainland many months later. Aborigines then kept Mrs. Watson and her remaining servant under surveillance until they eventually ambushed the servant, spearing him twice before he escaped back into the house under the cover of Mrs. Watson's gun.

Badly wounded, the servant helped launch a beche-de-mer boiling tub in which the three of them made their escape from the island. Offshore they became a plaything of the trade wind, which carried them to Watson Island after a worrying stranding and escape from a reef en route, where more Aborigines were encountered.

On Watson Island, the three perished from thirst, their bodies being found a few months later by the Aboriginal member of a passing trading schooner. They were interred in Cooktown, where a memorial was erected and stands to this day. The diary kept by Mrs. Watson during her last few days, and the tub, were sent to the Brisbane Museum where they can still be seen.

Sept.2:

Anchored off Night I., hearing Torres Strait pigeons calling "Boooo" on shore. Barely avoided a low-lying reef at the end of the island. Spoke to two ships (apparently pilots on board) today – the TNT CORNUCOPIA & the PACIFIC SPIRIT. Both very friendly. Second guy said I gave "a good strong signal" on radar.

7 p.m.:

Anchored (in near-dark) in lee of Lloyd I. after a fairly tricky 7-mile run between reefs through shallow Lloyd Bay. Took a million bearings & worried a lot, but it worked out OK. Wind light NE most of the day, gradually swung round to E. Managed to sail more than half of the day. Baked 2 loaves of stone-ground bread.

Sept. 3:

Anchored amid sleeping trawlers at Portland Roads after looking in vain for the fuel barge (it came in later, fed fuel to two boats and then left). Watched the brightly-lit trawlers leaving to begin their night's work, looking like spaceships from Star Wars.

Sept. 4:

Caught a fish! (Or most of one – tail was gone by time we got him in. Apparently a wahoo or narrow-barred mackerel, 20-25 pounds, a big one. Fish tonight, at last!

Sept. 6:

Cape York at last! Anchored here in a howling SE blow – flat sea but about a 35-knot wind in bullets. Lucas says this area has the strongest trade winds in the world. We'd planned to stop in Escape River, but were going so good we just kept on. Part of the route is 27 miles without markers, and it's so far offshore we could see no landmarks in the haze. Fairly tense for awhile, but a marker finally appeared.

Cape York is rocky, barren, a nice beach but not overwhelmingly impressive. Eborae Island & its lighthouse, just off the tip of the cape, was a notable turning point: the northernmost point of mainland Australia. Tomorrow, maybe Thursday Island.

9 p.m. (Underlined in red):

Suzanne says she doesn't want to stay on the boat. Likes me but not the sea life.

Sept. 7:

Despite a fairly high tide, we still ground our way over the sand banks w. the depth sounder reading 3.0, and SE wind bullets blasting us, moving too fast w. engine in neutral & no sails up. Anyway, we got into deep water & on our way, probably w. little paint left on the keel bottom. Weather forecast was for light to moderate SE – glad they didn't predict strong winds!

Raced across historic Endeavor Strait, heading for the Boat Channel. But changed my mind, thinking that the wind would pile up huge waves in the narrow space. Changed course & tacked under power assist around Horn I. & through Flinders Passage, narrowly avoiding Scott Rock, unmarked & just awash.

Powered slowly down & anchored off Horn I., amid wind bullets, along with all the other yachts visible (save one on the windswept Thursday I. side). Tidied up & then took the little yellow ferry to Thursday I. $4 each, one way) across to town. Got our mail, had free cold showers at the local Sports Complex, bought fruits & veg. off a truck, had 2 cold beers at the local pub & caught the 5:40 ferry (last one) back to Horn I.

56 miles, approx. – must have had a hell of a current, because we only traveled about 6 hours.

** Noumea, New Caledonia, to Thursday I., Australia: sailed 2,429 miles.

Horn Island became our home base, even though Thursday Island, about a mile and a half away on the other side of Endeavor Strait, was much bigger with Customs and Immigration, a shipyard, a post office, hotels and bars, a bank and shops, even a small marine supply store and the veggie truck. But it was out in the open, exposed to howling trade winds and swift tidal currents. And the anchorage had poor holding ground. Horn Island, on the other hand, had good sticky mud to grab an anchor and much less wind and current. And it did offer a public phone, one small grocery store and a pretty good restaurant with a bar and a much-used pool table, generally occupied by dark and rather surly-looking Thursday Islanders. (One more proof of my theory that even the most remote place will usually have a pool table somewhere.)

We spent most of our time on Horn, commuting to Thursday Island on the little yellow ferryboat for important business. I ordered charts of Indonesia, which had to be sent from Brisbane, and I arranged for a cruising permit for Indonesia, which involved hiring an agent and other complications.

I also had to prepare for the arrival of John Pierre Moolman, a young South African who was to replace Suzanne as crew. I had never met Moolman, but he had been highly recommended by a young crewman on another sailboat. He described

John-Pierre as 19, husky, and an experienced hand on fishing boats who wanted blue-water sailing experience. I looked forward to his help on board, but I knew I was going to miss the gentle company of Suzanne.

She left a week after our arrival and I was right – I missed her a lot.

Zara and I had an interesting day aboard the TORRES VENTURE, an old military landing barge converted to carrying cargo to islands in the Torres Strait. The mission that day was to carry supplies to Bamaga, an Aboriginal Settlement on the mainland about 15 miles away.

Russell, the captain, had extended the invitation to Zara, but I was allowed aboard too. I think Russell had a hankering for Zara, who was lithe and blonde and given to wearing revealing shirts with nothing on underneath. Gabriel, the mate and only crew, seemed interested only in fishing. He had a line and lure trailing behind on the entire trip, but he didn't catch anything.

We anchored and unloaded without a glimpse of the settlement, which was some distance inland. Our guidebook said the place had a "substantial supermarket" – something we could have used.

Young Moolman arrived several days after I bade Suzanne goodbye. He was indeed young and husky, blonde, good-looking and over 6 feet tall. He and Zara seemed to hit it off immediately – no big surprise. I felt a bit jealous.

John-Pierre struck me as somewhat cocky. On his first night he and Zara visited the Horn Island bar and when they returned, rather late, he reported ruefully that we now had a one-oar dinghy – somebody had swiped the other oar from the dinghy parked on the beach. They'd had a hell of a job paddling out to the anchored TURTLE DOVE with only one oar, he complained. I was quite unsympathetic, and considerably annoyed. This guy could turn out to be callow, careless and slapdash, I thought: in short, a pain in the ass. (And, no doubt, nowhere near as awed and impressed at my nautical prowess as my lady crew members had been.)

CHAPTER 15

Indonesia

Ambon kids, Maumere and Aladin, charter trip, Komodos.

1992

Sept. 23, 7:45 a.m.:

> *Departed Australia after vicissitudes. We leave with Zara Tremlett (new at Townsville) and Jean-Pierre Moolman of S. Africa, new at Thursday I. Left Horn I. yesterday & about 15 minutes later the engine overheated & quit. We tried lashing rubber dinghy & 2-horse Yamaha alongside, but it could do little in face of big tidal current.*

> *Hailed a passing skiff & he towed us against the current to Thursday Island, where we dropped anchor, & then a second anchor when the 40-pound Danforth failed to dig in. Finally stopped & then rowed a line over to a big mooring float nearby.*

> *We did our shopping & then had long hassles w. Customs & Immigration – both crew members' visas had long since expired. Finally got everything completed about 6 p.m. (Had spent the morning doing another oil change [10 days from last one] & also changing all fuel filters, inspecting salt water pump, etc. It appeared that I had not added enough oil Sept. 12, although I felt sure that I had.)*

Spent a rather uneasy night, up early & got the new big plow anchor up easily, but the big Danforth would not budge. Finally broke it loose by powering forward, but it came up with a huge bend in the shank – unusable now until we can somehow straighten it. Shit! Anyway, we finally got away w. a big outgoing current (it can run up to 8 knots!) shooting us along and now, at 2:30 p.m., we are well out into the Gulf of Carpentaria, sailing NW and bound for Ambon, Indonesia. Will be our first taste of the Orient, I guess.

I miss Suzanne.

Sept. 25, noon:

138 miles in 24 hours. A very good day's run.

John-Pierre was easing some of my misgivings. He volunteered to dismantle the salt-water pump, not an easy task in a fast-moving boat, to try to see why the engine had overheated at Thursday I. The pump seemed OK. When we tried running the engine it didn't overheat, but it didn't seem to be working very hard.

At sunrise on the 26th a small herd of pilot whales joined us. They swam smoothly alongside briefly and then disappeared. That night, still sailing well, we saw strange "looms" of bright bluish-green lights off to starboard. We thought they were big patches of sea phosphorescence, but they turned out to be big ships a long way off, probably tankers ablaze with lights and moving through distant haze. The wind was getting light and the weather hot. We were at 9 degrees South Latitude, sailing north toward the equator.

Sept. 28:

A quiet night w. light air. Shortly before dark a curious-looking native craft crossed our bow & then seemed to hover, waiting for something. Worried us a bit & we kept all lights off until long after dark. We even debated hauling down the radar reflector but didn't. Nothing happened & we didn't see them again. Seemed a pity that sighting another vessel should produce anxiety, rather than interest & joy.

Found two flying fish on deck yesterday morning. Fishing again, but no luck.

Sept. 30:

Another very hot day w. light steady wind from SE. Just kept chugging along under comfortable twin-jib setup. Made baggy wrinkle ("mopheads" of unraveled old rope tied to stays to prevent chafing of sails when they rub against the wire). Finally went up mainmast while underway to put it in place – turned into a difficult job, but managed to get it up there, at least temporarily.

Now (9 p.m.) about 30 miles off the isolated island of Manuk, reportedly home of thousands of seabirds. Had hoped to see it in daylight, but looks like we'll get there in the dark, so plan to pass to the north.

Log at noon next day (88 miles covered):

Just before dawn, after much peering ahead (no SATNAV fixes for 7+ hours) we made out the imposing cone of Manuk, the bird island, just about dead ahead. Passed it around 7:30 a.m. Pretty much a classic cone, 932 feet high, bare rock on top, trees below, steep rocky sides & thousands of birds roosting. Inquisitive boobies came out to inspect us, cocking their heads & staring boldly as they flew by. Honked the air horn, but the birds on the island paid it no mind . . . a lonely, mysterious place, about 200 miles from any other land.

Hot as hell again today. About 179 miles to Ambon.

We spent most of the next night hanging around a light at a spot marked Tanjung Nuranive, near the entrance to Ambon Harbor. We just wallowed in the small waves with no sails up, waiting for daylight. At last it arrived and we hoisted sails.

Oct. 2:

Reached up beautiful Ambon Harbor – past steep lush wooded hillsides w. smoke curling up, past funny little fishing-shack boats moored in DEEP water w. white & red flags bravely flying, past ships coming & going & past grinning fishermen in elegant little dugout canoes w. outriggers & tiny tattered sails. Very exotic, different & suddenly Asiatic.

Tried in vain to get a response from Ambon Harbor Control so kept on, looking for other yachts & a decent anchorage. But water very deep & ships anchored everywhere.

Ambon itself was overwhelming: thousands of people along the shore (a surprising number, we noted, balanced at the edge of the sea wall with their trousers lowered, facing inland and cheerfully shitting in full view), a constant din of honking horns, dirty grey concrete buildings, garbage & trash floating everywhere, and soon, small boys climbing aboard.

The small boys seemed to materialize from nowhere, with John-Pierre happily waving more and more aboard while we got the anchor down, much too close to the quay, and still in 40 feet of water. To add to the confusion, the temperature gauge for the engine showed that we were still overheating.

The log continues:

> *We collected ourselves as best we could, and I had John ferry me to the quay to start the process of clearing in. Went to a nearby cycle shop in an attempt to find somebody who spoke English. After much palaver found myself bombing off in a pickup truck and, after about 5 miles through the teeming city, landed at a big white office building loaded with uniformed smiling people.*

> *Ceremoniously ushered to third floor, where it finally turned out I was at the wrong Immigration office. So one guy came w. me – walking & then by bus! – to another building. More uniforms everywhere here, & a hot ping-pong game in progress in one office. After stopping at about 6 different offices we finally settled down in one, where John's S. African passport proved to be the biggest problem (followed by the facts that despite statements on my papers Suzanne was no longer with me, that we did not leave from Darwin, that Ambon was not on my advance list of places to visit, and that nobody spoke much English.)*

Everybody agreed on one thing – there would be no visa for John. I was learning that Indonesia and other countries whose citizens have dark skins were quite disinterested in any kind of cooperation with people from South Africa. Would have been pretty ironic, I thought, if John had been a *black* South African.

Back to the log:

> *At one point one guy said they'd have to keep John's passport till we left. We talked him out of that and then there was a big problem with copying my clearance paper – I had no Indonesian money to pay for copying and they had no copy machine anyway. They also wanted a crew list, but no one could supply pen & paper.*

> *It took a while to work through these difficulties, but we managed it at last. One official checked the exchange rate in the newspaper (1,470 rupia to one Australian dollar), offered to give me 1,400 to 1, & I gave him $50 Aus. in exchange for 70,000 rupia. Then I filled out forms & we (officials and all) took a cab to a water taxi (a huge dugout canoe) & then back to the boat, still overrun w. visitors.*

John was at the bow with a crowd of kids, happily drawing crayon pictures and showing them magic tricks. Meanwhile, hordes of other urchins were rummaging through the entire vessel. John was turning out to be a regular ambassador of goodwill, I thought. The steady din – a mix of kids' yelling onboard and the uproar of people and traffic onshore – made it almost impossible to think.

Finally, with the assistance of the Immigration people, we got the kids cleared off and sat down to talk. The officials told John he could not set foot on Indonesian soil, whereupon John informed them that he had a severe toothache and must see a dentist ("Doctor Geegee" in pidgin English). To my amazement, one of the officials immediately said he would return at 7 p.m. and escort John to "Dr. Geegee" – and this on a Saturday night!

With Immigration finally squared away and with Zara and me clutching our newly-issued visas, leaving John disconsolately on board, we adjourned by water taxi back to the pier and by land taxi to find Quarantine, another required stop. The log:

> . . . a very polite & friendly doctor who finally confessed that he had no staff to visit the boat, but that he would consider it OK if I checked in w. him on leaving. Next stop was Customs: again, lots of people (by now it's 3:30 p.m. Saturday) & finally a very affable gentleman who gave me two cups of water in neatly-sealed packages & chatted w. me about my travels for at least half an hour, finally calling in a grizzled gent who set off with me at a furious pace, first to a Xerox copy center for more photocopying, then a bus, then a water taxi back to the boat again (w. a stop on the way for him to line up a German tourist couple. "I'm Customs, and this is American man," he told them.)

Once aboard, our Customs man lectured us for not having a Bible on board ("I'm Pentecost," he said proudly.) Then he grabbed a purple Magic Marker and was about to inscribe some religious message on the side of the settee when we stopped him. He made a cursory inspection of the interior – "I'm sorry," he kept saying – and then departed with much hand-waving, apparently heading for the German couple who had been told to wait for him.

> Zara & I went ashore once more for beer & veggies & found an absolutely wild outdoor market w. thousands of food-sellers beseeching us & hundreds of kids peddling plastic shopping bags & baskets on poles to carry food. We bought fish, bananas, tomatoes, cabbage, had another beer & returned to the boat, where bedlam reigned once again. It looked like we were sinking, but it turned out to be the combined weight of what appeared to be hundreds of kids. About eight urchins wildly paddled our dinghy in for us & I upbraided poor John, who seemed to have become Big Brother ("Mista John") to every kid in Ambon. We cleared them off again.

At 6 that night the Immigration man showed up & took John away, who returned two hours later with his aching tooth drilled & filled, for $10 U.S. The Immigration man accepted a 10,000 rupia (about $5 U.S.) tip. Meanwhile, I discovered that about $200 in Australian money, carelessly left exposed in my forward quarters, was missing. Apparently one or more of John's young guests had made off with it while Zara and I were ashore.

I told John the open house had to cease. I also said I really didn't expect him to remain on board for two months – after all, he was white-skinned, about twice as big as the typical Indonesian, and blonde to boot. Not easy to disguise. He promised to sneak ashore only in less heavily-settled places and to take full responsibility if caught. Unlikely, I thought. But at least he was trying.

Oct. 4:

Upped anchor early & left Ambon Harbor-tired of seeing bare bums shitting over the sea wall.

* A total of 1,198 miles from Thursday Island to Ambon.

I soon abandoned trying to keep John-Pierre out of sight. As far as we could tell, everybody loved him. We stayed another two nights near Ambon, anchored off the friendly Tirta Kencana Hotel, and took off next morning for Flores Island, still part of Indonesia but almost 600 miles away. It took six days to get there, generally in light winds.

Oct. 11, 5 a.m.:

At first light there was Flores, just where it was supposed to be. This was the northernmost peninsula – we have another 60 miles to get to Maumere, which sits at the edge of a shallow bay. High (up to 5,500') volcanic peaks all around, and very few navigational markers. At 3 p.m. we're passing what appears to be an active volcano to port – much smoke & steam billowing out the side of a mountain along the shore.

Wind from the north, which doesn't give much protection for Maumere. Thinking of looking for an anchorage along southern shore of island of Pulu Besar, about 11 miles NNE of Maumere. Don't know if it will be shallow enough to anchor, though – the chart gives few clues.

Oct. 12:

Awoke at 5:30 a.m. after a night spent milling around, under light sail but w. almost no wind, in Maumere Bay. Couldn't find a decent anchorage off the island as it got dark – chugged up to one reef that suddenly appeared out of the depths, got scared & backed off. The bay is surrounded by volcano-like peaks & we kept seeing fires near the tops. Thrilled to think they were active volcanoes. But in the light of dawn we decided maybe they were grass fires – these hills have beautiful light-brown spans of grass mixed in w. dark green trees. Now passing log rafts lying in the water – saw one guy in one of the delicate little dugout canoes handling lines & a net. He was wearing a blue motorcycle helmet for some reason. Glad we didn't hit one of these rafts in the dark last night.

We arrived at Maumere City at 10 a.m., scouted the rather deep harbor for an anchorage, and finally settled in close to what appeared to be the town pier. Almost immediately we were visited by a smiling young fellow, dark-haired and slightly built, eager to act as a guide and anxious to show us the dog-eared notes of commendation he had secured from previous yachties.

This was Aladin (he told us his father had named him after a favorite radio, an *Alladin),* and he was to become a great help and a good friend. I was struck by his beautiful little dugout canoe and its anchor: two polished sticks of wood lashed together to form a hook at one end, with a flat narrow stone lashed on as a weight at the other. It could have been passed down directly from the Stone Age.

Aladin spoke some English and guided us ashore for beer, shopping and an encounter with the harbormaster, who wanted five copies of our papers. Later we visited Aladin's home and met his four sisters, his father and mother and two brothers-in-law. We were invited to a wedding party at the house next door that night.

Aladin's house was plain and small: three rooms for nine people. Two of the rooms had beds, but it looked as if people would have to sleep in shifts. The wallpaper was flattened sheets of cardboard. I saw only one attempt at decoration, a painting of two native women dancing. Zara made the mistake of admiring it, and I had a feeling that she had hit the Hospitality button. Sure enough, when we got ready to leave we were presented with the painting, carefully wrapped in newspaper. We tried hard to decline the gift, but it was impossible. We walked off with the only bit of art in the whole house.

I told myself to try to be equally generous with this family before we sailed away.

We saw more of Aladin's village that night when we returned for the wedding party. Maumere was a city of some size, but the village had a character all its own. Aladin's home was one of a string of little houses lined up in a double row close to the harbor shore. A narrow walkway led between the rows. There were no cars, and apparently no electricity. Almost every house had a kerosene lantern hanging by the door, and many had an open counter with food and other items on sale. In the dim glow of the lanterns and the quiet murmur of voices as people strolled along the pathway, the little street seemed to be an oasis of tranquility.

The wedding party was rather quiet too. The guests, none of whom spoke English, sat on the floor around a large colorful cloth laden with mysterious dishes. Apparently we were the honored guests – after a few awkward moments, with everybody smiling to the point of paralysis, we realized that we were expected to fill up our plates first. I was painfully conscious that these were poor people, now having to feed three rather large and unexpected guests.

We saw the bride and groom, a handsome young pair, only briefly. Since Aladin was the only one who even attempted to speak in English, there was little conversation but a lot of handshakes and smiles. I found these encounters difficult but also warming and gratifying. The immediate hospitality and kindness that these poor families offered us tended to leave me near tears.

We spent six days anchored here, with Aladin our regular guide to telephones, banks, grocery stores and town officials. First thing every morning we would see a long line of little fishing dugouts, like beads on a string, towed by a slightly larger skiff with an outboard motor, heading out to the fishing grounds. Each dugout contained a single fisherman, and the parade would veer toward us as they passed. Every fisherman grinned and waved and occasionally one would actually stand up and dance, somehow managing not to capsize his tiny boat. I think they enjoyed a glimpse of blonde Zara as much as we liked seeing them. And in the early evening the whole routine would repeat in reverse, this time the proud fishermen holding up samples of their catch.

Despite the language problem I became friendly with Aladin's father, who spent much of his time squatting near his front door making fishhooks out of bits of wire. I had never seen anybody manufacture his own fishhooks before. Aladin Senior took the big Danforth anchor that we bent at Thursday Island and had it straightened at a shop somewhere in town.

Getting ready to leave, we found we were stuck to the bottom once again. Since I had not been able to use the big bent Danforth I had set a smaller one, almost brand new, and I was determined not to lose it. We spent hours maneuvering the boat in all directions under power, trying to free it without success. The water was far too deep to swim down to free it.

We had to find a diver. The ever-agreeable Aladin was no help here – apparently he'd never had reason to deal with divers. (After all, if he needed a new anchor for his dugout all he had to do was find some rope, two sticks and a rock.) I was told there was diving activity at the Sea World Hotel, several miles out of town. There I found Flavia, a glamorous Swiss who was the hotel's activities director and dive instructor. We negotiated a price of $25 U.S. – a real bargain, and next morning, sure enough, there she was, in a hotel van waiting at the dock for our dinghy. Her driver helped her load the gear but he stayed ashore.

Apparently I was to act as assistant while Flavia dove. She stripped down to a brief bikini and assured me there was no need to worry. Her instructions were brief. "Keep the anchor rope tight and be ready to pull up when I pull on it," she said, and overboard went she, into about 80 feet of water.

Five minutes later I felt the yank, pulled up and raised the anchor, followed by a smiling Flavia. The chain attached to the anchor had been wrapped entirely around a big coral head, she reported. Mission accomplished, and that wasn't all. Over a cup of tea, Flavia said her hotel had a good mooring just off its beach, and suggested that we bring the boat up there for free. Furthermore, she said, she'd like to hire us for a day of diving. The hotel would supply lunch, drinks, all equipment and a guide, she said. We moved up to Sea World that very day.

What a comfort it is to be on a good mooring in a secure place! We settled in at Sea World and became part of the waterfront scene. We hung out at the hotel bar, occasionally bought a meal at the restaurant, and chatted with the guests. Meanwhile the hotel announced the forthcoming tour on TURTLE DOVE and almost everybody signed up. In the meantime we were Aladin's guests on a bus trip to Kilimutu, a triple volcano that is one of Flores's top tourist attractions. The passengers, most of them much younger than Aladin, were his classmates in an English-language school. The kids, a lively bunch, played guitars, sang lustily and had a fine time.

I wrote in the log:

> Up at 2 a.m. (!), rowed ashore & rounded up the sleepy hotel driver, who rushed us in to Aladin's village. He and his whole family were up & stirring. We then roused his cousin (pronounced "cow-sin") Dermon, age 13, & all shuffled back to the waiting van. Then whisked up to Aladin's school, w. two small buses & swarming students noisily waiting. Jammed all 40-odd people into the two buses & set off at a furious pace. (Later I learned that our driver had no lights on for a while.)

> Soon out into remote mountains, bouncing through tiny neat little villages. Driver turned on Indo. pop music, loud, & I discovered I was sitting under the bus's only loudspeaker. Fashioned earplugs of toilet paper & tried to endure. Knees hurting in cramped position. But the mountains are truly spectacular – steep, steep terraced slopes, bright green rice fields growing in cascaded terraces, each carefully watered w. elaborate irrigation systems.

> Took almost 5 hours to get to Kilimutu, which was magnificent w. its three crater lakes, each a different color. Kids played guitars & sang. Another 5 hours of torture heading back; returned to our hotel mooring around 9:30 p.m. A memorable day.

Next day was our charter dive trip – a first for TURTLE DOVE.

Flavia, again in her sexy bikini, lectured our eight hotel guest passengers sternly before we started. I had told her I wasn't sure our little marine toilet could handle such a crowd, so Flavia addressed that subject while reviewing the guests' training in SCUBA. "If you have to shit, you'll shit in the water!" she announced. The guests all nodded placidly, just as if they had been shitting in the water since birth. I had discussed this outing in advance with my crew members, and we resolved to give our guests a taste of smart boat handling: we would leave the mooring under full sail and without engine. We did, but the spectacle lost some of its pizzazz when I discovered our dinghy, quietly floating about 100 yards behind us. I had neglected to secure it to the boat. One guest immediately jumped overboard to collect it. Now we had two rescues to accomplish.

Dinghy attached and everybody aboard again, we anchored between two reefs guarding the entrance to a large bay, then had to move when the anchor dragged. We tried another spot and then moved again, but no problem: we had plenty of willing hands to raise and lower anchor and chain. Finally we settled fairly close to one village, over a fine sand bottom in beautifully clear water. Flavia handed around SCUBA gear and snorkel masks and everybody hit the water. We had lunch. The sun was hot, the breeze was cool, the sky was blue. If anybody shit in the water I was happily unaware of it. After a good lunch and more SCUBA action we hauled anchor, took off on a lively sail for several hours and finally motored home long after dark, with our guide directing us by flashlight.

The outing was a huge success. We had rave reviews written in the ship's log by hotel guests from Indonesia, Germany, Switzerland, Holland and Vermont. The glamorous Flavia wrote, "Jack, Thanks very much for the wonderful day and I deeply hope to see you once again. Be careful with your anker (sic) and lots of love." Wow!

Oct. 21:

> *Sailed back to Maumere & said goodbye to Aladin – gave him our small Danforth dinghy anchor and some money and took his picture; was really sorry to leave.*
>
> *(Years later I learned that Maumere had been nearly destroyed in a terrible volcanic eruption and tidal wave. Aladin wrote to say that his family had lost almost everything, but no one was hurt.)*

Oct. 22:

> *Becalmed, & suddenly two whales appeared (humpbacks, I think), slowly cruising along the surface, occasionally releasing a lazy blast of spray. They drifted across our path, nose to flank, maybe 300 yards away, stayed in view about 15 minutes, then flipped up their tails majestically in unison, dived & disappeared. Closest I've been to whales since the whale-watching trip off Provincetown, Mass., a long time ago.*

We were heading into exotic territory now: places with names like Komodo, Sumbawa, Lombok, and the tourist Mecca, Bali. Next would come the big island of Java, with place names like Surabaya, Malanga, Semarang, Cirebon, Bandung, and the capital of far-flung Indonesia, Jakarta, population 11 million. Then it would be on to Singapore (reportedly with the heaviest shipping traffic in the world) and the huge island of Sumatra, passing through pirate-infested Malacca Strait.

Our course would parallel the narrow length of Malaysia along its western coastline, past the capital, Kuala Lumpur, continuing northward along the even narrower stretch of land that is Thailand, to Phuket. This was another popular spot for tourists; it had an adequate harbor and was close to Phra Nang Bay, a spectacular cruising area.

I felt nervous and excited. I worried about the pirates, but I'd been told that they rarely attacked yachts because they weren't worth the trouble. These guys went after ships. Would I resist if attacked? Long before the trip began, I had decided that the answer would be no. The closest thing to a firearm on TURTLE DOVE was a signal flare gun – possibly of use to scare off dinghy thieves in an anchorage, but not much else. Americans, both sailors and landlubbers, often seemed surprised to learn that I went unarmed. My rationale (that the one or two firearms I could carry would be a poor defense against a boatload of guys with machine guns) often failed to impress.

I usually didn't even try to defend my other objection – I was not sure that I was prepared to kill someone who wanted my property. And if you carry a gun, I thought, you'd better be ready to kill with it. I had heard of several cases where a skipper or crew member had brandished a firearm at intruders, apparently intending only to scare them off, and was immediately killed for his pains.

There was still another reason. Most boat robberies occur in harbor, and harbor is where you don't have your gun because you had to hand it over for safekeeping when you cleared in. (The penalty for getting caught with a hidden weapon on board can be very severe.) You can only reclaim your arsenal, usually with considerable red tape, when you leave the country. These arguments made sense to me, but they often didn't seem to have much effect on the listener, particularly the American who liked weaponry.

Our first overnight stop after Flores was Labuanbajo, a village in a lovely harbor almost surrounded by islands. INTERMISSION, a yacht from San Francisco, was anchored there and we chatted with Jeff, her skipper. He recommended a spot to anchor in Komodo, where we hoped to see Komodo dragons, seven-foot lizards that could eat a deer (or a man, reportedly).

Oct. 27:

> *Departed Komodo, dragon-less, after a quiet night & a morning snorkeling in beautiful clear water. Fishermen on shore said the hills here too rugged to get to dragon territory, recommended we go back through the narrows into another bay. But the chart showed reefs everywhere & I demurred. We decided to have a lazy morning, then leave.*

Oct. 28, noon:

> *91.1 miles. Rather trying night – spent it trying to get by Sangeang, a 6,300-foot volcano. It's still visible but we're past it now. Wind light & variable, apparently currents setting us back, then a steady heavy rain that blotted out the stars and made the volcano invisible, though only 3-4 miles distant. Bobbed around most of the night, Zara getting thoroughly soaked on her shift. Morning dawned sunny,*

though, and wind came up from east. Now heading west along north coast of Sumbawa.

Next morning, 9 a.m.:

A very slow night, & at daybreak that blessed volcano was still visible!

Another volcano, the 9,035-foot Tambora, was coming up on our left. Our chart said this was an area of "magnetic anomaly," though our compass seemed undisturbed. We wondered if the volcano itself could throw off compass readings.

Oct. 30:

Another night of little progress. (We actually went backward 3-4 miles at one point.) Still passing Tambora Volcano.

Our destination was Gillie Island, just off the NW coast of Lombok and about 45 miles away. We suffered through another day of little wind and much motoring and finally anchored at the lovely little island of Gillie Air at 11 a.m. next day. Zara and John decided to spend the night ashore, probably because John and I had had a row over his dumping a used cigarette lighter that I thought might still be useful. (Obviously, we were getting on each other's nerves.)

I conducted a slow walking circumference of the little island, partly on a pony-buggy tourist track & partly along the beach. I stopped for several beers & chatted with a man building a dugout boat. He had primitive tools: a small crosscut saw, a couple chisels, a hand adze, a small broad axe with offset handle, a hammer and a small plane. He said he bought the hull in Lombok and was now finishing it. No motor, he said with obvious regret – he'll use sail. He spoke English pretty well and had a lot of questions about my boat.

Tomorrow we plan to sail overnight to Bali. Varieties of coral here seem almost infinite. I see great flat mushroom-like disks growing out of the bottom. And big gray half-rounds covered with deep wrinkles containing clam-like bodies that shrink down deep and even change colors as I swim near. And acres of large delicate spiral-shaped coral flowers, shades of brown & white, infested with little fish swimming in & out of the blooms. The bright electric-blue ones, tiny little guys who seem entirely unafraid of me, are my favorites. Looking astern I see only the horizon, as if we're anchored in the middle of the ocean. To my left, soaring above the clouds, is Rinjani Volcano, 12,222 feet high. And to my right, the perfect cone of Agungin Bali, this one 10,308. Looks almost exactly like Mt. Fuji, but without the snow cap.

This little island off Lombok was clearly oriented to attracting tourists, and there were many on hand. But the entire scene was low-key, physically beautiful and peaceful, and the local people seemed to be going about their own business in tranquility. I fell in love with the place immediately.

Things were different when we reached our next stop. Bad news was waiting there.

CHAPTER 16

Bali

Mom's death, Java, Crossing Line again, Singapore, Suzanne.

1992

Nov 4:

Arrived Benoa Harbor, Bali. Came ashore & found a printed notice with an American flag and my name in large print, telling me to call the U.S. Consulate. With sinking heart did so from Harbormaster's office and was told only to call "your brother, Chris."

Could find no long-distance phone. Full of foreboding, completed rounds of all five (5!) agencies involved in clearing-in, came back to TURTLE DOVE & then took a chartered bus into Kuta w. Zara. Found a postal agent – there were 2 letters from Suzanne, & one from Chris dated Oct. 20 saying Mom was dying. There also were notices that two more pieces of mail were waiting @ main P.O. in Denpasar, 8 kilos distant.

Took bemos (cabs) to Denpasar & got messages, dated later Oct. 20, that Mom had died. Took bus to Telecom office, finally got to a phone & called Jim (my brother) in SanFran, woke him up at 2 a.m.

Jim told me that he had flown to Florida and was with Mom when she died. She was 89.

I felt a hell of a long way from Florida, and I was glad to have Zara with me. Even though I knew my mother was in bad shape with Alzheimer's, it took most of the rest of the day for this news to really sink in. I realized that we had been almost completely out of touch with the rest of the world for several weeks; that during this time my mother's fragile condition had slowly failed, that my brother Jim had flown across the country to be with her, that my son Chris had had to enlist the help of the U.S. State Department to get the word to me, and that all this time I had been blithely enjoying my little sabbatical. I had allowed other people to take on a burden that rightfully belonged to me.

I was in one of the world's most exotic spots, and all I felt was stunned, confused, guilty and almost completely unaware of the sights and sounds around me. I didn't have a mother any more. It was over, finished. Following the careful instructions she and my father had drawn up years before, her body had already been cremated, goodbyes all said by those present. It was too late for me.

By telephone I thanked Jim for being with her. (Apparently brother Bob, true to form, had not been at the deathbed.) So once again Jim had taken up the slack. I felt awash in bad feelings and I really couldn't appreciate Bali.

We stayed there six days. At one point John and Zara planned to spend the day at a nearby beach. I foolishly agreed that they could take our elderly inflatable dinghy with its tiny outboard. This time, rather than just one oar, they lost the whole works. I was in the cockpit when I watched a big native dugout canoe steaming past with an extremely frantic-looking John-Pierre Moolman acting as bow lookout. Turned out he was hunting for our dinghy

"But don't worry," he assured me. "We're looking everywhere – we'll find it." "You'd better," I told him. But I had my doubts.

About two hours later he and Zara returned with dinghy and outboard, richer in experience but poorer in pocket. They had found the dinghy, pulled up on the beach and tended by a chap who calmly offered to sell it to them. When their protests failed to impress, John hurried off to find a policeman, leaving Zara to stand guard. He returned with a police escort, but the cop refused to hear anything about ownership, apparently seeing his job only as helping to arrive at a reasonable ransom. After much discussion John and Zara agreed to pay 31,000 rupiah ($15.50 U.S.). They dug up the dough and the dinghy was theirs once again.

Nov. 10:

Departed Benoa Harbor, Bali. Much hassle w. local bureaucrats, particularly over John's S. Africa passport, which they held while we were here. I'm still trying to adjust to the news about Mom, & the thought that I don't have to worry about her any longer.

Nov. 11:

102 miles at noon. As dawn broke I realized we were surrounded by maybe a hundred one-and two-man fishing boats, each w. an exaggerated swept-up bow & stern piece like a little Viking ship, all apparently working without lights. I wondered how close I'd come to them (we also were running without lights, thinking nobody was around) during the night.

Last night we had two separate visits by whales. First, two came by & stayed briefly – I could hear the WHOOSH! of their spouting very loudly. Then later one just sailed past, heading in the opposite direction. He (or she) came maybe within 100 yards. Eerie, but I wasn't really scared, just excited.

Nov. 13:

74 miles at noon. Another day of fluky winds. Started motoring just before dark, dodging fishing boats & nets which they had run out a quarter mile or so. Nets had floats & tiny twin lights near the end, but you had to be close to see them. And often it was hard to figure which net was attached to which fishing boat. So we dodged through them under slow power & somehow managed not to get entangled. Now we're making 0.0 again on the knotmeter. And it's bloody HOT.

Nov. 16:

78.4 miles at noon. A new obstacle: long heavy bamboo poles floating vertically as markers. Passed a no. of them – no flags or lights, & one floating at a 45-degree angle. In the dark they're invisible, of course.

We passed islands named Pulau-Pulau, Karimum Jawa, Karang Katang, and Krakal K, Kambar and Kumbang. Did not stop. Then on the night of Nov. 17 we had a truly close encounter.

Shortly before midnight a small freighter or tanker (maybe 150 feet long) passed us only feet away, so close that its bow wave threw us from starboard to port tack in one swoop, and its starboard side, steaming past, towered over us like a huge black wall. We had our proper lights on, and I had shined my lantern at him a number of times as he approached, but it got no response – he just kept coming on. The ship proceeded straight ahead, leaving us wallowing behind, thoroughly rattled.

I should have come about and gone off on the port tack as I saw him approaching. But all the way, until almost too late, I thought he would pass safely to port. He did, finally, but just barely. I wondered if the ship would have responded to a radio call. I probably should have waked John and Zara to man the radio. As it was, both of them came piling out into the cockpit, scared out of their wits, as the ship churned past us, making a hell of a racket. It couldn't have come any closer.

Nov. 21:

108 miles at noon – a good day's run, albeit not quite in the right direction. A night passing through the usual scores of fishing boats, a number of them showing a light only as we approached, and several ships which passed well off to port. One seemed to be headed for us as it passed through Liplia Strait & I feared another close call. Woke John, tried to call the ship on Ch. 16, no response, and flashed the 400,000-candlepower searchlight repeatedly at him & on our sails. But then he swung left down the shipping lane & all was well.

Nov. 24:

65 miles at noon. Last night pretty miserable: first a heavy squall about 5 p.m., then choppy lumpy sea & spattering rather cold rain. Wind totally wrong direction, TD refused to sail well because of heavy chop & light wind, & there were ships passing in every direction. But everything changes, & today is much better. I worry that we can't motor a lot because fuel is short.

We caught another fish yesterday: a fine mackerel about 7 lbs. I cooked him under difficult sailing conditions. Something romantic & vaguely threatening about the name "South China Sea" – connotes visions of pirates. So far only a lot of ships which, thankfully, seem willing to alter course to keep out of our way.

Nov. 25:

129 miles at noon. Found a little silver fish on deck yesterday morning. Was not a flying fish – did he jump up there? Would seem so. TURTLE DOVE has been performing handsomely, actually tacking within 100 degrees, according to compass readings. We're 150 miles from Bintan (still Indonesia, just south of the Strait of Singapore).

Nov. 26:

A difficult night of tacking against wind, current & heavy chop which tends to stop us cold. Around 3 a.m. a severe squall hit us & we frantically doused staysail & main in blinding, choking wind & rain. Today we're farther south of Bintan than we were yesterday, though we have moved west a fair distance. I'm getting very tired of looking at this one island, which has been in view for at least 24 hours.

Horace the swallow, who appeared yesterday & flew into the cabin, was back for a while this morning, perched on some books & snoozing with his head under his wing. He also likes to sit in the open porthole in the galley. We're now about 30 miles from the equator. King Neptune may have to make a night appearance.

Nov. 27:

120 miles at noon. *CROSSED THE EQUATOR at 12:06 our time. The SatNav read 00.00,84 N Latitude, 105.12,40 E Longitude. King Neptune appeared in traditional garb (flippers & snorkel, toilet brush as scepter) & administered Shellback oath to Zara & John. (This my second crossing – first was March 10, 1991, approaching the Galapagos from Panama.)*

Nov. 28, 4 p.m.:

Tacking north, trying to reconcile one chart which shows only half the area, combined with another chart which is a very poor Xerox of other Xeroxes. Can't read half of it.

Then Tanjung Penang at last! 1,801 miles and 18 days sailing from Bali. Finally found a channel with 9 to 11-foot depths. Chugged around looking for the alleged marina, trying to call harbormaster: no response. Finally anchored among large ships (shades of Ambon!). No other yachts or pleasure craft anywhere to be seen. Dinghied over to nearby Riau Holiday Inn. Marched through big empty hotel and out the front door into a kind of Arabian Nights: the night market, with hundreds of stalls & stands & little eateries all set up right out along the main street, with thousands of natives milling about.

Ate some very hot food, then walked back, stopping at a little outdoor park w. chairs & tables for more beers. Were joined by our waiter from the street stall & four or five of his friends, all pleasant earnest young guys who wanted to practice their English. Finally lurched back to TURTLE DOVE, somewhat inebriated.

(The waiter and his friends carried a stack of dog-eared Readers' Digest magazines. They were seriously trying to learn English. Several told us that they wanted to leave but couldn't, even if they had enough money. The Indonesian government would not give them passports, they said.)

That night the monsoon arrived. By 9 a.m. the dinghy was full of fresh water and it was still raining. Three days later we left Tanjung Penang, heading for Singapore, reportedly the busiest commercial port in the world.

Dec. 2:

Around mid-day the skies cleared & sun came out, but then the north wind started howling & we reefed again. Suddenly the entire clew of the jib ripped out. We hauled it in & set the old roller-reefing jib, but it flapped horribly in the gale & finally we took it in also. Next the block holding the staysail sheet broke & we had to replace that. Continued motor-tacking across the main channel, dodging scores of big ships (more than Panama!) & doing 7-8 knots.

We were heading for the Changi Sailing Club, which had several hundred sailboats on moorings. But we weren't at all sure we were in the right channel. Finally we hailed an approaching yacht and asked for directions. They turned around and led us directly to an empty mooring at the yacht club. Mark, our guide, invited us to dinner in the club restaurant and insisted on paying for everything. Next day I moved the boat off the borrowed mooring (we learned we were breaking one of the Sailing Club's many rules), and we anchored half a mile away amidst a crowd of non-members' boats. It was a windy spot with poor holding, and we dragged down on a steel yacht behind us. TURTLE DOVE's mighty locust-wood rudder hit the steel boat near the bow and inflicted a considerable dent where hull met deck. No apparent damage to us. I was aghast and finally located the boat's owner, a pleasant young woman. She said her boat already had a lot of dents and one more didn't matter much.

I had to hire a diver to untangle our fouled anchor, which had snagged somebody's anchor chain. It cost me about $100 U.S. "You're paying Singapore prices here," the diver said cheerfully.

Meanwhile, Zara and John had slipped seamlessly into the Singapore social scene and were preparing to leave. Suzanne was coming, and we planned to fly to Rhode Island for a Christmas visit.

My crew members moved off Dec. 5, the same day Suzanne arrived. We had a few days to see the sights of Singapore. It was fun for a while, though I found the place a strange mix of old-style British colonialism, monster shopping mall, and Brave New World.

It's a prosperous city-state now, but it has a bloody history. In February 1942, the Japanese captured Singapore from the British and ruled it brutally for the rest of the war. They killed thousands of citizens, particularly the Chinese, and jailed many Allied prisoners of war at the infamous Changi Prison, not far from my mooring at the Changi Sailing Club.

The *Lonely Planet Guide* says Singapore has the world's highest rate of home ownership. It looked to me as if most of the homes were in identical high-rise apartments buildings mushrooming almost everywhere we looked. How the average Singaporean can find his way home, especially after a drink or two, is a mystery.

Maybe they don't drink. The four million-plus inhabitants (76% Chinese, 14% Malay, and 8% Indian) appeared to be industrious, hurried but remarkably docile. They have reason to be: they are beset by rules announcing steep fines for Smoking in Public Places, for Jaywalking, for Littering, for Failing to Flush Urinal After Using, even for Sneaking Chewing Gum into the Country on an Airplane. Criminals can be lashed with the rotan (cane): it actually happened to a U.S. teenager who vandalized several cars. Topping the penalty list is a death sentence for drug trafficking. It's mandatory.

CHAPTER 17

Asia

Christmas, Singapore, Thailand, stolen sweets, Sri Lanka.

1993

U.S. Immigration in New York seemed to think Suzanne might be a terrorist. We had to clear in through separate lines, and she was questioned at length. Among other things, the authorities asked me whether we intended to marry. I said no, and almost immediately regretted it. Maybe I would want to marry her some day, I thought, and anyway it was none of their damn business. They finally let her pass through the sacred portals, but they didn't look very happy about it.

We stayed in Rhode Island with my son James for a while and then decided to see Bill Clinton inaugurated in Washington. We had a great time, even though we had to view the ceremonies from a considerable distance. But the happy, optimistic spirit of the crowd was contagious and inspiring. And we loved the free concerts and museums. Pretty nice place, we thought.

I sadly said adieu to Suzanne Jan. 24 and returned to Singapore three days later, alone. The plane rides seemed at least twice as long.

I spent three more weeks there, mostly because I needed to find crew. I talked to a few candidates who had advertised themselves at the Changi Sailing Club, but they wanted paying jobs. I had not paid anybody thus far, and didn't want to start now. So I wrote up notices and posted them at various hotels and backpackers' hostels, looking for more young folks like Zara and John who were traveling the world on a shoestring.

I finally came up with two: Petra Bul, 28, of Holland, and Iain R. Jones, 25, of England, separate backpackers who had seen the notice I posted in their hostel. Petra spoke English with a heavy accent and had no sailing experience: when she first approached the dinghy at the sailing club dock she stepped right out onto its tiny bow seat as if it were an ocean liner, and immediately found herself swimming. Iain had only a little experience with sailing yachts, but he said he liked windsurfing and was pretty good at it. I felt optimistic about him but was not so sure about Petra.

We left Singapore early Feb. 27 with the new Garmin GPS (Global Positioning System), acquired on my Christmas visit to Rhode Island, working nicely.

> *Marvelous to get position fixes whenever you wish*, I noted. *A lot of ships but no difficulties thus far. Now rounding the southern edge of Singapore, approaching Raffles Light, where you turn the corner and start heading northwest.*

Next morning I reported:

> *A pretty stressful night: first a thunder squall, w. a Singapore Police boat trying to question me in the middle of it (apparently bothered that I might be going to Indonesia – they waved & took off when I managed to convince them we were going to Malaysia. Then an incredible mass of ships all night long. For a while we were smack dab in the middle of a parade going both ways.*

March 3:

> *Now rolling heavily as we pass the pretty Sembilau Islands, about 9 miles off the coast of Malaysia. I always hate to go by islands without exploring. Petra very quiet this morning. So far, it seems to me she still hasn't a clue about sailing. Iain, on the other hand, has a natural curiosity, some mechanical aptitude & seems to be learning quickly.*

March 9:

> *Departed Langkawi, Malaysia, bound for Phuket (Thailand). Had a nice stop here – pretty well protected anchorage without roll, fairly easily-secured water & diesel, 50¢ transport to town & cheap food (Tiger beer about 40¢ U.S. per can – I bought 3 cases) & friendly people. Hated to leave, as usual.*

We reached Ao Chalong, the yacht harbor for Phuket, late the next afternoon. The harbor was crowded with boats, and so shallow that we had to anchor well away from shore, still only in about 6 feet. Dinghies had to be pulled up on the beach, right at the foot of a flourishing restaurant where you could sit at your table, have a quiet drink and watch the pounding surf turn your dinghy upside down. We soon learned to haul ours right up to the front porch.

Customs and Immigration was in town, several miles from the harbor. We took a Tuk-Tuk: one of the omnipresent little three-wheeled taxis named, I think, for the sound their engines make – and managed to work our way through the Thai bureaucracy. Fees were considerably higher than we had expected.

Two days later Petra and I took off for Phra Nang Bay and its spectacular scenery. Iain elected to head for Bangkok on his own. We were to meet him back in Ao Chalong.

March 14:

> Now anchored between three islands – Ko Yai, Ko Hong (Paradise I.) and Ko Na Khae. Scenery is incredible – I think it even beats Fatu Hiva. Sheer limestone towers rising straight out of the ocean, festooned w. stalactites that take every shape (including gargoyles). Earlier, we anchored off Ko Phanah to explore a cave that reportedly extends more than 200 meters & ends in an inner lagoon. But the cave was so big (and totally black once past the first corner), and our light so inadequate, that I turned the dinghy around & rowed out again.

> Now we're anchored in what looks like a Disneyland setting – spectacular islands & rock formations all around us. We did some dinghy exploring – went into one rocky little bay & finally through a short little cave, then out the other side of the island! Stalactites everywhere, even high up on the sheer cliffs overlooking the sea. A few fishermen in their graceful "longtail" skiffs, but we've seen only one other yacht so far.

(The longtails are long narrow wooden skiffs, powered by big air-cooled auto engines mounted on a balanced boom about 20 feet long. The boom carries a propeller shaft attached to a big three-bladed prop which extends far out behind and can be swung up to operate in very shallow water, or even lifted clear out while still running. These looked like highly maneuverable watercraft, but very dangerous with that big prop spinning out behind.)

March 15:

> An interesting day, though we only moved a total of 5 miles. Motored (after lounging several hours in our amazing anchorage & buying 4 crabs from some fishermen) 2 miles to an anchorage off Ko Phra At Nuni, a 378-foot-high island rising just about vertically out of a shallow sea. Chugged about a mile in the dinghy to a huge cave in the cliff wall, where we found two Thai guys digging & bagging bat-shit, packed at least 3 feet deep on the floor of the cave. Meanwhile, thousands of bats

squeaking & fluttering around the roof of the cave, which must be 100 feet high or more in spots. Supposedly, you can climb all the way up & look out the top of the island. We got about halfway up and chickened out. Getting down was harder than getting up, though one of the Batshit Brothers seemed able to walk up it, barefoot, almost without handholds. Iain would have loved it, I imagine.

Both guys were very agreeable – They had water & eating utensils with them, but no boat. Apparently one shows up periodically to haul away the bagged guano. The stuff had a penetrating smell but appeared relatively light & flaky, rather like coarse brown oatmeal. The cave was awe-inspiring. I wondered about the effect of breathing bat-shit dust all day, but these guys looked healthy.

Then we moved another 2-3 miles to anchor off Ko Thalu, a 100-foot island with spectacular sheer cliffs and another cave that reaches right through the island. One huge cliff was festooned with amazingly grotesque stalactites dripping down from the overhangs, some of them weighing tons, hanging there precariously. The local fishermen pull their skiffs under the overhangs and tie up to the stalactites to snooze in the shade. I wondered if the stalactites ever broke loose and landed on them.

March 19:

Underway out of PhiPhidon harbor, heading back to Ao Chalong. Supposed to get a call there from Iain at 4 p.m. Sorry to leave PhiPhidon & its topless tourists – interesting viewing for a sex-mad old person like me.

After Thailand we have a long straight run ahead of us – about 1,200 miles across the Andaman Sea and the outer edge of the Bay of Bengal to Galle (pronounced "Gaul") at the southern tip of Sri Lanka.

(I decided, reluctantly, to skip India altogether because I was told that the Indian Customs wanted a list of every item (including every sewing needle, every knife, fork and spoon) on board, and were wont to seize whatever didn't get listed. Never did learn whether the report was true, but it scared me off.)

Our route to Sri Lanka would take us close to the Nicobar Islands, which looked inviting on the map but were barred to visitors. Reportedly the Indian government wanted the islanders left in their uncivilized state.

We collected Iain and departed Ao Chalong March 22.

March 25:

Night sky filled w. stars – easy steering w. Big Dipper & Polaris in the north and the Southern Cross in the south, with Orion overhead, all at the same time, & distant lightning flickering far off in the distance.

March 26:

Rounded the corner about 7 last night, keeping well south of the Nicobars, w. just a hint of Great Nicobar I., about 20 miles north. Iain says he saw a light for maybe half an hour, also one ship heading east, well to the south. Our fears (about pirates) proving groundless, so far at least.

On March 27 I was steering, staring at the sea in my usual half-trance when two killer whales slowly rose out of the deep indigo, close together and glistening black with big patches almost blindingly white, silently looking me over. They hung there, almost motionless, for two or three minutes and then slowly sank out of sight. I wasn't scared; they were too beautiful.

March 28:

Lost a fish – apparently a big one because he broke our 80-lb. test line. At same time a flock of dolphins appeared, flashing & frolicking in our bow wave. Much picture-taking.

March 29:

130 miles, an excellent run. Iain lost one fish very early but shortly afterward caught another. Tomorrow is his 26th birthday. Petra plans on attempting a cake.

March 30:

119 miles at 12:30 p.m. (We'll turn the clock back 1 hour today – we're now 6 hours ahead of GMT.) Big birthday celebration at midnight when Iain started his shift – I arose from my bed (having previously decorated the place with our one paper streamer while Iain slept) and we had coffee, tea, whiskey (Asian Mekkong) and the famous cake, painstakingly made with preserved fruit bits picked out of our Muesli cereal & baked in the frying pan (didn't do the plastic handle a lot of good). Iain received a wrapped can of fruit for his gift. Good time had by all.

Petra very quiet these days. But she worked hard for Iain's birthday.

April 2, 7:45 a.m.:

Landfall! Dondra Head Light (& a ship) off to starboard.

** Total miles – 1,059 from Phuket to Galle. Total engine hours – 13.

The Galle inner harbor was small and populated with a half-dozen yachts. Peter of the yacht SAMARANG, out of Sydney, helped us tie up by dinghying our stern line back to a big floating drum. Our first visitors were a health officer and a man with the unlikely name of Goonch. Goonch was representing the shipping agent Don Windsor, now deceased, who seemed to have corralled all the business with yachties visiting Galle. Goonch immediately invited us to a party that night to note the first anniversary of Don Windsor's death. We were told that the affair would go on all night, and promised to attend.

I wondered how much we would see of Petra, who seemed to have grown steadily more morose – she had started packing when we were still miles out to sea, and she and her bulging backpack disappeared almost immediately after we reached land. I wasn't sure what the problem was, but I had an unhappy feeling that part of it stemmed from The Great Candy Theft.

I was the culprit here. One night, while on watch in the small hours, I discovered a small package of hard candy, obviously stashed away either by Petra or Iain. Thinking "They won't miss just one, will they?" I stole a piece and then, overcome by animal lust, I devoured the entire package.

I didn't get away with it. "*Did You Eat My Candy?*" Petra demanded shortly afterward. She was clearly enraged. On an ocean passage everything is finite and everything is rationed, except maybe sea water. You don't take more than your share of the common stores, and if you have secreted some private goodies somewhere, they should be *yours* and nobody else's. I had stolen her stash and broken the rule.

I told her I was sorry, that I wasn't thinking, that I would make it up to her as soon as possible. This did no good. My guilty apprehensions proved right: she was not present at the Windsor bash, and I did not see her again. Iain would be leaving too, but I knew he would clear out properly. I wasn't so sure about Petra, especially when I heard she had taken up with some local guy. This was a worry: if she turned out to be a problem or a burden on the community she would be my responsibility – I brought her in, after all. I had heard many horror stories of skippers being held liable for the antics of errant crew members.

There didn't seem to be much I could do about it though, except to watch for her and try to get her to sign out officially if she was leaving. I wondered if she really understood the spot she had me in, and if she was truly pissed at me. If so, I might be paying a large price for a handful of lemon drops.

Meanwhile, I explored Galle and environs. I hiked into town along the long curving beach, past little fishing shacks and huge dugout fishing boats and men mending nets under palm trees. They usually waved or smiled as I trudged by. I visited the historic fort, built by the Portuguese, enlarged by the Dutch and finally occupied by the British, that protected the west side of the harbor. Within the fort I found a complete smaller town that included banks, a post office, hotels, gem dealers, wood carvers, and souvenir shops.

I did not take a room at the historic New Oriental Hotel, but its brochure was fascinating. A sample:

There are many tales these rooms tell of the hilarity of the parties to an occasional suicide of the occupant. Ghosts? Well that has to be experienced!

Galle was a comfortable place. I tried to chat with the toothless old man who turned up every day, slowly paddling a battered dinghy among the anchored yachts while he cast a very thin line for tiny fish. I dickered with a young guy who paddled out on a chewed-up plastic surfboard to tell me that his wife made courtesy flags. (I visited them in their home near the harbor and bought a bunch of beautifully-handsewn flags for the countries still lying ahead.) One day I took the train to Colombo, the capital, about 70 miles away. But the city seemed too busy, too noisy and too crowded for me. I returned the same day. Though my train was called the Colombo-Galle Express, it seemed to stop every few minutes for passengers. Another day I went to a dental clinic to get a filling replaced. I was ceremoniously ushered in to the dentist, ahead of a roomful of waiting patients. I felt that I should apologize to them. The dentist charged me about $10.

I hunted for crew. I hiked around the harbor with my hand-printed notices, trying to explain my plan to hotel and beach-bar managers who seemed completely baffled. I did manage to post notices in two hotels, but I was sure that any hopeful applicant would be hard-pressed to get his questions answered there. All I could hope for was that he would be able to find me on the boat.

I often drank beer with two brothers who ran the little store where I bought most of my provisions. The time passed pleasantly, but my search for crew seemed to be going nowhere. And I was determined to go to the Chagos Archipelago, reportedly the sailors' heaven out in the middle of the Indian Ocean.

What about going alone? A neighbor yachtie told me he had learned to sleep 20 minutes at a time while sailing single-handed: he figured it took about that much time for the average ship to reach you once you spotted it heading toward you on the horizon. He had a little egg-timer kitchen gadget with a bell. He'd set it for 20 minutes, go to sleep, wake up and look around the horizon, set it again and go back for another 20 minutes' sleep if the coast was clear.

"After all, it isn't written in stone that you have to sleep four or six or eight hours at a stretch," he said. "Look at animals – they don't do it."

Well, I told myself, I have a timer, if it comes to that. And it did. I left April 15, heart in mouth and all alone, at noon. That morning I wrote these impressions in the log:

The logo/symbol of Sri Lanka probably should be the outstretched hand – a lot of people, particularly kids, ask for money or freebies. The other night some Customs guy pursued me, requesting a can of beer. And young guys are constantly attaching themselves to me, wanting to be "guides," usually in exchange for beer. But the people are warm & friendly & gentle, despite their rather aggressive hustling. Bandula & Mike, brothers who sold me most of my provisions, are intelligent and seem genuinely friendly. They had me over yesterday morning to sample their traditional New Year's Day food (also punctuated by many firecrackers set off at certain propitious times, like 6:09 in the morning).

Sri Lanka is apparently one of the most heavily-populated countries in the world, & it certainly seems crowded – narrow roads absolutely teeming with people, bicycles, motorcycles, Tuk-Tuks, cars, huge trucks & buses, plus crude wooden-wheeled carts drawn by water buffalo, plus many lone cows meandering, the only things not in a hurry. And, one day, even a huge elephant gliding along, tended by several important young men.

This was my first single-handed voyage of any length and I was feeling pretty scared.

(Years later, the Sri Lankan coastline, the harbor of Galle and the little train I rode to Colombo were all wrecked by the Christmas tsunami of 2004. Thousands died.)

CHAPTER 18

Solo

1,400 tough miles alone to Chagos Archipelago.

1993

April 15, 4 p.m.:

> *Well, I'm underway – and I do mean "I". It's the big solo voyage. I feel more than slightly apprehensive, wondering how this will go and whether I really know what the fuck I'm doing. Well, guess we'll find out, won't we? Spent most of the day yesterday dealing with the bureaucrats; found out that the elusive Petra had come and gone 2 days ago. She did clear out properly, anyway, which saved me some grief. Wind is light and dead on the nose. Now motoring with autopilot making its little squawks. Guess I'll be listening to that a while – I hope. I really didn't have much choice about the single-handed sailing. Absolutely nobody responded to the two notices I posted. Shit. Getting sleepy already and it's not even 6 p.m. yet. May as well try a 20-minute snooze, I guess.*

April 16, 6 a.m.:

> *Well, I survived the first night but I didn't do much sleeping. Lots of ships passing, and thunderstorms finally caught up and passed me. Not much rain, but horrendous columns of brilliant lightning. Wind shifted completely around as it passed, then*

moderated. About 2 a.m. I finally got up courage and energy to hoist reefed main, jib and reefed mizzen, then turned off the engine at last. Set timer at 20-minute intervals. Woke up at one point to find jib aback and us traveling northeast, heading back to Sri Lanka!

7 p.m.:

Shuffled out from one of my many half-hour naps and was surprised to see lights way off to port – a ship sailing my way; first all day long. Then a little rainy squall came through so things got lively for a while. Ridiculously enough, we seemed to be on a collision course (just the two of us preparing to crash way out here?), so after a while I turned away. We passed, green to green, and I went back to 216 degrees.

April 17, 7 a.m.:

A pretty good night last night – wind moderate and steady enough so no sail changes required until early dawn. At least twice I slept right through the rather loud chime on the kitchen timer, set for half-hour. Probably slept at least an hour each time – not so good. Maybe I'll get more used to this business. Otto has done very well so far – I wish I had an extra. I keep thinking he will burn out at the first real heavy drag on the tiller. I'm beginning to appreciate how nice it is to have something other than me on that tiller.

April 18, 6 a.m.:

A somewhat frustrating night, with wind almost non-existent. Tried to sleep in cockpit to tend Otto, who kept beeping his alarm in frustration. Awoke three times to find us heading (or at least facing) north with all sails aback. Had to jibe around to get back on course and last time took forever, with me pushing on main boom trying to get sail to jibe back. There was just enough wind to make this very difficult.

Have now worked out on the trombone two days in a row. Can't do it long – lip gets tired. Have had a number of very vivid dreams every night.

April 19, 6:15 a.m.:

A fairly tough nite, with steady strong SW winds. Had jib, reefed main and mizzen up . . . we must have inadvertently come about 6 times during the night, and each time I had to wrestle in the jib and start over. With the chop we were tacking in about 130 degrees, not good at all.

Noon:

86 miles. Weather is not improving, despite a pretty good barometer (29.78 and rising) & occasional sunshine. Waves continuing to build. This weather is getting uncommonly tiresome. During the strongest part of the blow I saw jumping porpoises, maybe 5 of them just soaring out of the waves. Looks like they like the rough weather. It's fairly calm down below with this sail rig, though pretty hot. Almost all the ports & hatches are closed to keep out spray. Now & then I find myself wondering if I'm really doing this. The frequent dreams seem so real, things get confusing.

Last night the $10 patch-filling on my front tooth, attached in Sri Lanka about a week ago, quietly detached itself. So much for that dentist & his Kings College, London, credentials.

April 20:

Our track for the last day and a half looks like an exercise in frustration. Once again I slept through a no. of bells on the timer. But I woke & emerged just as we came about. Apparently I'm fine-tuning my sense of what TURTLE DOVE is doing, even when I'm asleep. Put jolly old Fats Waller on the tape today to celebrate the wind change.

April 21, 2:30 a.m.:

Fourth squall in less than 12 hours. And since we were sailing 270 degrees at times, and never less than 180, I thought we'd get west somewhat. But just got a new fix and our only progress was due south, moving steadily away from our course line of 216. Well. Have to move west at some point. In the middle of the hullabaloo I saw the lights of a ship, far off to port and moving north. First vessel sighted in two days.

9 a.m.:

Finally managed to sleep a while. And there were two more flying fish waiting on the deck this morning.

Noon:

Wind still blowing steady 25-30, and 40 when the rain squalls come over – I've stopped counting and don't even go out in the cockpit; just hover in the companionway, ready to luff the main when we get hit too hard. Think we'll be ready for a new jib when this is over.

We have made a little westing in the past few hours – that gives me a little encouragement. For some reason I keep singing Waller's "I'm Gonna Sit Right Down and Write Myself a Letter" – it's driving me nuts.

. . . Only 11 miles north of the equator now, but no Crossing-the-Line ceremony is scheduled. This will be my third time (twice heading south, once north).

April 22, 1 a.m.:

I'm passing a ship! And I actually talked to him on radio, although not much of a conversation. He sounded Japanese, requested my position, then said something like, "Impossible to talk by radio."(Is there another way we can talk that I don't know about?) and signed off. Ship past now – I wonder what it's like on board. Very different from here, I guess. First conversation I've had with anybody in six days, and a pretty unsatisfactory one. Well, at least I know that the radio works. I wonder – whatever happened to the Fraternity of the Sea?

3:15 a.m.:

Well, the jib just ripped all to hell. Proceeding under staysail till morning. I'm going to bed (I hope).

5:20 p.m.:

Now proceeding with double-reefed mizzen (first in a while), double-reefed main, staysail and ridiculous little jib. Boat is balanced and doing 4-5 knots, sailing comfortably. But pointing ability appears to have fallen off – we're pointing about 205 degrees, and actually doing about 175. Could be hitting current, too. The chart says current ½ to 3 knots toward the east, worse luck, along here.

Caught another fish, or at least part of a fish, this afternoon. When he hit he was so heavy I decided to tow him a while. So after about 15 minutes I hauled him in, with some difficulty. I found I had the head, and only the head, of a big tuna, maybe 20-30 pounds. Sharks or something had left me very little. In Australia, at least, we got about half the fish! I managed to cut out a few morsels and had them for dinner – right tasty with a bit of soy sauce.

5:45 p.m.:

Two boobies flying against the setting sun, wheeling, soaring, gliding, almost touching the sea, almost touching each other, bodies perfectly streamlined with their feet tucked up behind them, turning their heads to take sly little peeks at me as they soar circles around us. Made for this element. Later I see them afloat, riding the choppy seas with nonchalance, looking for all the world like ducks in a city park.

April 23, 1:15 a.m.:

Wind suddenly gone light . . . Very quiet down here without the crash of waves against hull, creaking and banging of blocks and lines on deck.

The wind – its presence, occasionally its absence or contrary direction, is always there, always the first consideration. When it blows hard you can't eat soup or salad in the cockpit; cabbage blows out of the bowl and soup blows off the spoon. When it's light I feel anxious as I watch the Southern Cross gradually swinging to starboard, meaning we're getting farther off the course. And if we do go off course, what does that mean? Maybe an extra day or two to get there. Time to quit fretting and nap again.

April 24, 10:15 a.m.:

Last night, to anyone cruel enough to watch, our path would have looked like this: (Crude drawing of corkscrew path with five complete loops, drunkenly heading northeast: wrong direction). *We did at least four complete 360s when TURTLE DOVE came about and I elected to jibe around to get back onto anything like our course. I was determined to stay on the port tack all night, to see how it would go. It went badly – we went NE instead of SW and lost maybe 12 miles. Whether it blows hard or light, the wind want to come from the wrong corner.*

I was thinking about the absence of bugs (except my own stable of cockroaches, of course) – no flies or mosquitoes out here. And then I saw a lone dragonfly flitting around, about 350 miles from the nearest land. How?

5 p.m.:

A while ago I dropped one of my two hideous purple plastic bowls overboard. Decided to try to get it. We came about, then jibed around in one of the 360-degree maneuvers I've been practicing . . . TURTLE DOVE swung around slowly in a perfect circle, came up alongside the bowl & I scooped it up with the landing net, first try! A pretty neat maneuver. (Of course, Man Overboard tactics aren't all that useful when you're sailing alone.)

April 25, 8:15 a.m.:

Last night I discovered I'd left the anchor light at the top of the mast turned on, all day. And I kept wondering why the batteries weren't charging. This morning

I left the same light on again for more than two hours . . . Seem to be making a lot of stupid mistakes lately.

And this morning I found a fresh rip in the bottom of the furling jib – probably ripped while I struggled with it last night. I fear it's rotted by sun, but will try to sew on a patch.

1:30 p.m.:

I realize that in these days alone (how many? Nine?) I have come to move w. exaggerated caution: stooped over, always one hand holding onto something, moving slowly like wading through knee-deep water. I try never to run, no matter how great the crisis.

Last night, in the dark, wind & rain stinging my privates as I moved naked around the deck, I suddenly had a vivid picture of me going over on a sudden lurch, the last grab slipping, the boat rushing away as I'm enveloped by this warm water more than two miles deep, and TURTLE DOVE churning on, really on her own now, diesel engine chugging away at 1,000 rpm, the AutoHelm chirruping and squawking throatily to itself as it makes tiny little course corrections to stay at 250 degrees, Antarctica the next solid land. How long would she go? Diesel tanks close to full, she might run quite a while till somebody saw her – after all, I haven't seen a ship or a plane for two days. "A whole lotta nuthin' out here", my daughter used to say.

Not the worst way to go, I'm sure. (But then I think of the tuna I caught two days ago. By the time I got it in, only the head was there.)

April 26, 12:15 a.m.:

Arthritis bothering my right hand considerably the last two days. Even writing is painful. Seems that in a crisis (halyard jammed at the top of the mast, say), the adrenalin takes over & I work away full strength without feeling a thing. Then, afterwards, I have trouble picking up the sugar jar.

Eleven days now – at the moment, at least, I'm in no great rush to get there. It is, after all, just another stopping place – "Wherever you go, there you are." I will be glad to see other yachties, but I guess I'm gradually getting over at least some of my earlier anxieties. Have been thinking about a better rain-catching system – maybe a kind of canvas skirt hanging below the main boom. Barrels of water landed on this boat today, enough to fill the tanks many times over, and I caught only a pitiful 2-3 pails full. (And some of that probably flavored with WD-40, where it ran off the main gooseneck fitting.)

April 26, noon:

Slept much of the night away last night – I know we did several 360s in the non-existent wind. At one time during the night we had a passenger – a booby balancing on the overturned dinghy on deck, head tucked under his wing. I shone the flashlight on him and he woke up, turned & stared at me in what looked like indignation. He didn't move & neither did I.

April 27, 2:30 a.m.:

Just realized that I'd let TURTLE DOVE's birthday get by – she was launched April 23, 1988. Will have to have a ceremony tomorrow. Also realized how much more attention I'm paying to the boat & the environment, now that I'm on my own. I can tell our compass course pretty closely at night just by looking at the Big Dipper to my right, the Southern Cross on the left, and Orion up ahead. And tonight I decided that the vertical axis of the Southern Cross acts like the hour hand of a clock, as it rotates around the heavens.

3:15 a.m.:

Rain started in earnest & I out on deck, naked, collecting water. Got the 5-gal. plastic jug and two pails full & felt good about it till I realized I'd left the main hatch open. Cushions inside soaked. Crept outside & emptied water into tank through the deck fill. Makes me feel like the thrifty squirrel. The fresh rainwater tastes delicious – surprisingly cool.

11:30 p.m.:

Awoke a little while ago, came up, looked around blearily, & there were the lights of a ship passing in the same direction, 4-5 miles off to port! First ship sighted in a number of days. I wonder if he saw me. I tried to call him on VHF but got no response. Would have been nice to talk to somebody.

April 28, 3 a.m.:

Awoke to find TURTLE DOVE aback as a major squall hit w. heavy rain & strong wind. Made the necessary adjustments for port tack, let main luff (already 3 sail slides torn loose by flapping) and then stood helplessly in companionway hoping nothing blows out (thinking of that elderly midget jib flogging away up front).

I hear birds crying overhead, close by. Those two boobies that seem to be traveling with me, maybe. Were they birds, or something in the water – maybe porpoises? I heard them again, twice more, as I struggled w. sails. Managed to drag the main down w. considerable difficulty, it was blowing so hard. Decided to leave midget jib, staysail & miz up to give us some stability. Besides, I was soaked, cold & beat. Also scared – I kept thinking it was going to get worse. After I got the main lashed up I just went to bed.

In the early hours we drifted NE (damn!) and are now approx. where we were at 10:40 last night. This is getting depressing. The only good thing I can think of to say about it is: "Well, I'm collecting drinking water!"

* From Sri Lanka to position at noon 4/27: 939 miles sailed.

April 28, Noon:

53 miles. I just decided what to do – probably shut down engine & just drift, if we must. Don't have the fuel to keep motoring indefinitely. Trouble is, motoring seems to be the only way I can move westward.

April 29, 12:15 a.m.:

Was awakened by the agitated bangs & rattle & rushing noise that spells squall. Scrambled out & into slicker but hated to get out into it. TURTLE DOVE just tucked her shoulder down & plowed on through it, heading NW, with no help needed from me. Pretty good boat. Now things are calming down & I can see stars out ahead. Will go check my rainwater pails. They're hanging under the main boom, rather like maple-sap buckets.

Noon:

55 miles. We're almost exactly where we were at 6:30 a.m. today, which is farther EAST than where we were at 10:30 last night!

April 30, 7:15 a.m.:

Awoke this morning to find a large tanker already past me to starboard. Called on radio and got a response, though a laconic one. I asked if he'd seen me on radar & he said, "Oh yes, we saw you." He said they were headed for Brazil from Singapore. Asked me no questions and I seemed to run out of conversation, so we wished each other a good journey & signed off. First conversation w. anybody in a long time.

April 30, Noon:

Carefully taped duct tape over my stitching on the rotten roller jib. Tape seemed to start detaching itself the minute I got the sail up. So far the stitching is holding but it hasn't blown very hard yet.

1140 p.m.:

Second squall to come through tonight since dark – in both cases I awoke feeling the boat was racing ahead, lunging & plunging. I got halfway out of the companionway & eased the main sheet till the main was pretty much straight with the wind, luffing & flapping like hell. Not very good for the sail, I guess, but what else to do? With this one I was a little scared, wondering what to do next if the wind kept increasing. It didn't, or at least that's what I persuaded myself to think.

In the daytime (if awake) I can see these squalls coming & at least be psychologically prepared – not at night. So far this is turning out to be a tough night. Fortunately I have a pot of pea soup to sustain me.

May 1, 1:40 a.m.:

Awoke with the familiar "squall coming" feeling, but so far it's mostly rain & only a small increase in force of wind. I was dreaming I was with some friends & we were waiting for my father to arrive in an unfamiliar car. I went to the front porch to look for him & there he was, just pulling up to the curb in front of our house. He was wearing a hat, some kind of light straw fedora, the kind he always favored, and he had his glasses on and was slightly hunched over and was staring ahead intently, but he was talking to somebody much younger. And suddenly in the streetlight I saw him laugh at something the other person said, a quick genuine but slightly abstracted laugh, so real.

So real. And I remembered what a good guy he was, so alive and alert and responsive before he got old and forgetful and vague and confused. I miss him and wish I had been more appreciative & responsive to him in those days. He was a very good Dad.

1 p.m.:

Boat rolling heavily & everything banging & crashing. If this is "transitional" weather, I don't much like it. Nowhere to go but up, I guess.

May 2, 5 a.m.:

> *I'm up, with another howler coming through. Even with only two little sails up, I've got too much – TURTLE DOVE heeled over most cruelly and racing along. Am now within a few miles of my detailed 'local' chart. Timing is good – I'll have a full day to negotiate, but weather is bad for dealing w. reefs. I'm wondering if I dare try to enter an atoll under these conditions.*

7 a.m.:

> *It's light outside & what I can see is pretty dismal. Some lighter clouds up to windward, but the wind is hitting us hard, waves are big & rough & everything is shades of gray. If I must go on without stopping, I figure to pass between Blenheim Reef on the right & the Salomon Islands on the left – passage is about 6 miles wide & 30 miles ahead.*

Noon:

> *Trying to thread our way through & can't see beans – it's pouring rain. GPS, don't fail us now! Looks pretty doubtful for a stop here.*

(At this point it was too rough, and I too tired, to make log entries any more. We were hit by squall after squall and finally it turned into a real storm. I started pulling down sails – first the main, which came down readily, to my great relief. But I had a battle with the jib, which bellied out madly and threatened to pull me overboard as I struggled with it at the end of the bowsprit, now and then plunging waist-deep into the sea.

(I got it in somehow but I heard a rip when it caught on something. So now we had just the little super-heavy staysail up. But it was shaking crazily in the wind, and the light at the top of the mast was vibrating so fast it looked as if it would disintegrate at any minute. Then the *real* wind hit. I lashed the tiller in place with rubber strips, to keep us moving more or less west, and crawled below. Later I felt the boat rolling heavily, climbed out and saw the staysail was lying on the foredeck, still hanked to the stay. The top of the sail, where the clew ring had been, looked as if somebody had taken a big bite out of it. The ring had been torn out and was still attached to the halyard, three-quarters of the way up the mast.

(We needed some sail, so I dragged out the storm trysail, made new for me in 1987 and used only once before. To get this sail on the mast track you must open a little gate in the track above the furled mainsail. This is held in place by a bit of wire, like a cotter pin. With the fitful light of my headlamp I was working on this tiny wire when the boat took a fearful roll to leeward. Clutching the main halyard for dear life, I swung out over the sea like a kid on a rope at the old swimming hole, then back in as the boat rolled back, smashing my left thigh hard against the mast. I was wearing my safety harness but I hadn't snapped it onto anything, so it did me no good at all.

(Seriously shaken, I fell down on the cabin top, sat there recovering for a few moments, snapped myself to something & finally resumed working on the trysail. I got it up at last and it steadied the boat surprisingly well. It stayed in place for the rest of the night and most of the next day.

(Now my main concern was to move west, or at least no more south. I was worried about tiny Nelson's Island, a little rocky 4-foot flyspeck on the fringe of the Great Chagos Bank, about 22 miles south of the Salomon Islands, where I was trying to go. I had been forced south to within about 3 miles of the island. I speeded up the engine and we managed to claw off more to the southwest.

(Later the storm eased & the wind shifted enough to allow me to turn back northeast. We had come almost in a perfect circle. By first light I had decided that I must skip Chagos & press on to the Seychelles. But around 9 a.m. I suddenly realized that I was looking at land, off to the northwest. And the storm was pretty well past – some sunshine was squeezing through the clouds. So on I went, finally taking in the trysail and motoring into the wind, up over rollers maybe 20 feet high and a quarter-mile apart that seemed almost benign. Close to the islands, I tried to call any boat nearby on the VHF but got no response. When I looked up the mainmast I could see why – the radio aerial had blown away.

(The pass into the atoll looked OK – there were rollers bracketing the entrance, but they were not breaking heavily. So in I went, after battening down the companionway in case a following sea came aboard. None did, though TURTLE DOVE got thrown around a bit. I could see a bright blue-white sand bottom through the clear water in the pass. The water was 20 feet deep. All was calm inside the atoll and I motored slowly across, heading for a dozen sailboats anchored on the far side. As I neared them, a guy in a dinghy sped out and came alongside, introduced himself as Brendan from South Africa, and guided me through the coral heads to an anchorage among the other boats.

(I was so tired I was having auditory hallucinations – I could clearly hear a radio playing and a man and a woman having a lively discussion in some unknown language. This, and a strange sinister scuffling sound on deck, continued even after I turned the engine off and welcomed Brendan aboard. I could kill for a cold beer, I thought.)

I was snug and safe within a ring of tropical islands, all of them breathtakingly beautiful. Chagos at last!

This was one of the toughest ones, I wrote in the log. *But I feel great having done it.*

- 1,419 miles traveled, Sri Lanka to Chagos
- Sailing hours 350; engine hours 82, total days 18.

CHAPTER 19

Chagos

Five weeks in Paradise.

The Chagos Archipelago is a collection of tropical atolls in the middle of the Indian Ocean, about 1,000 miles south of India. Each atoll is a ring of little coral islands. The northernmost atoll, the Salomon Islands, is a cruising sailor's dream. About 130 miles to the south is the biggest island in the entire archipelago: Diego Garcia, about 17 square miles of coral, sand and palm trees with a magnificent natural harbor. It has become one of the world's most secret military bases.

The British acquired all of the archipelago in 1965 from Mauritius, which had ruled the islands for more than a hundred years. Then, in a secret deal, Britain leased Diego Garcia to the U.S. All 1,200 inhabitants of the entire archipelago were resettled – some to the Seychelles, but most to Mauritius, more than 1,000 miles away.

The islanders, called Ilois or Chagossians, had been there for centuries. They tried to fight their removal but so far their objections have not prevailed, even though in May of 2006 a British high court ruled that the Ilois have every right to return home.

Much evidence of those who lived here years ago still remains. On the island of Boddam in the Salomons several buildings are hidden in the undergrowth, including the remains of a chapel and a graveyard. One building, which still has a roof, has become the cruisers' Yacht Club, decorated with painted yacht names and even with a visitors' book. Nearby is a huge rusty iron tank holding rainwater with a hole cut in its side, stopped with a wooden plug. Pull the plug and you get a shower, if there's been rain lately.

Both Boddam and the island of Takamaka, on the other side of the atoll, have wells with a limited supply of drinking water. Reportedly you can find little lime trees still bearing fruit, though I never did.

Since the Salomon Islands form a circle two to three miles in diameter, anchored yachts can switch sides to get good shelter from wind and waves when storms come through. This was why I found almost all the yachts clustered near Boddam, at the sheltered side of the circle, when I arrived after the storm. Skippers said several boats dragged anchor but were not damaged. They reported winds of up to 50 knots.

There were few restrictions to visiting most of the Salomons, except for Diego Garcia. Yachts could stop there only in dire emergency. B-52 bombers took off from Diego Garcia to attack Iraq during the 1991 Gulf War, and again to bomb Afghanistan in 2001 after the September 11 attacks in the U.S. Reportedly, suspected al-Qaeda terrorists have been held and interrogated there. Most recently, the military base was in the news because it survived the great Christmas 2004 tsunami with relatively little damage.

Every few weeks a military ship from Diego Garcia visits the Salomons. It's too big to enter the pass, so British and U.S. personnel come in on a launch. They check passports, deliver and collect mail, and reportedly will assist in an emergency. Most important, they also bring in, prepare and serve a sumptuous shore dinner for the yachties.

I was lucky – the ship arrived just two days after I did. I had recovered from all my vicissitudes, and thoroughly enjoyed the grilled hamburgers and chicken, the potato salad and cole slaw, the cookies and cake and *the cold beer.* It was the first – and likely the last – time I would find Customs and Immigration people treating me to anything.

Aside from these sporadic visits, our little Chagos home was totally isolated. It was a community made up entirely of transients. Some people had been there for months, though there was supposed to be a time limit. It appeared that the only real limitation was the prospect of running out of food, and since there were plenty of fish and coconuts, ships' stores could last a long time.

On Chagos there were no laws, no elections, no mayor or government, no military, no police or fire department, no chapel or town hall, no Wal-Mart (in fact, no store at all.) This was a society continually being reborn – a sociologist's dream, or maybe nightmare.

I was told that generally everybody got on well. There were frequent potluck dinners and other get-togethers with everybody invited, and daily volleyball games on the beach. But I also heard of a few ugly moments. One yachtsman reportedly had tried to claim ownership of a plot of land (chasing others off where he was operating a marijuana farm), and finally had to be forcibly dissuaded. And I was told that another time there was a dramatic fist-fight on the beach over a woman, (presumably somebody's wife or crew member), where the combatants had to be separated before one drowned the other. In these and less serious conflicts, I heard, cooler heads had stepped in and harmony prevailed once again.

If leaders were needed at Chagos, they must emerge spontaneously, like crocuses (croki?) popping up through the snow in spring. And the process would have to keep repeating itself as new resident arrived, stayed awhile and then departed. So I regarded my fellow yachties with particular interest. Which were the wallflowers and which the croki?

There were about 40 people and 17 boats when I got around to counting – six vessels from the U.S. or Canada, three from Australia, two each from France, Germany, South Africa and Holland, and one from Hong Kong. There was an elderly French couple, probably well into their mid-80s, who had been sailing their big shabby wooden ketch for 40 years. There was a 75-year-old grandmother who traveled alone on a little sloop. There was an electronics wizard who seemed able to fix anything. There was the burly American Burt Reynolds type who owned the volleyball and net and organized the daily games.

There was an American couple who had had their yacht shot to pieces around them in Aden, South Yemen, but were still cruising on a new boat. There was the diffident family who had taken an incredible 84 days to arrive from South Africa, running out of almost everything en route. There were a number of male-female couples, one gay male couple and several lone bachelor types. (Reluctantly, I listed myself in the last category.)

All these people had at least one common interest: they all had sailed at least 1,000 miles (and in many cases, much more) to get to a place where they were on their own. There was a lot of communication within this little enclave. Six mornings a week there was the regular radio net, where every boat tuned its VHF short-range radio to exchange information about weather, special events, arrivals and departures, particular needs or problems. Most boats left their radios on all day. I used mine, and got immediate help, when I stuck a fishhook into my right forefinger. First Andre from SIRIUS arrived and cut off part of the hook, then the ever-helpful Brendan of CHRISTINA (he who welcomed me when I first arrived) came on board and pushed the cut-off hook through the skin and out. It hurt like hell. As he bandaged me up, Brendan told me he was accustomed to giving first aid to injured workers on his farm in South Africa.

There were barbeques, breakfast parties and a book swap. One high point was the First Annual Chagos Fishing Tournament, conducted in the lagoon with a number of outboard-powered dinghies. There were prizes for most fish, biggest fish, smallest fish, prettiest fish, ugliest fish. I won the prettiest fish competition with a coral trout of about five pounds – a handsome creature with beautiful rose markings. The lagoon was alive with fish, so many that you could start fishing shortly before mealtime and be pretty sure to produce the specified dinner in time.

Not long after my arrival most of the boats moved back to a favorite anchorage off Takamaka Island, at the northeast corner of the atoll.

When you think of the words "tropical paradise" you are describing Takamaka. It is a small island, next to an even smaller island that makes up part of the coral reef that rings and protects the atoll. A pristine beach rims the inner side of the island, which is heavily wooded with coconut palms loaded with fat green coconuts. The base of each tree is mounded with fallen nuts, many turning brown and sprouting strong green shoots: future palm trees.

The beach at the island's southern end is just big enough for volleyball. Occasionally the ball goes into the narrow stream separating the two islands, but recovering it gives a perfect excuse for a quick swim. When there is a tidal current in this stream you can float face-down in waist-deep clear water and slowly drift out to the guardian reef.

The reef is rough black coral, high enough to block the big Indian Ocean waves pounding in across a thousand miles. It is populated by tiny fish and strange oyster-type shellfish that live in cracks in the coral and slowly close their shells as a swimmer approaches. Their fluted lips are black, bright blue or orange in a wiggly zigzag pattern. They are smaller versions of the "giant clams" that invariably snapped closed on some poor native diver in old movies.

Inshore from the beach at Takamaka there were little clearings where cruisers had constructed primitive tables and chairs out of sticks and branches. The place looked like a Flintstone encampment.

The yachts were anchored near the beach in 10 to 15 feet of crystal-clear water where the white sandy bottom seemed to glow in the sun. Weather was warm and sunny but not hot. There was almost always a cooling easterly trade wind. There were no mosquitoes. No wonder the unfortunate Ilois objected when forced to leave Chagos.

I loved the place. In between the volleyball games and the beach parties I even did some work. Using the dry concrete floor of the little building next to the "yacht club" as a sail loft, I re-sewed the ring into the top of the staysail and stitched new patches on three jibs. I paid Sandy, mate on the American boat ZARANA, to use her onboard sewing machine to stitch over the extensive patches I had put on the old furling jib. It looked a lot better and I hoped it would hold up for the next leg.

I worried about the next leg: about 2,000 miles of solo travel to Kenya. Unless I stole a wife or a crew member from one of the other boats, the pool of possible crew candidates in Chagos numbered zero. And I had a scant 20 gallons of diesel fuel in my tanks. There would be little motoring on this leg, I vowed. There should be lots of help from the trade wind, which had blown steadily from the east since I arrived, and the chart showed favorable currents along the way. Hopefully, this should be a lot easier than the solo trip from Sri Lanka.

So, after almost six weeks, leaving behind a limitless supply of fish and cocunuts in paradise, it came time to depart.

CHAPTER 20

Solo II

2,100 easy miles alone to Kenya.

1993

On June 12 I motored (for one hour only) out through the pass, shut off the engine and hovered. It was a beautiful day but there was almost no wind. After all the goodbyes, it was embarrassing to sit out there in a flat calm, in full view. Finally a gentle east wind came up and by early evening I was working my way past Peros Banhos, a slightly bigger atoll about 25 miles to the west.

> *Last land I'll see for awhile,* I told the log. *Still feeling pretty disoriented – the usual beginning-a-voyage malaise, I guess.*

Three days later I had traveled about 270 miles and noted:

> *It is once again pouring rain & I am sitting in this boat, rocking & rolling and going almost nowhere. Can't use electricity because batteries are down, w. little likelihood of charging them by solar panel, since there's no sun. Seasickness some better, but still feeling rather queasy. Had planned to get a noon fix w. the GPS, but it's raining too hard to take it outside. Have filled every available container w. water. One fairly bright spot: so far, at least, no apparent water leak.*

By the 16th I was getting out of the gloom, in both mood and weather. I was finding that with a strong steady breeze directly astern, and with the tiller lashed at a certain angle, TURTLE DOVE would steer herself with just a small jib on each side of the bow. Things settled down so well that this was the only crisis noted that day:

> *Read Jimmy Breslin's Forsaking All Others and liked it – then found, on page 453 or so, that the ending was missing. GAWD!*

Three days later:

> *Shit! Just lost a fine big yellowfin tuna, plus one of my last few remaining lures & hooks.*

June 19, midnight:

> *Constant irregular rolling is a pain in the ass . . . I got thrown off balance while standing in the companionway & banged my left elbow in exactly the place where I hit it on our maiden voyage. Worrisome.*

Noon:

> *We're a little better than halfway to the Seychelles now.*

(The Seychelle Islands were lying right on my projected path, but I had heard that they charged yachts $100 U.S. just to anchor overnight, so I decided not to stop there.)

June 21:

> *Have seen no vessel or plane since leaving Chagos 8 days ago.*

June 23, midnight:

> *Tonight I could see: The Big Dipper; Scorpio; the Southern Cross; the False Cross (part of two subdivisions of The Ship); and Corvus (The Spanker). Later I should be able to see Orion, pretty much dead ahead to the W. I've read that Orion is the best natural navigating object in the heavens. It's my favorite.*

June 24:

> *Just found two flying fish in making my morning rounds. Will eat 'em shortly . . . I seem to do almost nothing but read, eat & sleep. Still have seen no ships or planes.*

Forgot to note that early this morning I emerged into the cockpit & saw a very bright orange light on the horizon, coming up dead astern. At first I was sure I was looking at a ship about to run me down, but finally it turned out to be a planet. Don't know which, but I'd guess Mars or Jupiter. It was incredibly bright. By 6 a.m. it was pretty much overhead & still glowing brightly after the stars had faded out altogether.

June 25:

Most of the time these last few days, I've been on pretty much a minimum use of electricity – no knotlog, no SatNav (just GPS for a few minutes twice a day), no running lights (just the little kerosene lamp in the galley at night), no compass light, no reading lights at night (just headlamp or flashlight), no tape deck. With this regimen, and plenty of sun & adjusting the solar panel during the day, I've actually managed to gain on battery-charging. Whatever you do you have to pay, though – now I'm beginning to run short of flashlight batteries and kerosene. (And books, as well.)

Psychologically, I feel better when I'm being at least slightly productive. I caught a fish yesterday and I practiced the trombone & woke up in the middle of the night singing to myself & feeling particularly cheerful.

June 26, 2:45 p.m.:

The waves roll in, choppy & frothy and white-fringed along their tops w. an occasional flash of blue-green as the sun strikes through a crest. But that's on the surface – supporting & carrying this is an immense moving wall, ponderous but rapid, powerful, inevitable. The wave slowly rears up as it swings down on us; now I look up along the dark purple wall & see white flat blankets of foam spilling over its lip, jagged & tossing little peaks along the upper edge, I hear its thunderous muttering.

Now, just as the crest rears up above us, our stern lifts smoothly, daintily, slews off to starboard for a moment, hesitates. The entire boat swings longitudinally, and green water rushes down the starboard side deck. For an instant we seem to hang suspended at 45 degrees; then we swing upright and the giant wave, almost as if it had been trapped under our keel, now rushes on past us. It seems to accelerate as I see its great blue humped back racing toward the setting sun. I look back astern, and another big one is gathering itself together, coming on.

("Mother, Mother Ocean," Jimmy Buffet sings. "You've seen it all.")

June 27, 6 a.m.:

Still blowing hard, maybe harder. Just had one wave across the cabin top that dumped about a bucket of seawater through (or under) the main hatch, despite the hatch's being closed. First time that's happened since New Zealand. Will have to try to lash it down as soon as we get a little more light. Meantime, I have a wet bed. Damn!

10 a.m.:

I now have 13 pieces of fish strung up beneath the mizzen boom, all spinning around wildly in the gale. I'm told that it's wind, not sun, that preserves & dries the fish. So far, the pieces I've tried to eat looked and felt (and to some extent, tasted) like discarded shoes. But there's good nourishment there, I believe, and it helps flesh out the never-ending rice and noodles.

. . . Relatively quiet & peaceful down here below – it's always a surprise when you stick your head out & find that the wind is howling & the waves are BIG.

June 27, Noon:

97 miles. Wind unabated – we just took part of another wave over cockpit & cabin top – once again a bucketful through the hatch & my sheets, which had dried, wet once again. And this time I was out in the cockpit digging around in the lazarette, looking for a cleat. Cockpit half full of water & both me & the lazarette well drenched . . . Some of these waves are truly immense.

June 28, Noon:

112 miles. Moving right along, despite the one teeny sail. Have rigged a shelter half over the starboard bunk, using the cockpit awning. Pretty ridiculous, but maybe it will keep me dry. Right now I'd say the bigger waves are 20 feet high from trough to crest, and a remarkably long distance apart. They look a lot like the waves on the Fiji-to-New Zealand run. They are most impressive, but generally not menacing. Now & then another one (usually smaller) will run somewhat crosscurrent and smack the port side very loudly, causing me (inside the drum) to jump about 3 feet. These are the ones that try to come inside.

June 29, 12:05 a.m.:

Well, slept about three hours pretty solidly & awoke w. wind howling once again. Am beginning to think about arriving in Africa w. this kind of wind pushing me – could be hairy. Well, it's still 480 miles away.

June 30:

Have been working on a start for the new great novel, though I still can't figure out a good ending. Beginning is pretty good, I think.

I find myself dreading the upcoming landfall in some ways – must be getting more like Moitessier, who won the first single-handed round-the-world race but decided to keep on going, passing up the prize. Will turn into a hermit if I'm not careful.

July 1:

Threw the big kettle overboard – I'd already patched one hole in it & now there was another. Last seen bobbing astern, nicely upright. Will soon fill & sink in 14,000 feet of water.

July 2:

Starting to get excited about landfall. Jittery too . . . Africa scares me a bit. Partly, I guess, it's that Kenya is next to Somalia. I want to stay away from there. Makes me feel guilty, though, thinking of those poor suffering people.

July 4, 8 a.m.:

Happy 4th of July! A rather rough night. It blew hard all the way through & we raced along at 6-7 knots, water running down the side deck & around the water jugs. Lost the water out of one when it came adrift. I slept some, but not very well.

July 5, 1 a.m.:

Awoke w. godawful diarrhea – undoubtedly the can of Ma-Ling Stewed Pork, very greasy. Now maybe 35 miles east of Pemba I. and 2,000 miles from Chagos, heading in a pretty good direction . . . Just realized that we had no 4th of July observances – oh well. I had thought of firing off a flare but decided that would not be wise. Despite seeing nobody for 22 days, somebody might see that.

10 a.m.:

Now on a latitude north of Pemba I., moving about 310 degrees but pointing maybe 280-290. The current worries me – think I'll try to head down more, playing it safe. Don't want to get there too early. Reaching Mombasa at first light tomorrow would be about right, I think. A whole new continent – AFRICA! – about 45 miles off now.

4 p.m.:

A ship – my first in 24 days! Tried to call on radio – no response. He is crossing my bow, heading NE along the coast, apparently. We now are about 22 miles offshore. So far I have run engine 1 hour in 24 days. I hope & pray the dear thing will start. Can't seem to sit still. I realize that I am tremendously excited (and nervous) about this landfall.

8 p.m.:

A second ship close by – talked to him on radio, he a friendly Filipino. His ship "just drifting," he said (at 7 knots!). He passed close to me, assuring me that he could see my light. He said (when some distance away) that he did not see me on radar. Disquieting. He is waiting for instructions to enter Mombasa.

July 6, 3:15 a.m.:

Well, despite much effort we may miss Mombasa and Mtwapa – we're almost there & it's still at least 2 hours till daylight. The current has carried us north at close to 5 knots, which is about 3 times faster than I'd figured. It's possible that there's less current close to shore, but I don't want to get very close in the dark. We're about 6 miles out now – lots of lights on shore.

7:15 a.m.:

Well, it's light and I can see it – rolling hills & trees & nice-looking houses – but I can't get to it. We were 6-8 miles north of Mtwapa by the time I turned on the engine – even so, it was still dark for an hour, and I made almost no headway battling south against big waves and strong wind & current. Tried for about 1½ hours & then quit. So it's on to Kilifi. We better do better there.

Noon:

Well, we did it, thank Gawd. I navigated by GPS, plotting the point to run through the pass into Kilifi Creek & then steering to that point. After that there were two easy ranges to deal with, and then we were in the river. I had everything battened down for the pass, because we had taken some hellacious rolls out in the deep water. I figured the pass would be worse yet. But it wasn't.

What I see of the countryside looks green & beautiful. I'm on a mooring at a sort of marina – one of the workers waved me over as I came in. Don't know what it will cost but it's worth it. Just opened all the ports & hatches – first fresh air down here for awhile. I think I'm going to like Kenya.

** 2,122 miles, Chagos to Kilifi.

25 days (24 without seeing a ship or plane), 5 engine hours.

CHAPTER 21

Africa, East

Mary P., new crew, Yemen, Red Sea crash, Egypt, Suez Canal.

1993

What a huge blessed marvelous relief it was to be in calm water, surrounded by rolling hills and green trees, seeing that friendly little black guy take my mooring line!

I had first planned to make Mombasa my landfall. But it's a big city and then I heard about Mtwapa, just a bit north of Mombasa and reportedly much nicer. So I collected charts and information about Mtwapa and then, almost at the last minute, learned about Kilifi farther north, just a possible fallback if worse came to worst. I knew that the next possible stop after that would be Mogadishu, Somalia, and I did NOT want to go there. Mogadishu had become a lawless part of the world ruled by rival warlords. When the current took me past Mtwapa and I couldn't fight back against it, I made up my mind that it would be Kilifi. I figured I'd rather be wrecked on the Kilifi reefs, if it came to that, than be dodging bullets in Mogadishu.

My home-drawn chart detail, a gift from other cruisers, showed two range markers to show the passage through the reefs and, lo and behold!, there they were, just where they were supposed to be. I aimed at a point in the center of the opening and chugged through with no trouble at all. Kilifi Creek was more like a river, wide and deep, studded with little fishing boats. One difficulty appeared immediately: a big highway bridge spanning the river and not shown on my home-drawn chart. It appeared that I must get under the bridge, and I could see sailboats anchored in the distance. Some seemed to have masts as high as mine. But were they really? I couldn't tell for sure.

I motored close to a fisherman and asked whether I could pass safely under the bridge. He smiled, laughed, nodded yes. Did he understand me? Do natives speak English in Kenya? I wasn't sure. I headed for it, as slowly as possible, and passed under with room to spare.

And here was a man in a skiff working on a mooring float! He waved to me and pointed to an empty mooring. "You can tie up here!" he said in perfect English and with a big smile. And so I met James, the boatyard boss. He asked if I had a Kenya courtesy flag. I said no and he offered to get one for me. "The colors are red and green and black," he said – and he held out a sinewy forearm for my inspection – "The black is like the color of my skin you see," he said. I could have kissed him.

I had arrived at the Swynford Boatyard, a family-run enterprise that included about 20 deep-water moorings, a rather primitive marine railway, a small bar and restaurant, and curry dinners on Sunday afternoons. About 10 yachts were moored there, most of them owned by cruising yachties who had taken jobs with various UN relief missions in Africa.

Five of the yachts had residents: Annie of Australia, whose husband was off with the UN; Debbie of South Africa, likewise; Jane and Eric of England, both recently returned from UN jobs, Poone of Sweden, a quiet towhead sailing alone, and Paul and Gwen of the U.S., a hard-drinking pair whose yacht seemed to reflect their own personalities. It was named UPYURS.

I stayed in Kenya about 10 weeks. I dickered for native carvings in Minerani, a little native village about a half-mile away, reached by walking along the sandy shores of the creek where native boatbuilders were working. I bought groceries in Kilifi, a bigger village across the bridge. I made several hair-raising trips to Mombasa on a *Mutatu,* one of the native-owned cab-vans.

I joined, reluctantly, the expatriate British gentry who turned up regularly for the Sunday-afternoon curry dinners at the boatyard bar. And I corresponded with Mary Pagano of Cranston, R.I. I had met Mary on my visit to R.I. while the boat was in New Zealand and had asked her then, half in jest, if she'd like to join me. She said no – she had pets to look after at home. But much later I asked again and she agreed. A friend would look after the pets for two weeks, she said. She would fly to Kenya to get a taste of boat life without actually voyaging (she had no sailing experience), and we planned a visit to a game preserve. I tried also to suggest that I hoped there would be romance involved, and she seemed agreeable.

We met in Nairobi Aug. 25, both of us nervous as newlyweds. We had a private stateroom that night in a sleeping car on the train heading back to Mombasa. This was a marvelous slow old train where our names were posted on the outside of our First Class coach, where courtly old black waiters in spotless white coats gravely inquired whether we wished the First or Second Seating in the dining car, where the conductor wanted to know when he should awaken us as we neared Mombasa, and where the toilets had little trap doors that opened directly out onto the roadbed below.

Back in Kilifi, we explored the shops in town and the unpaved single street in Minerani village, where free-lance tailors set up their foot-powered sewing machines in front of their houses. We chatted with the native boatbuilders working along Kilifi Creek. And we signed up for a safari in the Maasai Mara Game Preserve, for Mary's final days in Kenya.

The safari (in Africa, a trip of almost any distance is a safari) was a huge success. We traveled in a small van driven by Richard, a knowledgeable and friendly guide, with three young couples – Jens and Lone of Denmark, Robert and Gudrun of Germany, and Steve and Rachel of New Zealand. We slept in a tent, dined in an outdoor mess hall serving enormous meals, watched native Maasai dancers and spent almost every waking moment driving across vast rolling plains, gaping at animals everywhere. We saw thousands of migrating wildebeest and zebras, plus elephants, lions, rhinos, cheetahs, ostriches, hippos, giraffes, gazelles, topi, hartebeest, impala, Cape buffalo, baboons, monkeys, warthogs, one jackal, buzzards and countless other birds. We watched a lioness single out an old wildebeest, then stalk and kill the animal in a silent slow-motion ritual that seemed almost bloodless. We felt enormously lucky to have seen the place before a growing onslaught of tourists changed it forever.

Mary flew back to Rhode Island from Nairobi on Sept. 8. We had indeed become lovers and we planned to be together again, probably after I reached the Mediterranean. We agreed that final arrangements would have to wait until my plans were more definite – I still had no crew lined up for the leg through the Red Sea.

I took a bus back to Mombasa, very watchful of my fellow passengers. (Poone, the young Swede moored at Kilifi, was returning from a trip to Europe on a similar bus a few months earlier when he accepted a piece of candy from a seatmate. He woke up two days later, stumbling around Kilifi in a near-coma, bereft of everything he had been carrying, including some expensive electronic navigational gear he had purchased in Sweden for other yachties. He had no recollection of arriving in Mombasa, and he never found out who or what had knocked him out.)

No one offered me anything on my bus ride: my seatmate was a nun who silently puffed on cigarettes all the way to Mombasa. Safely back at the boatyard, I concentrated on the search for crew. I had been corresponding with Jim Bushby of Vermont, a man of about my age who operated an inn in Vermont. He had seen my ad in Cruising World magazine and wanted to try a different kind of life. I decided to take him on.

It looked as if it would be just Bushby and me, and I worried about that. By all accounts, the Red Sea was going to be close to 2,000 miles of strong headwinds and heavy shipping in confined waters. Bushby apparently knew almost nothing about boats in general, let alone ocean sailing.

But a young backpacker from Zimbabwe turned up at the boatyard while I was off on safari. He was looking for a crew spot and my fellow yachties were much impressed with him. Fired by their enthusiasm, I signed him on. It was a serendipitous decision. The new arrival was Justin J. Thornycroft, 19, a brand-new graduate of what sounded like a very posh private school in Zimbabwe. He let me know, in his soft-spoken way, that he had been the top student leader there. It seemed evident that he came from a wealthy family, but I could see no arrogance or snobbery in him. Like many European young people, he had decided to take a year out of school to see the world and try to decide a future for himself.

We left Kilifi Sept. 18. Right away I realized that the pesky current that had been so difficult on the approach to Mombasa was now going to be an enormous help.

Sept. 19, noon:

> *147 miles – a strong start for our first day's sail. Did most of it under reefed main & jib only – barreling right along under a steady SE wind. New crew doing well – captain seemed the most seasick but is recovering now. We are now off Somalia, trying to keep well off. Equator about 140 miles north.*

Sept. 20, 10:30 a.m.:

> *About 15 miles S of the Equator. There will be a ceremony for my two Pollywogs.*

1:30 p.m.:

> *Motor Vessel USSER passed on port bow – talked briefly on radio just as we crossed the Equator and did our swearing-in. She heading for Zanzibar.*

Sept. 23, 6 a.m.:

> *Jim saw a whale & says it bumped us. If so, it was a light bump, thank Gawd.*

Noon:

> *124 miles (in water) – About 205 miles over the ground!! All hail the current!*

Sept. 26, 8 a.m.:

> *Rounded the Horn of Africa! Steep high cliffs, 2,000 feet or more, silent and rutted in the haze: a magnificent headland. Wind light and from the east – a big change after days of hard south-westerlies.*

* Approx. 1,150 miles (over bottom) from Kilifi to Horn in 8 days. Works out to 143 miles a day (with the huge help of the current). A tremendous run for TURTLE DOVE.

6:30 p.m.:

In contrast w. previous days, we have sailed just 9 miles in the past 6 hours. Pretty well becalmed off this beautiful headland. We seem to be out of the shipping lanes (have seen a number of ships farther out), and it's a pleasant respite after the last few days.

. . . Had to interrupt dinner to haul in a nice yellowfin tuna, maybe 10 pounds. Fish (including one frantic marlin) have been jumping & feeding all around us since we entered Gulf of Aden.

Sept. 28, 10:30 p.m.:

Since we turned the corner around the Horn it's been HOT – nobody has worn a shirt since then, even at night. Before, running under strong SW winds, we were bundled up in slickers & long pants – I even wore a wool hat! Amazing change.

Sept. 30, 2:30 a.m.:

A beautiful full moon on this last day of Sept. More ships passing now – for the first time on this leg we were bracketed with a ship on each side, fairly (but not dangerously) close. Broke out the harmonicas & played a bit tonight.

Oct. 2, 3:30 p.m.:

Anchored in Aden, S. Yemen, among ships but at what seems to be a good anchorage, close to Customs & Immigration and easy rowing distance to shore. Went ashore & were immediately taken in tow by a gent named Omar, who led us to Customs (everybody chewing huge cheekfuls of what was described as Ghat (sp?), which "makes you feel good."

Customs excitable but friendly – wanted donation to have a drink "for Christmas." Also wanted to change our money, to which I first agreed & then changed my mind. Then to Immigration, which took our passports & gave us "gate passes." Then to Sailors' Club Motel for free shower & expensive cold beer – delicious. Local brand is SEERA. Then guided by Abdul, who apparently is rival of Omar, to a local outdoor restaurant, very good & cheap ($6 for the three of us) & a brief tour of downtown, which was not too impressive – a lot of dusty buildings in disrepair.

Jim liked Omar & we liked Abdul, which created some tension. Finally decided to go today without a guide. We want to buy fruit & groceries & do a bit of sightseeing.

*** Total of 1,446 miles on knotlog, Kilifi to Aden. About 1,520 miles measured on big chart. Ran engine approx. 7 hours.*

Aden was my first contact with a fundamentalist Arab nation, and a very primitive one to boot. We saw few women, and those few who had to venture outside looked like moving black pillars with feet. Apparently they could see through those veils, but the outfits must have been stifling. Curiously, we saw little girls wearing Western garb, with bare legs and arms and faces. Apparently this kind of freedom doesn't last very long for them.

The males, on the other hand, were everywhere. And almost everybody, from the age of about 10 on up, had a huge wad of *ghat* stuck in his chops. At first I thought they all were afflicted with some weird facial disorder. Then I discovered that the swelling was removable.

Aden seemed impoverished, somnolent, slightly decadent, incredibly out-of-date. One of the biggest downtown banks was a dim, dirty cavern, noisy with veiled women clacking away on old manual typewriters – a scene out of the '50s. And when I presented my trusty credit card to the cashier (male, of course), he held it aloft, stared at it and turned it round and round and over and over, as if he'd never seen such a thing before. I didn't get any cash. We had to resort to our dwindling stock of U.S. currency, which was readily acceptable. But every bill above a dollar had to be held up to the light, turned over several times and examined at great length. Apparently counterfeiters were rampant.

TURTLE DOVE was the only private yacht in Aden harbor, which had a coating of heavy black oil and was littered with half-sunken vessels. This was where Richard and Kathy, my friends from Chagos, were shelled and had their boat sunk by a government gunboat.

(The name of their ruined yacht, amazingly, was INNOCENT BYSTANDER. Richard said the two of them were on the boat when they saw two gunboats moving into the harbor, the first towing the second. To their horror, the crippled craft suddenly started firing at them. They cowered on the floor while their boat was torn apart over their heads. Somehow they survived. They said their efforts to get some sort of reparations had failed thus far, nor had they received an apology or even an explanation. Apparently the gunboat crew just decided it was time for some target practice, they said.)

We left Aden Oct. 4, five years to the day from our departure from Wickford, R.I. *The start of a long journey, indeed,* I wrote in the log. *I'm glad I did it.*

Oct. 8, 6:30 a.m.:

Wind pretty strong, from NNW last night & the dreaded steep chop built up, making for fairly tough sailing: beating, heeling well over w. considerable spray (suddenly, TURTLE DOVE seemed to be a wet boat). But then, around 11:30 as the moon rose, the wind died, leaving still the chop & much rolling & banging.

6:30 p.m.:

Anchored in southern bight of Harmil Island in 22 feet of water, just as darkness falling. Were beset by birds: scores of little swallows that were entirely fearless, flying in & out of the cabin, even allowing themselves to be picked up. They were all over the place. Had to chase 'em out w. the broom!

Oct. 11:

Hawk perched on mizzen spreader for last 6 hours or so – he just shit on my head while I was lying in cockpit talking with Jim . . . . Jim says he will leave boat in Port Sudan. "Our lifestyle too basic" for him, he says.

Oct. 12, 5:30 p.m.:

In a rising SE wind we negotiated a slightly tricky pass, took several doglegs to avoid coral & anchored close to Farajin I., basically a sand spit 5 miles long & half a mile wide. Nobody on this island, but we saw lights on the far side of one nearby last night – the chart says there's a fishing village there with "WELLS CONTAMINATED." I continue to be amazed at the places & conditions in which people live. Here there seems to be nothing but sand & salt water & contaminated wells – and fish of course.

Jim seems to have gone into a silent & passive role almost entirely – initiates nothing, says almost nothing, but will do whatever he's asked. Spends most of his time reading "Fire in the Belly," a book on being a man. Irony everywhere these days.

Oct. 16:

Motored about 6 hours in stifling heat & flat calm to Port Sudan inner harbor. We found one small sailboat & three charter boats, tied up together. French (?) guys aboard, skinny in bikini bathing suits, directed us to anchor nearby. Did so

& waited for doctor to give health clearance. Finally went ashore to talk to white-shirted agent who said we must hire him for $50.

I doubted it, but as usual Jim wants to do it. He wants out of here on the first plane, which leaves for Cairo maybe tomorrow night. Spent most of the day, in company w. agent (finally agreed on $35 fee), trying to get cleared in. Visited by doc on board, then harbor master, then made THREE trips to Immigration plus Security, finally begging a ride in a dinghy to Customs on the other side of the harbor, bringing Customs guy out here & then back.

When it was all over they had my documentation papers, plus our passports, and we had stupid "shore passes". Worst procedure I've hit yet, I do believe.

The Immigration office was a scene out of Kafka. It was part of a complex of one-story concrete structures in a courtyard jammed with people, all wearing white robes and expressions of almost stupefied boredom, baking in the heat and apparently waiting forever to talk to some official, presumably about getting the hell out of there.

Jim and I joined the waiting throng and eventually were directed into a miserable little one-room office with an open door (as usual, it was stiflingly hot), an open window, a ramshackle desk, three chairs and every bit of wall space jammed with dog-eared paper file folders. They looked as if they had been there a hundred years. Maybe they had.

A dark-skinned thin gentleman wearing some kind of naval officer's hat, heavy with gold braid, sat in one of the three chairs. The second chair had no seat, but I chose to sit down very gingerly in it because I noted that the third chair had only three legs. Jim tried to sit in that one and immediately pitched over backwards. I couldn't keep from laughing.

I found myself fighting hysteria throughout our interview, because people kept walking through the office and climbing in and out of the window. Our interlocutor paid no attention whatever to this. At one point he left the room for a moment, leaving his gold-braided cap on the desk. I grabbed it and pretended to hide it in my backpack.

Jim looked as if he was about to have a heart attack. Poor Jim. I don't think I ever saw anybody so eager to flee. The thought that somebody might do something – anything – that could delay the process threw him into a panic. When we finally got through it he rushed off to find a hotel room – no need to stay on TURTLE DOVE anymore. We arranged to meet for a farewell dinner that night.

Justin and I went walking. Port Sudan was big and busy, with thousands crowding the streets. As in Aden, most of the people were men, but here women were allowed to show at least part of their faces. One young guy walking toward us started laughing and talking to me from 20 feet away. "Blue eyes!" he shouted, in great delight. "*Blue eyes!*"

He was Tariq, a young Ethiopian stranded in Sudan. He brought us to a magnificent open-air market where we gawked at fresh-ground peanut butter piled up on tables in great mounded heaps, and bought huge pink-fleshed grapefruit, ripe tomatoes and green veggies. We ate at an open table in the market, with stray cats jostling for scraps around our feet. There was more than cats under the table, we discovered – one of our bags of freshly-purchased food disappeared while we sat there. We were pretty sure the cats hadn't taken it. Fortunately, we kept our backpacks on our laps during the meal. Tariq seemed genuinely mortified when we discovered the theft. He had successfully defended us against a number of hustlers already, but somebody had outwitted him here.

I wrote in the log next morning:

> *Said goodbye to Jim at the Sea Scouts Cafe last night. We had several blowups yesterday – he was hell-bent to get out of here & immediately took a hotel room. I was pissed off & told him so. We parted more or less amicably – he apologized, said he was disappointed & sorry. I said the same. But I was thinking that now the son of a bitch has his hotel room, it wouldn't occur to him to offer us the use of the shower, would it?*

> *. . . . Justin is still aboard, thank Gawd.*

Oct 20:

> *With Agent Samkary, completed the clearing-out process:*
>
> 1. *To Harbor Control, for papers showing how long we were in harbor.*
> 2. *To Port Accounting Dept. (miles away) to get a bill of $32.50 ($8 a day), for use of the port.*
> 3. *To El Nilein Bank (miles away) to pay bill.*
> 4. *Back to Port Accounting, (more miles) to show receipt from bank.*
> 5. *To Customs (nearby) for clearance paper.*
> 6. *To Immigration (Kafka Hq.) to turn in shore passes & retrieve passports.*
> 7. *Back to Harbor Control to retrieve ship's papers.*
>
> *All this cost $92 U.S.: $20 for two shore passes, $35 harbor dues and $37 to the agent, (he'd added $2 to his fee and I didn't have the energy to argue about it) plus taxi fares.*

Oct. 21, Noon:

> *81 miles. A difficult starting day yesterday – dead calm, gales, thunderstorms with spectacular lightning, like fireworks exploding across the sky. Plus a touch of seasickness.*

Oct. 22, 9:30 a.m.:

Calm persists. I believe we have Egypt on our port hand now, w. Saudi Arabia to starboard as the Red Sea narrows. We could see the faint loom of Jeddah far off to the east last night. This morning we had a lovely escort of 11 porpoises – small guys with grey racing stripes, twisting & turning in our bow wave. They seem able to propel themselves without visible movement.

The lightning, night before last, was like watching glass breaking – a shattering explosion across half the entire sky.

11 p.m.:

Around 2 p.m. we passed NAM, a German (?) sloop heading south from Suez. Spoke on radio – he said he'd been having NE, E & SE winds like us. Advised us that Endeavor anchorage is good – said Ibrahim at Port Suez (Trans Ocean Club) is a good agent to hire for the canal transit. Didn't seem much interested in my negative views about Port Sudan, where he plans to stay. Destination is Thailand. We are now better than halfway up the Red Sea.

Oct. 24, 4:45 p.m.:

Temps getting cooler now – I don't use the sweat rag constantly. We're almost at the 24th parallel of latitude, about that of the Bahamas & Florida Keys. Chart shows what it calls a 'political boundary' between Sudan & Egypt at the 22d parallel. About 80 miles farther north is an 'administrative boundary.' Is that 80-mile stretch in between a kind of No Man's Land?

Oct. 25, noon:

95 miles. Were buzzed by a four-engine U.S. Navy plane, same as off Panama. Spoke briefly to them on VHF – they said they are stationed in Brunswick, Maine. Didn't say what they are doing in the Red Sea. At noon we put out lure & instantly hauled in a baby barracuda. Apparently the place is alive with them.

Oct. 26, 3 a.m.:

About 1 a.m. Justin woke me to look at a mysterious vessel lying off our port side, a few hundred yards away. Long & low, dead black in the moonlight, a single red light forward & several small white lights at the stern. J. said it had come racing up from behind, then settled in alongside us. Looked like a gunboat or patrol boat – quite menacing. Makes you realize how vulnerable we are here.

Oct. 27, 7:30 p.m.:

Had a calm around 2 p.m. and were visited by maybe 50 porpoises, playing all around the boat, surfing in the rollers, diving deep, slapping their tails on the surface, one leaping far out twice. Justin wanted to swim with them, and finally I said OK. When he came out I went in w. face mask. A great experience – water a deep blue and porpoises all around, just keeping their distance (6 feet or so). Lovely to dive down and look UP to see them. They seem such beautiful happy creatures.

Oct. 28, noon:

Motored 9 p.m. to midnight, when NW wind came up strong. Tied one reef in main, then big jib ripped – on both sides of my new patch. Took jib in, then took in mizzen and put 2d reef in main. Now under our "heavy weather rig," which is hopeless in going to windward. We back-tracked our path, came about and backtracked again! Tacking 180 degrees – Jeez!

Struggled on through the morning, again w. our huge porpoise escort. They were with us at least 6 hours, having a great time surfing the rollers.

Oct. 30, 6 p.m.:

Stayed over on Tavila I. (Endeavor Harbor) – changed oil & main filters, went to top of both masts, decided to replace shiv (pulley) at top of mainmast . . . Didn't go ashore today, except to deposit Justin for diving this afternoon. He didn't return till after dark, causing me some worry. Found myself wondering how & when to start searching for him. Very glad when he turned up.

Possible story ideas: (1) Couple anchors off deserted island, wander off, make love, etc., return to find boat gone. What happens next? . . . Or (2) Young crewman disappears, as I feared Justin did. Skipper has to search for him, can't find him, finally takes boat to nearest settlement, runs into incredible hassle w. bureaucrats, returns to island, finds evidence of struggle but no sign of him . . .

Standing in the middle of this island is like standing on the moon, if the moon were scraped flat . . . There is absolutely nothing here.

Oct. 31, 3 p.m.:

Last night was Halloween, I believe. My grandsons probably had a grand old time. Right now I'd like to be home.

Nov. 1, 1:45 p.m.:

Anchored in Tor Harbor around 9 a.m., to get out of the wind & try to get diesel & water. A guy in a camouflage suit (Army?) beckoned & we went in w. 5 diesel jugs. Next a young guy in civvies showed up, said he was from Intelligence, asked for our passports and took us in a truck to see the General. But the General was not available, & we're back on the boat w. him holding our passports – worrisome. And no diesel. And I don't even have the guy's name.

5:30 p.m.:

Well, everything worked out. Mohammed Fouad, the young Intelligence guy who took our passports, turned up on the dock & called me in. We had a huge discussion about diesel. I had only 35 Egyptian pounds and it would take 40 pounds to buy 100 liters. Seemed to be an impasse till M. called his General, who arrived shortly afterward. We decided I could get 80 liters (four jugs) for 32 pounds. And he looked at the passports and gave them back, much to my relief.

Then he wanted to know if I liked tea, and how many sugars! Soon I was having a glass of tea w. them. The general refused any extra money or cigarettes. Next they invited us to eat w. them. I came back to collect Justin & we sat down on a blanket for a meal of rice, fish & tomatoes. Pleasant conversation in very halting English ("America is beautiful" – "Egypt is beautiful, too," etc.) At one point a soldier said something confidentially to the general, who then asked me to uncross my legs. I was wearing shorts, and apparently the sight of my bare crossed thighs (or maybe my privates were showing, for all I knew) was bothering the military. Different strokes, right?

Nov. 2, 1:10 p.m.:

Up early to empty water jugs into mysteriously-leaking main tank, & then Justin rowed in against the rising wind to fill them, twice. Dock crowded w. tough-looking "fishing-mans," (Mohammed's term), all of whom seemed quite friendly. Would rather hate to see some of them in a dark alley, though. Then Justin brought out Mohammed & his friend Yasser to see the boat. They tried our tea (they each had three sugars) & didn't like it.

Not looking forward to tackling the Gulf of Suez, reportedly dotted w. abandoned oil-drilling rigs standing in the waves like huge steel spiders, and BIG choppy waves and howling head winds.

Nov. 3, 7 a.m.:

Departed Tor & immediately found ourselves battling big breaking rollers coming in from NW, despite a moderate breeze from NNE. Pretty uncomfortable. Kept engine running – otherwise we'd be stopped dead.

Tried to go into town last evening & were stopped by our friendly soldier. Apparently the General had said no.

5:30 p.m.:

Anchored (or rather, moored w. great difficulty) at Rae Gharib anchorage after battling a strong NW wind & big seas almost all day. We're on somebody's mooring here. Hope it holds. Had a hell of a job picking it up in the wind & waves. First tried to anchor – it dragged. Then got hold of mooring but had to let it go; couldn't hold it against the wind. Managed to hang on, with great difficulty, on the 2d try. Arms are aching now.

Nov. 4, 4:45 p.m.:

Crises, crises. Awakened by a big bang last night at 1:30 a.m. – rushed out to find T.D's bowsprit crashing against a big steel work boat – hard enough, I thought, to smash it. But it held, though one whisker stay broke. Our line to the mooring buoy had chafed through in 6 hours. We took off under engine, nursing our wounds. Backstay ominously loose – still don't know extent of the damage.

Then, about noon today, the staysail stay broke clean off! Managed to rig a short length of wire to it & got the stay set up again. With the other damage, I was afraid the jib stay might go, & with it the mainmast. But we're still intact, more or less, motoring toward a distant anchorage under double-reefed main alone. Wind 30-plus, on the nose, and BIG waves. Not a pleasant day.

(This episode with the mooring, like losing the rudder in Australia, was the result of my own stupidity. I knew it was bad business to tie a rope, no matter how thick and strong, through the steel eye of a mooring buoy. The reason is chafe: the steady rubbing away of something soft against something a lot harder. The way to handle this, I knew very well, is to feed a short length of chain through the mooring eye, and shackle both ends of the chain to your mooring line, which has a steel thimble spliced into its end. You thus have steel working against steel. But here we were, knotting a 5/8-inch soft nylon line through a rusty old steel eye at the top of a big mooring buoy.

(The only excuse I can offer is that we were worn out when we reached the anchorage, and even more exhausted after the struggle to get attached to the mooring. When we finally managed it we just stumbled below, fell into bed and slept like the dead. The anchorage was hardly sheltered at all. We pitched and rolled heavily, and every movement rubbed away a little more nylon. Soon it parted and the wind swept us away, right down on this ugly old work boat, while we slumbered down below. Still half asleep, groggy and scared shitless, we had to get the engine started and get the hell out of there, into the wind and the waves and the dark.

Nov. 5, 5:30 p.m.:

> *Anchored – AT LAST! – at Mersa Thelemet. So far I guess I'd have to say the Gulf of Suez is the toughest I've encountered – steady howling wind smack on the nose, working oil rigs (with huge flares) and abandoned ones (with tiny flickering lanterns), a lot of shipping, even one area prohibited because it has mines! We had a collision w. a workboat, broke the staysail stay, broke the staysail boom & winch, had two engine failures (but got going again both times). Even the companionway ladder broke, & we chafed through the ties on 5 slides on the mainsail. A rough trip so far. I reckon we'll stay here a little while.*

Nov. 7:

> *Well, in the last two days we have:*
> *Checked bowsprit for damage. (Seems OK.)*
> *Repaired broken staysail stay.*
> *Repaired broken whisker stay.*
> *Repaired broken staysail boom.*
> *Checked bobstay for damage, tightened backstays.*
> *Re-sewn five slides on mainsail.*
> *Repaired companionway ladder.*
> *Repaired light in head.*
> *Re-wired stove solenoid, by-passing broken switch.*
> *Tightened wedge on tiller.*
> *Secured 10 gals. diesel, free.*
> *Dealt w. police bureaucrats who wanted to kick us out.*
>
> *Police Intelligence here is represented by Yousri, young and friendly but in fear of his captain, who wanted us to leave. (Harbor not open to foreigners, says captain.) Much examination of our passports & head-scratching. Finally we are allowed to stay until 6 a.m. tomorrow.*

Yousri gave us 10 gals. diesel from his private stock, refusing any payment. Finally he visited the boat, where I gave him 3 books in English. Very nice guy. Local crab fishermen also friendly. Village has about 30 people & six full-time police, said Yousri. Most desolate forsaken place I've seen. Not a blade of grass or a tree – only two forlorn little bush-like things struggling out of the conglomerate rock & coarse tan-colored sand. Hills in background, major Cairo-to-Aswan highway running just behind a handful of squat flat-roofed stone buildings.

Nov. 9, 8:45 a.m.:

Approaching Port Suez after a long night of tacking under sail w. inadequate lights. Found our 3-way light broken off & dangling by wire from main mast top yesterday. Hoisted poor Justin to the top in choppy seas – best he could do was tape it to a stay. (He could barely hang on, never mind doing any real repair work). Then, just at daybreak, we ran into heavy fog – first in 5 years. Crept along under power till it cleared at last. Found lots of ships around us then. Also found turnbuckle body had disappeared from newly-repaired whisker stay. Difficulties seem to come in bunches.

11 a.m.:

Arrived Port Suez Yacht Club, where we were taken in tow by Abdul, the friendly agent. He agreed to get visas, clearance, canal transit, etc. for $250, but then had a problem w. Justin's Zimbabwe passport. Finally got us both "Quick" visas, good for 72 hours. We're to go to Cairo pyramids on Thurs., day after tomorrow. He drove us into town for a beer & a meal. Right now I'm so tired I can't see straight. But glad to be here.

The Cairo tour was compressed into one very long day. In a hired taxi we drove through the desert past innumerable military outposts and finally entered the huge sprawling city, capital of Egypt. We passed an enormous ancient statue planted smack in the busiest part of the city – a benevolent Pharaoh Ramses gazing calmly down at teeming busses, taxis, bicycles, pedestrians and shops all around him.

We visited the National Museum, a huge building displaying what seemed to be hundreds of mummies in various states of repair. Then we crossed the famous Nile on a rather ordinary-looking highway bridge into Giza for the pyramids and the Sphinx. The place is awash with souvenir shops, hustlers and native guides, but all this doesn't really touch the impact of these mammoth structures, thousands of years old. We had our pictures taken, Justin on a camel and me on a horse, and then entered the Great Pyramid.

"Entering" means crouch-walking down a very long narrow tunnel that gradually descends into the center of this enormous pile, lighted only by some rather puny bare electric bulbs, and then walking up through an even narrower tunnel that angles up into a tiny room in the very center of the structure. I'm not ordinarily claustrophobic, but by the time we reached this dark little room I was all too conscious of the thousands of tons of cold ancient rock pressing down all around us. I had to get out of there. The hot dry air outside felt wonderful.

We stayed late that night to see the light show. The three enormous silent pyramids and the battered but still-serene Sphinx seemed even more commanding in the darkness. There was a spoken program that went with the presentation, but the words didn't impress. The sight, and the sense of overpowering antiquity that went with it, is there to stay.

Nov. 14, 9:30 a.m.:

> *Waiting to start through the Suez Canal – pilot is on board (a dour small dark guy who immediately said he hoped for a good tip & asked for cigarettes), said goodbye to Abdul, our friendly agent, and are waiting for four ships to pass, when we will join in at the end of the convoy.*

Noon:

> *Well on our way up the Suez Canal, under a hard bright sun & facing a very cold north wind. Desert scenery; occasional military outposts. Our pilot seemed totally nonplussed by the tiller when he took over steering briefly. In sign language he conveyed that he is used to wheel steering.*

Nov. 15, 9 a.m.:

> *Departed from overnight anchorage in Lake Timsah, Ismailia, which we reached just before dark last night. A quiet night, broken by a vast chorus of muezzins (sp?) at the usual muezzin-hour of 4:30 a.m. Despite word that the new pilot would appear at 5 a.m., he didn't arrive until 9. But he's a younger guy named Aloo Mohammed Ali, and a big improvement over his idiotic predecessor, who drove me crazy with his nervousness & irrelevant hand-flapping signals.*

> *Aloo arrived w. a smile, an English-language newspaper and a briefcase full of skinny loaves of Egyptian bread. And he speaks a little more English, too. I'll give him a bigger tip – maybe $15 U.S., plus our lone leftover Egyptian pound.*

1 p.m.:

Motoring steadily along w. about 20 miles of canal to go. With luck we might be out of Port Said before dark. Scenery a little more interesting – less desert, more trees & settlements, still many bunkers & military installations and VERY heroic war memorials popping up. (You might think it was Egypt that won the war.) Little green car-and-people ferries churning back & forth across the canal, plus many fishermen in rowing boats with huge heavy oars and nets. They don't mind setting them right in the middle of the canal, between passing ships.

CHAPTER 22

Med I

Cyprus, Bordeaux & Suzanne, Barbara & Turkey, crew for Greece, Malta.

1993-94

Nov. 15, 6:30 p.m.:

In the Med at last! Unloaded our friendly pilot, made one stop for a police check (more cigarettes handed out), got a brief escort out by a pilot boat, & now clearing the last two buoys of Port Said.

Nov. 16, Noon:

155 miles, est., from Port Suez. Would like to make Larnaca marina in Cyprus, though it's supposed to be full. (I think we'd be harder to turn down in person.) Haven't quite got it in my head yet that we're actually sailing in the Med – a significant accomplishment. Pretty damn cold outside – wearing three layers under my foul-weather jacket and am none too warm. Hard to believe that a few weeks ago we were sweating bullets.

Nov. 17, 3:30 p.m.:

Running downwind w. jib on boom and 1-reef main w. two preventers, rolling horribly. Just fixed myself a nice cuppa, took one sip and had it go flying into the cockpit. Just caught a nice little dorado! 'Twill make a fine dinner for two.

Nov. 18, 7 a.m.:

Now hovering outside marina entrance, waiting for office to open at 8 (we've talked on VHF to somebody), & hoping to get a spot. Wind calm, sun warm.

10 a.m.:

Have docked, been visited by Three Spirits (Health, Customs & Police, Immigration), have turned over our passports to them (which I hate), and have checked into the marina. Praise be – they've found us a spot!

Nov. 19:

Wind howling & BIG waves crashing where we were tied up yesterday in outer harbor, dealing w. Customs. We got here none too soon. Will cost about $500 U.S. to stay here 6 months, and so far it looks to be well worth it. Town about the size of Whangarei – just right, w. lots of restaurants. Prices close to U.S. but tolerable, I think.

** Aden to Larnaca, Cyprus: 2,156 miles sailed.

Almost the first person we met at the marina was Gerald Webb, an elderly elf-like little guy of great sailing experience, incredible energy and unlimited generosity who lived with his wife Wendy and their cat Topsail on JEEONA, a little double-keeled British sloop. They were to become great friends. Gerald introduced us to several excellent local pubs: the marina dwellers had an active social life. There were weekly Quiz Nights (a favorite English activity) at the Personality Pub in town, and the yachties even had their own clubhouse, provided by the management. There wasn't a lot of time to enjoy all this, though. Justin was leaving to travel Europe on land. I hated to see him go, but I had plans, too – I was going to spend Christmas with Suzanne in Bordeaux, France.

Suzanne planned to rent a friend's house in the city while the friend was away. The friend wasn't leaving for a day or two, though, so we had overnight quarters in another friend's place – an unoccupied old brick farmhouse in the middle of a vast and wintry vineyard. The house was heated only by a large central fireplace downstairs. We settled in front of it, stoking the flames with heaps of dry old grapevine. The vine wood burned briskly and that was fine, but the upstairs bedroom must have been close to zero. We piled on every blanket we could find, but still it was a long night.

The Bordeaux house had a fireplace, too, and we made regular trips out into the woods in Suzanne's little Peugeot to gather fuel for nightly fires. But we also had central heating, and we were quite cozy there. We visited points of interest in the old city, like proper tourists. We shopped for food, watched a little television and talked and talked and talked – about politics, the state of the world, the French and English languages, childhood experiences, France and the USA.

Jan. 19, 1994:

Returned to Larnaca via TAROM (Romanian Air Lines) out of Bordeaux & Paris, w. a three-hour layover at Bucharest International Airport: huge, cavernous, dimly-lighted & COLD (only warm bright spot was the duty-free store where I bought 3 bottles of relatively cheap booze). Toilet had no lock on the door, no seats, and no toilet paper. A forlorn bar at each end of the terminal, where silent travelers sat wearing hats, coats & gloves, morosely watching CNN News broadcasts, in English. Glad to get out of there and back to Larnaca, where it is sunny & relatively warm.

Two memorable meals in Bordeaux:

1. *Xmas Eve, at home of Bernard & Marie Follain of Camblauer, near Bordeaux:*

A dozen raw oysters w. rye bread & Sauvignon dry white wine; foi gras biscuit (half-cooked) w. toasted bread & 1938 Sauterne sweet wine; stuffed roast capon w. dressing, green beans & baked scalloped potatoes, served w. decanted Graves red wine; cheese (goat, Roquefort & hard) w. wheat bread & green salad, plus more red wine; assorted small chocolate cakes from Antoine's, (best patisserie in Bordeaux), then dry champagne & lychee nuts.

2. *New Year's Eve party at home of Suzanne's friend Katherine in Bordeaux:*

Cocktails of champagne, lemon juice & Cuacao liqueur; smoked salmon on toast w. warm blinis, green olives & pistachio nuts; Raw oysters w. lemon & two white wines – one dry, one Sauvignon; Crepinettes (roasted pork grilled over grapevine fire); home-made fish pate w. white wine; Magrets (duck breasts grilled, with two red wines – St. Emilion and Medoc '88; salad & assorted cheeses w. more red wine; Chocolate Marquera (choc. cake & fresh raspberries w. cream, then more champagne.

The bash finally ended around 7:30 a.m. with Tourin – traditional onion & tomato soup. A hell of a party. People in Bordeaux talk about wine the way Americans talk about sports. I learned at least a little about it during my visit – could hardly do otherwise. And I never let on that I often bought the stuff by the gallon jug or (worse yet!) in a cardboard carton. Suzanne would have been horrified.

On Jan. 22 I noted in the log:

Very slowly getting back to work on the boat – I have a long list of chores to do. Feeling pretty lonely so far.

I really wasn't alone. Gerald, who had run his own car agency and was an expert mechanic, seemed willing to help with any tricky job. And his wife Wendy invited me to dinner a number of times. I made other friends among the cruisers, too, but Justin was long gone and I still felt a little bereft. A month after I returned from Bordeaux I wrote this to my ex-wife Ellen:

I feel pretty pleased with my accomplishments. I've raised a family, loved several people, held a number of different jobs, built a boat and sailed it to far-off places (with good help, of course), now have written what I think is an amusing and entertaining novel, and am considering another. Generally, I think, I've been considerate of other people. I have some true friends. And I've done what I wanted to do, most of the time. I've paid a price for this, of course – in relationships where I couldn't seem to bend enough to hold the thing together, in the resulting loneliness & occasional depression when it seemed there was nobody to hang onto.

As noted earlier, everything changes. A month later I wrote:

Now planning to take Barbara Roberts sailing w. me. She a long tall US lady, 54. No sailing experience, but agreeable.

Barbara was slim, 5 feet 11 inches tall (at least 2 inches taller than me), an avid tennis player who knew nothing about boats and somehow had never learned to swim. She taught English as a second language at the International School in Larnaca. Through her church she had met a British sailor on a boat in the marina, and through him she met Gerald and Wendy and other sailors, including me.

She was not getting on well with the British sailor, who was a heavy drinker. As our friendship developed she broke off with him. I began spending nights in her apartment in Larnaca, and after a while I wrote to Mary Pagano in Rhode Island, telling her about it. She finally replied, telling me she was hurt and disappointed but leaving it at that. She seemed to be saying she might hang on and await developments. I did not object.

In the meantime I was enjoying Larnaca, playing trombone very badly in a makeshift but enthusiastic band (clarinet, trumpet, occasional sax and a washboard bass) that performed at clubhouse parties. After my first appearance, giddy from a number of strong drinks and applause that I certainly didn't deserve, I packed the trombone in its case, balanced it across the handlebars of my bicycle, and set off at a fast pace in the dark, down the hill that led toward my boat in its slip. But the road took a sharp turn at the dock at the foot of the hill, and I didn't make the turn. I flew off the dock – bike, trombone and all, and landed in a boat slip that fortunately was empty. The bike sank immediately. The trombone in its case floated, as did I. I paddled ashore with the instrument, chagrined and wet but unharmed. All this occasioned much merriment among the boaters, some of whom got up early to watch me fishing up the bicycle next morning.

Despite all this activity I managed to find time to post Crew Wanted notices, and this time several applicants responded. The most promising were Ron Bieri, a young Swiss, and Gabrielle Green, his Australian girlfriend. Neither had sailing experience, but they were smart and fit and seemed excited at the idea of boat travel. Barbara liked them too. We talked several times and I agreed to take them on.

April 24, 10 a.m.:

> *Departed Larnaca, bound for Antalya, Turkey, amid much fanfare from some great friends. Everybody somewhat seasick at start – heavy rolling in choppy waters hitting starboard side, but seem to be recovering now.*

April 27, 6:50 a.m.:

> *Wind came up yest. afternoon, dead on the nose. Barbara announced that she was scared to death & would be off the boat the minute we reached Turkey. Seemed serious.*

We had a pleasant stay in Antalya. Barbara and I took a 3-day tour to Cappadoccia, an ancient underground city about 400 miles inland. The place is fascinating and amazing – a human anthill with 9 known levels (and more still unexplored) of rooms, corridors, deep air shafts, shops, etc., all carved out of soft stone. Then there were the "fairy chimneys" – huge natural stone columns carved by wind & weather looking very much like erect penises, with rooms and even churches carved out inside them. The trip through the Turkish interior was fascinating too – rocks & snow-capped mountains, flat fields w. women tilling the land, deep green valleys w. cows & sheep. People very friendly everywhere.

Sadly, Barbara left to return to Larnaca and more teaching, by way of Marmaris, Rhodes, and maybe Athens by plane. We spent a lot of time trying to figure a more direct route and couldn't – It was almost a "you can't get there from here" situation because of the never-ending enmity between Turks & Greeks in Cyprus. I contined on with Ron and Gabrielle.

May 7:

Arrived in Cineviz harbor after heavy beating in fairly strong S wind, scattered rain & rather miserable conditions. Several goulets (Turkish charter sailboats, built of wood & beautifully maintained) & small inboard fishing boats were there – 6 in all. During the night everybody but us dragged anchor at least once, & the biggest goulet gave up altogether & just charged around the harbor, anchors dragging. Very fierce gusts (maybe 50?) hitting us hard. Started motor & grimly steered in gear through wind, heavy rain, lightning & thunder, even hail at one point. Things finally subsided somewhat long after midnight, & we got a little sleep. Clothes well soaked – a difficult night indeed. But Cineviz is truly spectacular, almost surrounded by lovely mountains.

May 8:

Shook hands w. a fisherman & left in bright sunlight & what seemed to be a light N wind. But once out in the open we found big swells & the same old south wind, w. ominous clouds approaching. Decided the hell with it & put in to Cavus Liman, about 7 miles south. A big curving bay w. small fishing boats moored close by, no larger craft. Looks good. Restaurant ashore, according to the guidebook.

7 p.m.:

No chance at the restaurant – howling gusts developed, just like the previous evening, and we started anchor dragging. Ended up anchoring FIVE TIMES – a new record, the last two times w. 2 anchors. Finally the gusts stopped, just as abruptly as they started.

May 9:

Anchored in Kekova Roads, entering a long narrow bay w. a bottleneck, beautifully protected, passing a marvelous old castle w. crenellated walls, high up on a hill. Anchored near a little village, waited for the wind to die, rowed ashore for a good fish dinner at a friendly restaurant owned by the genial master of Lucy, a weird little short-legged brown dog who likes to lie on her back & bite her own tail.

May 10:

Fired up the outboard & motored over to the other village to visit the castle. Besieged by female scarf-sellers, particularly one old lady who became more & more incensed when we wouldn't buy, and finally wound up spitting at us! Beautiful view from the castle: thousand-year-old stone tombs, olive groves, farmland, harbor & islands & complex waterways. Then motored across the main channel to see the "underwater city" – walls & tombs & foundations right at the edge, all thousands of years old & underwater. Water rose? Land sank? Nobody seems to know for sure.

Returned to boat, had big lentil lunch, took Gabrielle & Ron ashore, returned to boat, put gas in outboard & managed to lose gas cap overboard. Fashioned a cockamamie gas cap out of old jerry-can cap & extra washer. Now must keep eyes open for a Yamaha outboard store.

May 11:

Departed Kekova, heading for Kas. A quiet night, w. pattering rain which left red dust all over the boat. (Africa?). Sailed along very happily in a nice following breeze; decided to go past Kas because we going so good. Shortly afterward, big black clouds came up astern & then we saw two waterspouts, then two more. Doused the mainsail & shortly after the jib, when the wind did a 180 & started blowing hard from the NW. Motored the remaining 8 miles to Yisilkoy Bay & tried to anchor in a cove in NW corner, but it was deep almost right up to the edge. Then crossed over to Kalkan Harbor marina in the NE corner & entered, heart in mouth. Dropped the small Danforth as a stern anchor & tied up w. bowsprit 2 feet off the pier – very neat, for a first attempt. Paid 300,000 lire ($10 U.S.) for a night, plus 30,000 for a shower. Nice to be snug & out of the wind.

May 12:

Departed Kalkan after being awakened at 6:10 by the big goulets on either side of us firing up their engines & leaving, apparently w. all passengers snoozing. Found toilets ashore were locked; used homemade "holding tank" w. only partial success.

(TURTLE DOVE did not have a real holding tank. Ours was a 5-gallon jug marked "TOILET", assembled in hopes it would meet Turkey's strict anti-pollution laws. In Larnaca I had heard horror stories about huge fines being levied against offending yachts visiting Turkey. We planned to flush our illegal pump-out toilet only when out of harbor, and we never flushed toilet paper. Until now we had managed not to use our "holding tank.")

9:30 a.m.:

Turned back (NW wind) & hid out in beautiful little cove in NW corner of the big bay. As usual, the big Danforth dragged & we had an interesting time. Ron said he could row, & I tried to send him ashore in the dinghy with a bow line. Turned out he couldn't row – he just floundered around helplessly while I tried to steer the boat near him. Finally the elderly skipper of the HAKU BABA, *a little party boat tied up on shore w. four Germans aboard, swam out to us and took the line in. Pretty embarrassing. We'll have rowing drill later today.*

Wind persists – heavy bullets coming off the mountains in front of us, a sea of whitecaps farther out in the bay. I'm feeling annoyed @ Ron for telling me he could do something when he couldn't. I would have tried something different if I'd known.

May 14:

Arrived Gocek after a pleasant sail. Anchored beside STORYVILLE & said hello to Nick the clarinetist from Larnaca. (Nick was the star of the yachtie band.)

May 15, 7 a.m.:

Departed Gocek, homemade "holding tank" unused. But toilet pump busted; used bucket. (No-toilet-dumping law applies only to protected bays and harbors – we're told it's OK to dump out in the open Mediterranean.)

7 p.m.:

Arrived Marmaris after a great all-day sail past many islands. This country is even more beautiful than the coast of Maine. Had a fish on – our first! – approaching Marmaris but lost it. Anchored west of a big marina off a little park & among six other yachts. Quiet night.

May 18:

Departed Marmaris, sailed wing & wing for a while, thought we had a fish which turned out to be a big piece of plastic, then turned in to Bozuk Boku & were greeted by a guy in a small rowboat holding up a mooring float. Tied up there & talked over future plans. Decided to leave Turkey from Kusadasi or Cesme, then angle SW across Greek islands past Peloponnesus to Malta, have our mail sent there, then maybe on to Tunisia and the S coast of France. Then called over our host, who took us to shore & a dinner w. appetizers, beer, salad, fish & tea. About 200,000 ($6 U.S.) apiece. Very nice. Then a quiet night, except for dogs barking on shore.

For the next week we made overnight stops at little Turkish holiday coastal towns with curious names – Bozuk Boku, Keci Buku, Kargi, Aspat Bay, Turk Buku, Cukurkuk – coping with erratic winds and dragging anchors and gawking at incredibly beautiful scenery.

May 24:

Anchored in Cukurkuk, a beautiful little sandy bay, welcomed by a friendly bearded fish farmer. He speaks English pretty well & invited us to his house for a fish barbeque tonight. We'll report there at 7 p.m.

May 25:

Went ashore for our fish barbie; tried unsuccessfully to catch the sea bream raised by the fish farmer in a big pen – we finally hauled up some of the net that formed the pen itself to catch our dinner. Met a large florid German from Hamburg & his Turkish wife, who came in after us on another boat. The German turned out to be a world-class asshole & a racist, bragging about his 500-hp Wellcraft speedboat ("50 miles per hour – one hour from Kusadasi!") & getting steadily drunker through the evening.

Had a good dinner w. bread, olives, salad, pickles & peppers & fish & beer, & sat around the fire w. the fish farmer & two of his friends who arrived in a 1960 Ford Falcon station wagon. Got more & more annoyed w. the German & finally left, after paying our friendly farmer 1 million Turkish lire, which was about twice what I'd expected.

1:40 p.m.:

Tacking through Samos Strait . . . A beautiful sunny day.

May 26:

Arrived Kusadasi Marina yesterday, visited ancient Ephesus today and were much impressed. Marvelous marble buildings and statuary, much of it still in excellent condition. An enormous temple, most recently rebuilt in the third century B.C.! Place was crowded with hundreds of gawking tourists, us included. I had no idea that Turkey has such a wealth of antiquity – seems that it really rivals Greece, which gets most of the publicity.

May 28:

Departed Kusadasi. Had our final dinner out last night & found we didn't have enough Turkish lire left to pay the bill. Somehow the meal was 1 1/2 times as costly as the same food in the same place the previous day. They finally settled for all our lire, though we were about $1 short. So we walked home, w/out even enough money to pay for a pee in a W.C.

Probably won't make Khios (Greece) today. Cleared out yesterday – Immigration, Harbormaster & Customs in town, then Customs Patrol at the marina. All OK, it seemed.

May 29:

Awoke in Kavikal Limani (still Turkey) at 2:30 a.m. w wind howling & anchor dragging. Started engine & fought off from rocks, hauled up anchor & spent the next 3 hours motoring around the bay. Wind was fierce but moonlight helped. Finally w. daylight we re-anchored, this time. w. two anchors. Wind increased & I tried to sleep but couldn't – decided to row a line to shore. But I was halfway there when our TWO anchors dragged. Rushed back to TURTLE DOVE & we motored up to N shore & Ron swam ashore w. a line. Fastened it to a big rock.

At 3 p.m. the wind shifted & started pushing us close to the rocks. While trying to set the big anchor Ron dislocated his shoulder, which has a pin in it from an old injury. Finally got big anchor set & we seem to be in better shape. Ron nursing his shoulder now.

May 30:

Chugged into the big harbor of Khios, Greece. A friendly Customs guy directed us to tie up along the big concrete pier – no anchor necessary and, apparently, no charge. Filled out a form & crew list, then walked to the Customs & Immigration office nearby, then to Port Authority. Everybody very cheerful & accommodating. Only bad news is that I must pay 8,000 drachmas (about $32 U.S.) for a transit log to show my proposed route through Greece.

June 4:

Departed Khios in a flat calm – big change after being wind-bound for three days. Have decided to press on to Tinos.

June 5:

Finally anchored, bow-to, in Tinos after interminable tacking into an infernal south wind that started around 11 last night. Took us a long time to work our way down here, especially the last bit through the strait between Tinos & Mikonos. When we got here we had to anchor & wait for a spot at the marina. Finally a big power boat pulled out, snagged somebody else's anchor and then ours. Finally got free & left, and we gratefully slid into the empty slot.

(We now found ourselves grappling with the "Med mooring system", in which your boat approaches the pier, turns 180 degrees and heads away, drops a bow anchor and then backs into the dock, where it ties up with stern lines. It's a tricky maneuver, particularly when it's windy and you're trying to squeeze into a narrow space between other boats.)

June 7:

Arrived at the beautiful little natural harbor of Port Vatki, Milos. Dropped big Danforth & immediately had run-in w. German couple who complained that we were too close. Moved to another spot, then moved again when it seemed we were too close to another boat. Finally anchored & then rowed out to anchor smaller Danforth. Half an hour later a storm came thru w. thunder, lightning, rain, hail & fierce wind gusts. Dragged both anchors (2 other boats dragged, too.) Spent at least an hour struggling to recover both anchors, which were fouled w. weeds, tried unsuccessfully to re-anchor, were pelted w. wind & rain & hail & were freezing, during which this ridiculous German was shouting at us & honking his boat horn every time we dragged past because he thought we were menacing him.

"You're a bad sailor!" he yelled at one point. What a jerk! We finally gave up the fight and nosed into the pier next to 10 Austrians on a charter boat & tied up w. a stern anchor. Trying to tie more bow lines, working from the dinghy in the swell, I fell overboard & had to be hauled out onto the dock by Ron. What a day!

Later had a very jolly dinner ashore w. the Austrians. (I wondered what would happen if the German showed up – I figured Ron would try to strangle him. He didn't appear. Just as well.

We spent another week exploring the Greek coastline, stopping one night between Manolini Island and uninhabited Poliagos, another in the lovely little harbor of Kapsali Bay on the island of Kithera (where we had to move to keep clear of a big freighter tied up alongside), then several days at a big-ship pier at Kalamata, where we cleared out for Malta, about 400 miles away.

June 16, 6 a.m.:

Finally tacked after 273 miles w. wind from starboard. Moved steadily WNW till about 2 hours ago, when wind fell off & we started heading S. Will see how we do.

June 17:

Just passed the new tug MUSAEA, bound from Malta to Port Said & on to Kuwait. Spoke briefly on radio to skipper, who invited us aboard for a cold beer.

I declined (thinking of difficulty tying up alongside at sea), but now I regret it. I seem to have that New England diffidence or stand-offishness; wish I didn't. I'd have liked to see the tug up close – it looked powerful & beautiful, too. And a cold beer & a chat would have been nice. Skipper sounded British.

June 18, 10 a.m.:

389 miles sailed (& motored) to date – distance is right, but we're still about 100 miles from Malta. For a little while last night we had a S wind & could actually sail our course, 280 degrees, but not for long – it swung back into the WSW & we had to resume our port tack, now about 350 degrees, or almost due north. A bit frustrating.

Caught another tuna yesterday – maybe 8 pounds, far more than we needed. Ron & Gabrielle made a rather indifferent fish curry, cooked w. their usual agonizing slowness & w. twice too much rice. I find myself getting impatient w. them – not really fair, I know. Too much proximity. But these two do everything together (except shit, I guess, & that's probably because they haven't yet figured out how.)

Just started The 13-Gun Salute, by Patrick O'Brien. He writes w. a lovely precision & irony. I'll read more of this series when I can find them.

June 19, 6 a.m.:

Started motoring at 8 last night & still at it, weather still calm. Had to divert around a mile-long string of lights, apparently marking a huge tuna net, around 4:15 a.m.

10 a.m.:

Stopped engine to unwind a piece of plastic tape from prop & have a brief swim. Sailed across a second long net this morning, passing between its buoys without mishap. Seems strange to have big nets strung out in the path of ships.

3 p.m.:

Sighted Malta, dead ahead.

* 511 miles (est.) sailed & motored, Kalamata, Greece, to Malta.

CHAPTER 23

Med II

Mary P. and Tunisia, Sardinia, France, good ship STRIDENCE, Spain.

1994

Malta is an independent republic with a history going back at least to the 9th Century BC, when the Phoenicians landed there. Rod Heikell, author of our excellent cruising guide, writes that Malta is "a stepping stone between the two continents" of Europe and Africa. It has been fought over many times.

In World War II, Italian and German bombers "reduced the Maltese to living in rubble-strewn towns in near-starvation conditions," Heikell writes. The siege was finally broken in August 1942 when the American tanker OHIO, though badly damaged by bombs, managed to reach the islanders with a cargo of oil. The British government, which then ruled Malta, collectively awarded all the islanders the George Cross, honoring their bravery.

We stayed on the island a week and liked it. There were several friendly and lively bars close to our anchorage, and the natives were cheerful and accommodating. The scenery, with its rocky cliffs and harbors within harbors, was fascinating.

June 26, 10:45 a.m.:

> *Departed Malta after a lovely week's stay, bound for Tunisia. Malta very exciting visually: magnificent natural harbors surrounded by huge forts & churches, all of*

a sandy brown stone. Impressive public buildings on the hilly streets of Valletta, the capitol. Old busses (back to the 50s, at least) all painted green & blue & looking in excellent shape. Friendly people & efficient authorities, a little cafe overlooking the harbor.

June 27:

Rigged our very light mizzen staysail as extra jib; around midnight it ripped straight across. Not much sleep; feeling grouchy.

June 28:

Just before total darkness we arrived in fishing port of Kalibia (Tunisia) & tied up alongside a nice new wharf in the last remaining place (so we do get lucky once in awhile). Seems to be a good spot. A lot of fishing boats here, plus the biggest Travelift I ever saw – 250 tons. Visited by Customs (who actually inspected the boat), Immigration & other unnamed officials; filled out identical form twice. Gabrielle, with her Australian passport, has to go off to buy a visa. Why, I don't know.

July 1:

Still in Kalibia – had planned to leave today but wind still strong. Yesterday took a cab to Kerkouane, an abandoned 2,500-year-old community not discovered until the 1950s. Walls, streets, thousands of rooms, hundreds of bathtubs. A very nice little museum, beautiful buildings & gardens. Then stopped in town at a hammam, a public steam bath. Big steam room, then little cubicles where you dipped water over yourself. Liked it.

July 3:

Arrived Bizerte & tied up, bow-to, at Yacht Club. Since it's now 7 a.m. Sunday, there's almost nobody here, but someone did direct us into the dock & helped w. lines. Smells unpleasant – burning garbage?

We stayed in Bizerte four days. I located a little man in a little tailor shop who mended the mizzen staysail. This was tricky work, because the sail was made of very light nylon that was hard to handle. He did a good job, to my great relief. This was our only light-air sail and we needed it.

The other noteworthy event was that we kept hearing what sounded like a rooster crowing – but at a marina? Turned out to be real. A rather strange English lady, apparently alone on a big powerboat nearby, told me the rooster was hers. She had bought it in hopes it would devour all the cockroaches on board, she said. She seemed uncertain about the success of the experiment. Meanwhile, the rooster marched around her deck and inside the cabin, crowing lustily at all hours.

I never did locate the source of the burning-garbage smell.

July 7, 11:30 a.m.:

> *Departed Bizerte, heading for Cagliari, Sardinia (Italy).*

July 9:

> *FINALLY – tied up in Cagliari w. other yachts alongside a big stone pier, draped w. an enormous chain which threatened to chew up TURTLE DOVE – strong NW wind (and big wake from ferries barreling out of the inner harbor) blowing us hard against it. Fended off w. all our bumpers & two tires, plus another tire liberated from an old wreck against the outer dock. (Don't like using tires because they leave black marks on the hull, but we had no choice.) This wind had plagued us for two days – blew out the mizzen sail, put a new rip in the jib, and had us creeping along under just 2-reefed main & staysail for much of the way. A really tough trip; Ron was actively sick & Gabrielle & I both very much under the weather.*

> *All we did was sail & sleep – I had one peach, one cookie and several cups of tea, total, during the entire 46 hours. Mighty glad to get here, even if we are pinned against the pier.*

> *Cleared Immigration with a jolly gent who took us to a nearby bar & bought us coffee & beer!*

There were to be changes here – Ron left to return to Switzerland, where a job was waiting for him. And Mary Pagano arrived, some hours late, because a strike had shut down the Rome Airport for a while. When she learned that her flight out of Rome had been canceled she burst into tears in the airport, which apparently produced results – they found a way to get her to Cagliari. She was still fuming when I met her, because the strike had been scheduled well in advance and nobody told her about it. This was to be her first real sailing experience – we hadn't left the mooring in Kenya while she was there.

One morning the skipper of a neighbor yacht told us that his boat had been robbed during the night. While he and his family slept on board, somebody crept in and made off with cash and other valuables. As he related this tale, I realized that I had seen Gabrielle's pocketbook lying on the companionway steps that morning. I thought she was getting pretty casual with her valuables. But now we checked the contents and sure enough, some cash was missing, though her passport was still in the purse.

And when I looked through my wallet, carelessly left out on the navigation desk, I found that two U.S.$10 bills had disappeared. The wily thieves had visited us too, even though we were sleeping peacefully within arm's reach. We were discussing this as we walked down the pier, when a gypsy woman approached and asked to tell our fortunes. We declined, but she persisted, speaking in very good English. "You really should do it," she told Gabrielle. "I know a lot about you: your name is Gabrielle – " The rest of the pitch was lost in our amazed responses. How could she know that?

We marveled, but we still said no and continued walking. The gypsy had long since disappeared when the light finally dawned: she must have looked at Gabrielle's passport when she sneaked onto our boat as we slept.

We never saw her again.

On July 16 we rounded rocky Cape Teulada, the southernmost point of Sardinia, and proceeded cautiously up the shallow San Pietro Channel, between the islands of Sant' Antioco and the San Pietros. We anchored in nearby Carloforte with three other yachts. The finals of the World Cup, with Italy facing off against Brazil, were to start in a few hours and we figured Italy would go mad if they won. We went ashore to an inviting restaurant and found the entire street closed off, with hundreds of chairs set out in front of a large television set on a table. By the time the game started the street was packed and the crowd was at fever pitch. The game went to double overtime and Italy finally lost, 3-2, in a penalty shootout when their star player inexplicably missed scoring. The crowd slowly evaporated in near-total silence, obviously crushed. It was a lively evening for us, but we felt saddened at the end.

July 22:

> After prolonged tacking, arrived at last in Porte Conte, a beautiful enclosed bay guarded by the mighty rock of Cape Caccia, rather like the Rock of Gibraltar. A light on top, 600 feet up, guided us in along w. the light of a full moon. Anchored near two other yachts in Cala del Bollo, a bay within the bay. Went to sleep & awoke to view the end of a long-distance swimming race.

July 24, 5 a.m.:

> Off to a VERY early start (still dark), trying to get through Fornelli Passage in daylight, bound for Port Torres, Sardinia. That magnificent rocky cape with its big lighthouse & the light slowly sweeping the sky was a great sight as dawn slowly appeared. Passed a few fishing boats w. their distinctive lateen rigs – I have yet to see one of these boats actually under sail.

2 p.m.:

> Arrived Port Torres after all-day motoring in calm weather. Were through Fornelli passage by 11 a.m. – so much for early rising. Tied up in a marina, about $26 U.S. per day. Snoozed & walked around town & observed the Sunday-night promenade

w. thousands of dressed-up teenagers in the streets. Dined out in a tratorria & had veal w. mushroom, excellent but minuscule.

July 27, 7 a.m.:

Arrived at Vieux Port Marina, Ajaccio, Corsica (France!) – tied up to pontoon & waited for marina to open. Learned it would cost about $70 US for one night (!), so adjourned to an anchorage just outside another marina, Port de la Amirante. Went ashore to a bank & Immigration. Had to wait till 2 p.m. for Imm. man to appear, but when he did he stamped all three passports (including Gabrielle's, who was supposed to buy a visa for 200 French francs).

July 28:

Departed Ajaccio, passed between Pt. de la Parata and Ile de Pirri, motor-sailing. Anchored at Cargese, near three French yachts just outside the little harbor. On the way here a sailfish suddenly jumped near us three times – a beautiful fish. (Mary swore he winked at her.)

July 30, 1 p.m.:

Arrived on Sunday in the crowded harbor of Calvi. Anchored in clear green water over clean white sand, 11 feet down. Went ashore & located a dentist, Dr. Bazzali, who arrived in shorts & sandals with his little boy, apparently having interrupted a trip to the beach. He removed my front tooth, broken 2 weeks ago & getting looser & more painful ever since. Now I really look like a Jack O'Lantern, w. two front teeth missing. But I can eat & talk a lot better now. Dentist's bill (and on a Sunday, too!) was 150 francs: about $30 U.S. When we went to pay, Mary discovered her wallet missing – apparently left in the phone booth where we had been calling trying to locate a dentist. She rushed back to the booth and found the wallet, intact.

Departed in early p.m., motoring past the magnificent ketch WHITEHAWK & a fully-rigged sailing cruise ship. Now motoring in the usual absence of wind, heading for mainland France.

July 31, 8:30 a.m.:

Motoring again in a confused, choppy, rolling, uncomfortable sea. A night of varied weather: thunder & lightning & a front rolling through that had us down to 1-reef miz and staysail only. But by first light there was no wind & much sea. Mary fell in the cockpit & landed on her tailbone. Says she's OK. I hope so.

Aug. 1:

Sailing in moderate SW wind w. long tacks along coast. Lost a big tuna last evening. Got him right up to the boat & he straightened out the hook & broke the leader. Fine clear night last night . . . Lots of boats enjoying the French Riviera, which we are by-passing.

Aug. 3, 7 a.m.:

Chugged into Golfe de Fos, surrounded by petrochemical plants & refineries w. big tankers anchored, waiting. Motored down a canal to Port St. Louis, France, and tied up in a marina. Walked into the little town for dinner later.

* Corsica to Port St. Louis – 220 miles sailed.

Port St. Louis was a friendly little French town. The only difficulty here was the continuing absence of a big package of mail that Harrigan had sent, well ahead of time. It never appeared, thus weakening my confidence in the reliability of the Poste Restante system, at least in France.

We stayed in the marina a day or two and then moved to a freebie spot, alongside a stone wall at the entrance to the lock leading into the Rhone River. There was another sailboat tied up there and we talked to the skipper, a young Englishman. He seemed very casual about the arrangement and said he saw no reason why we couldn't berth there also.

Just opposite the lock entrance was a little traveling circus operated by a sturdy dwarf man and his family, which included a full-size (actually quite large) wife and a little dwarf son who looked exactly like his father. The father dwarf become enamored of Gabrielle, and took to planting himself on his stomach on the grass next to our freebie berth. On arising first thing in the morning, climbing the companionway ladder and sleepily looking out over the wall, we would find the dwarf's face, about three feet distant and staring directly at us all. He didn't seem dangerous, but it was an unnerving start to the day. Not much to be done about it, I thought – he had as much right to be there as we did.

Meanwhile I was exploring the idea of a side trip up the Rhone River in our 8-foot rubber dinghy with its 1 1/2-horse outboard, but met with discouraging reports. We were told that the river was too big, with a lot of shipping and many enormous locks: we would either be arrested or die horrible deaths in one of the locks if we tried to negotiate them in a tiny raft with its dinky outboard.

I was about to give up the idea when Mary chatted with Capt. Al Mackin of Belfast, Ireland, who was in charge of a small freighter tied up next to the lock. Capt. Mackin said he could take us and our rubber boat up the river to Lyon in his ship, but he was leaving within the hour. So in a great rush we collected our gear and the dinghy, lugged everything over the closed lock gate, put dinghy & all back in the water & motored to the ship, where the crew carried everything up on deck. We waved goodbye to Gabrielle on shore, who had agreed to tend TURTLE DOVE, and we were off for two days and two nights.

In the meantime, Capt. Al had received a change in orders. He was now to go to Privas and Valence, about two-thirds of the way to Lyons, where he would take on grain, then return down the Rhone & carry the grain to Crete. Because of the change, his vacation in London would be delayed about a week, a development which annoyed him greatly.

His ship, STRIDENCE (the company's names for all its ships ended in "ence," for some reason) was registered in Nassau, the Bahamas, but was owned by a British concern. She was 300 feet long, 45 feet wide, and made for river travel with hydraulics that moved the entire bridge deck up and down like an elevator. The ship didn't even slow down as she approached a low bridge – the bridge deck would silently drop down, as if by magic, she would sweep underneath with inches to spare, and the bridge would rise up again without anybody (except us) batting an eye.

STRIDENCE had a complement of six (Capt. and mate were English & Irish, the others Polish), plus Marco, the French pilot, who steered all the way and spoke hardly at all. Capt. Al drank beer and tossed the empties out the porthole into the Rhone, all the while telling us that the company allowed neither alcohol nor passengers on board. ("If either of you gets killed I don't want to hear about it," he remarked several times.) We had barely settled in when he suggested that Mary might like to join him in bed. When she demurred he persuaded her to iron five of his shirts: that apparently would be our fare for the river trip.

It was very hot in the ship. We slept uncomfortably on sticky plastic sofas in the crew's mess. But we really liked the food, prepared by the friendly little Polish cook who was eager to have us test his sauce.

The locks in the river really were formidable – great gaping concrete structures with towering walls and deluges of water pouring down as they filled. Mary said we must have been insane to think of tackling them in "that little rubber boat."

At Valence the ship tied up at a large grain elevator and we clambered down it, with some difficulty, for a brief visit ashore. Next morning the crew helped us unload our rubber dinghy, the outboard motor and all our camping gear, and we motored to a marina and camping area nearby. The official campground was fenced off from us at the river. So we ignored the "No Camping" signs and pitched our tent among others on a lawn at the marina side. The other tents were occupied by people with little hovercraft boats who were holding a rally of some sort.

Mary had been having a persistent internal bleeding problem, so next day we took a cab to a local medical clinic where the doctors conducted a number of tests. They prescribed medicine but suggested that she go home for surgical repairs. We got on the telephone and scheduled a flight home in two weeks from Barcelona, our next major stop. Next we went off for dinner and returned to our tent, full of accomplishment and fine food.

We found my backpack open and all my French francs, worth about $600 US, missing. Passport and credit cards were intact. *A major bummer.* Mary was convinced that the thief was one of the hovercraft crowd – an American girl she had seen near our tent. But the rally was over and the entire crowd was gone; ours was the only tent left on the lawn. And the marina manager chose this moment to tell us to clear out, immediately.

Both of us were distraught enough over the theft to see this as the last straw. We told the manager that we had just been grievously robbed; we strongly suggested that one of his "guests" had made off with our money, and we insisted on more time to get cash and rent a car. He relented a bit: we could stay till morning.

We rented a car, got some more money and prepared to leave in the morning. We did not report the theft to the police – we decided it would be a wasted effort. Somehow, we crammed everything (including the tent, the rubber dinghy and the outboard motor) into the tiny rental car, motored north on pretty back-country roads through Lyon, and found a lovely free campground on the River Seille, just where it joins the Saone. We spent four idyllic days on the river, chugging slowly in the dinghy through four small locks (three of them self-operated), past lush meadows with grazing cows and sheep and little French villages.

The little locks were lovingly decorated with flower beds and just big enough to enclose the tourists' canal boats that moved up and down the river. We pitched our tent along the riverbanks and the weather was perfect.

On a Sunday we stopped near a small village to get more gas for the outboard. A man on the other side of the river began shouting at us and I (remembering all the tales I'd heard about unfriendly Frenchmen), did my best to ignore him. Next thing we knew, the guy arrived on our side in his car. Turned out he wanted to help. He took me and my empty gas can on a long ride through the countryside, trying to find an open gas station. At last we found one. I filled my gas can and another one, supplied by our new friend. He refused to let me pay for it. (So much for the unfriendly-Frenchmen reports.)

We returned to Port St. Louis to find TURTLE DOVE back in the marina. Gabrielle had been caught by a strong wind that pinned the boat to the side of the lock. She recruited the marina manager to help her get the boat through the lock & back into the marina – this time stern-to, tied to mooring floats near our favorite bar.

We left Port St. Louis Aug. 22, after a two-week stay. We really liked the place, even though we never did get the mail package. This time it was just Mary and me – Gabrielle had left to visit Ron in Switzerland and would not be back.

Aug. 24, 3 p.m.:

> *Got our socks knocked off last night. Motored in almost flat calm till around 8 p.m., when light northerly started. Before I could get the jib untied it was howling. Pulled everything down but the staysail & chugged crosswind for almost 12 hours w. wind roaring, seas breaking & TURTLE DOVE rolling most horribly. With*

just this tiny sail we covered about 70 miles (in the right direction, even!) in the 12 hours. Damn uncomfortable, though. Left the anchor light on & popped up every 10 minutes to look for ships. Passed one, fairly close.

By 7 a.m. we could see Cape San Sebastian, the other side of the Gulf of Lions (aptly named!), and by 11 a.m. we were in the lee & running slowly & shakily under staysail & jib. Never saw so strong a wind come up so fast.

Since this was the first really heavy weather Mary P. had experienced, and since we were now down to a work force of two, I would not have been surprised to see her bail out at the first opportunity. But though she said she had been sure she would perish during the night, she made no mention of leaving. That was admirable and encouraging.

By late afternoon thunderclouds were gathering and we decided we'd had enough. We located a small and very crowded marina in Blanes, Spain, and persuaded the management to squeeze us in at the gas dock, the only space left. The guy at the dock refused to take our mooring lines, leaving me standing in the cockpit forlornly holding out a rope, like an idiot, until we agreed to pay the asking price. Not a very warm welcome to Spain.

Aug 25, 3:50 p.m.:

Turned into Port Olimpia, the new marina in Barcelona (built for the Olympics) & found good prices (about $20 US a day, dropping to around $9 on Sept. 1), & many empty spots. Settled in to explore Barcelona.

Now we were tourists, riding the Bus Turistic to see Gaudi's incredible unfinished cathedral Sagrada Familia (I actually managed to climb all the stairs to the top of one of its fantastic towers), strolling down the famous street Las Ramblas with its shops and "living statues", sampling the many bars and restaurants surrounding three sides of the marina, with a lovely beach and lovely topless bathing beauties just next door.

Mary left for the doctors at home after five days. I was on my own now and I noted these impressions of the city:

Cosmopolitan, busy, well-planned, clean, devoted to the Good Life. At 3:30 a.m. today the sound of the discos around the marina was like a huge machine, pulsating, throbbing, but in control. Seems as if everybody stays out all night, but you don't see any drunks. (I wonder how anybody manages to get up to go to work in the morning.) Plenty of parks & water fountains, but very few public WCs. They are in all the bars & cafes, though, & nobody objects if you use them w/out buying. I really like this place, but I'd have to learn Spanish if I were to live here.

I was getting ready for another run on my own.

CHAPTER 24

Solo III

Alone with the Guardia, Barcelona, Duquesa.

1994

Sept. 10, 8:20 a.m.:

*Departed Barcelona, after a half-hearted and unsuccessful effort to find crew.
Captain: J.T. Crew: Ditto.*

Sept. 11, 7:30 a.m.:

*Spent a rather fitful night w. sails up but just drifting in no wind. Shut off engine
at 6 p.m. & had about an hour's slow sailing before wind died. Started engine
again when it got light, now motoring w. about 100 miles to Ibiza. Feeling sleepy
& cranky. GPS getting more & more balky. Dismantled plug end where wires
are spliced (during which I cut through a tiny black wire, killing GPS altogether,
but refastened it), thinking the fault might be a bad connection. But apparently
that's not the problem. It just loses power & goes blank – often just before it can
come up w. coordinates. Very frustrating and alarming – I really depend on that
little sucker.*

7:30 p.m.:

Went to pull in fishing line before dinner & found I was dragging a baby tuna, about 9 inches long. Maybe my lure is a bit small. I had him for dinner. Only a few fishing boats seen today. So far I don't seem to have attained the peace of mind I had the last time I sailed alone. Takes time, I guess. And there are a lot more ships here to worry about. Haven't got the catnaps down pat yet, either.

Sept. 12, 9:30 a.m.:

Wind came up last night & held pretty steady – best I could tack was pretty much WSW, so worked my way back toward the mainland. Slept fairly well, about half an hour at a time. Saw no ships, but could see a big light (35-mile range) marking the Columbretes Islands with a 3+1 group flash.

Spent most of the night creeping by that one. With first light the wind died. Started the engine but soon stopped it when wind shifted around to the NW – a reaching breeze, at last! Now aiming at a point just off the turn at Cape de la Nao, about 70 miles away. Looks as if I may give Ibiza a miss after all.

6 p.m.:

Still blowing pretty hard, still hoping it will calm down. My fix puts me 11.8 miles east of 00 degrees Greenwich, beginning of the Western Hemisphere. It will be a first when I cross it, but if I do it now I'll have to cross back again to clear Cape de la Nao. It's 45 miles to the cape from here.

Sept. 13, 8 a.m.:

Rather difficult last night, though it turned out to be more bluster than anything else. With first dark around 9 p.m. I was about 25 miles offshore & could see lights everywhere – even a fireworks display! But also Mother Nature's fireworks – a truly awesome lightning storm over the land, with massive jagged bolts crashing down one after another. Finally decided to reduce sail & took everything down but the double-reefed main. Then just waited, barely moving. Lightning went on all night. At 3 a.m. I discovered I was moving NE rather than SW, so jibed around & went back to sleep. Storm finally passed overhead around 5 a.m. – some rain, big lightning & thunder, no wind. Now skies are clearing, wind light from NW – good!

8:40 p.m.:

Just gave the tiny little contact plugs in the GPS a shot of WD-40 & swabbed them w. cotton & got 2 good readings! YAY!

10:50 a.m.:

Just hauled in a small dorado! Perfect eating size, too. But he was so pretty – a brilliant green/blue/gold color – that I let him go. Hope he lives. (Besides, I already had one fish today – a baby tuna, slightly chewed up but still tasty.) My lure seems to attract the little guys.

4 p.m.:

Had a light following N wind right to Cabo San Antonio, where it died altogether. Had lunch, started engine & immediately it came up from the S. On the nose again, pretty hard. I realized I was really tired so came in to Cala de la Fontana, just beyond Puerto de Javea. It's a little beach resort & I found buoys set out partway across the harbor mouth. So, with some trepidation, I anchored just outside the buoys. So far nobody's bothered me. Want to go ashore to buy more little batteries, but I hate to wrestle w. the dinghy (lashed on cabin top). Maybe I'll swim in in the morning if I feel energetic.

Sept. 14:

At first light I saw the "sausage-shaped clouds" noted in the guide: a sign of strong Levanter winds coming. Then SW wind died & we rolled even more. I decided to get the hell out. Got anchor out of the mud w/out much trouble, but I farted around w. the chain attached to it & in the process banged the anchor against the bow, putting a big gouge in the planking.

Finally got it on deck, & in that short time it was blowing hard from the N. Chugged out, turned off engine & drifted while I started tying things down. Wind picked up steadily & quickly to maybe Force 8: could barely stand up in it. I went under bare poles, (no sails up at all), and am still that way, with everything battened down.

Boat doing well – barely moving but that's OK because I'm still in some lee from Cape de la Nao. I poke my head out of the hatch now & then like a turtle, then retire below again. I seem to recall reading that these Tramontanas can last three days! Geez. Spectacular coastline along here – sheer headlands, caves in the rocks, mountains. But hotels everywhere.

8 p.m.:

Well, it's now 12 hours since the wind started howling & it hasn't quit – in fact, at the moment it seems stronger. (Did abate a bit when I put up sails, but not for long.) I'm able to make about 180 degrees from Cape Nao – in fact I wanted around 215. Oh well. Three cruise ships have passed – I called the first one, who seemed to be heading toward me, & asked if he could see me & he said, "Of course I can see you." Sounded about 18 years old – supercilious little bastard in his big fat comfortable cruise ship.

Sept. 15, 9:30 a.m.:

Well, the wind finally eased off around 8 a.m. after 24 hours of strong stuff – hopefully it will remain this way. I finally ventured out on deck. Still windy (but better), but a nasty confused chop remains & we're in for a period of heavy rolling. Soon I may actually put up a bit more sail. Took 2 GPS fixes, one at 1:25 a.m. and the other 7 hours later. We covered a big 14½ miles during that period. But at least it was in the right direction.

Just before the earlier fix I poked my head out & found myself staring at a huge tanker, passing very close on the starboard side, big & black & menacing in the bright moonlight, rushing silently past. I assume he saw me – I didn't see him until just then.

A cool 65 degrees inside this morning – I even have sox & shoes on!

Noon:

Fix puts us six-tenths of a mile into the Western Hemisphere – first time in several years for TURTLE DOVE! It will be West Longitude from here on in – I must get used to counting from right to left.

Small plane, apparently private, just buzzed me 3 times, close. What an idiot! Tried to call him on VHF, got no response. I'm about 30 miles offshore.

Sept. 16, 8:30 a.m.:

Am now south of Cape de Palos, another major cape. Will stay on this tack a while more, to get well clear of the land.

Sept. 17, 9:30 a.m.:

Weather here is unbelievable. Have spent two days tacking against a steady SW wind (exactly where I want to go). At about 3 this morning it was calm for half an hour, then started blowing from the NE – a 180-degree turnabout! Am now running before it w. just staysail. Doing OK but didn't get much sleep last night. Just caught 45 minutes or so & will try for more. Discovered I'd left the anchor light on an extra 2 hours. Lack of sleep catches up w. you.

Sept. 18, 6 a.m.:

Two rude awakenings today: the first was at 4 a.m., when a bright light & 2 blasts of a horn scared the hell out of me, snoozing down below w. just the staysail up. I stumbled out in the dark & found four guys on a big black Customs boat staring at me. I waved, they looked a little longer & then took off, running without lights. I set the alarm for 5 a.m. & went back to bed.

When the alarm went off I got up (lucky I did – I don't always make it) & found myself looking much too closely at a large hotel, & us almost on shore. Just as I got turned around and heading back out to sea, here comes Customs again – with a second boat, this one white and also without lights. Both boats came close, no doubt thinking I was an escaped maniac, & asked me something: I think, "Where are you going?" A fair question, under the circumstances. I hollered "OK!" and "Gibraltar!" and "I don't speak Spanish!"

They looked me over – rather dubiously, I thought, probably wondering how I'd managed to get this far, & finally took off. I sure hope I don't see them again.

When I shakily did a G.P.S. fix I found I was in the one lousy section (about 20 miles across) that I hadn't been able to get a chart for. No excuse, of course; I simply had let the wind carry me off course while sleeping, but an unnerving experience. Maybe I am getting a little too cocky.

I now have engine & autopilot on. Dare I sleep again? Probably.

Sept. 19, 9:30 a.m.:

Well, finally found an anchorage – Ensenada de la Herradura, described in the guide as "magnificent", & rightly so. By the time I got here the howling E wind had subsided & I found this a lovely spot, even with the ever-present vacation apartments, water skiers & jet skis. No such thing as an isolated anchorage around here. So I've had a much-needed sleep and feel much perkier this morning. Decided to press on, rather than go ashore. Estepona not too far away now.

8:30 p.m.:

Stopped at Marbella Marina – swell was too great to anchor outside. Somehow managed to enter, turned 180 degrees and backed into a slip, without assistance & in the dark: a rather desperate move that worked out. 1,870 pesetas for the night, not too bad. Was visited by two ladies who seemed to be asking if I'd like their company. Declined. Disco at night, but it really didn't bother me.

Sept. 20:

I do believe I'm looking at Gibraltar! Looks like a great grey island from this distance. It's a beautiful clear day, & I'm pretty sure that's it – it's the gateway to my home ocean!

Just checked out Estepona. Looks pretty good, though town is a little distance away from marina. Nice mix of fishing craft & yachts there. I may come back to it. But I've heard good things about Duquesa, another 5 miles or so. Will see that first.

I have routinely been dodging fishing boats and nets as I run along the coast here. But when I went below to make tea (Otto was steering) I almost didn't dodge one. When I came up with my tea, there, smack in front of me, was a brightly-painted red & white fishing skiff whose lone occupant was desperately trying to start his outboard to keep from being annihilated. I threw myself at the tiller, swerved to port & just missed him. The fisherman said not a word – just stared at me and put one finger to his eye as if to say, "Keep a lookout, you dumb bastard!" He had a point. Can't imagine where he came from; when I went below I hadn't seen a soul.

These recent misadventures are directly related to sailing alone. They wouldn't be happening if there had been someone standing a watch.

No question now that I'm looking at Gibraltar. It's beginning to look just like the Prudential logo.

545 miles from Barcelon to Duquesa in 10½ days; approx. 45 engine hours.

CHAPTER 25

Strait

Estepona, Paris, Morocco, busking vs. Elvis.

1994-95

I left the boat in Port Duquesa for a month while I visited Mary Pagano back in Rhode Island. I had decided to move the boat to Estepona, and she was to join me there in February.

Estepona, Nov. 17:

> *Well, I moved here yesterday. It's probably better – close to town, sailmaker & bicycle shop, etc. I have some friendly neighbors – an English couple working hard on their big ketch. One difficulty, hopefully temporary, is that my right hip & leg have been plaguing me greatly. This is the third day when I couldn't walk, or even stand, for any length of time, & it bothered me much while trying to sleep. Spent much of the day in bed. Found myself thinking positively of a 2d hip replacement.*

Nov. 19:

> *Hip still bothering me, though it felt a bit better this morning. Been pretty much incapacitated since arriving here.*

Got pedals & a rear brake put on the bike – works much better now. (It was a
freebie from the discard pile at the Duquesa Marina.) Took a little bike tour of
Estepona this morning – it's really a charming town. (And a lot easier biking with
at least one brake.) Feeling pretty lonely, though.

I was alone on the boat in Estepona for almost three months, except for a two-week visit with Suzanne in France over Christmas. We went to Paris and stayed in the home of another absent friend. This time it was a cozy little apartment on the fifth floor of a lovely old building in the heart of Paris. The trouble was that this lovely old building, like many others in the city, had no elevator. You got there by slowly climbing four long flights of a spiraling staircase. It wound its way up around a vertical shaft that looked to be about 15 feet in diameter. The effect, looking down from the fifth floor, was dizzying – the proverbial bottomless pit. When you left that place for the day you tried very hard to bring along everything you could possibly need. Just carrying up the groceries for the evening meal was a real workout.

(Suzanne's friend had arranged for a new hot water heater to be delivered while we were there. The guy who brought it carried it up all four flights, somehow managing not to have a heart attack en route.)

We had a good time in Paris, but I missed the camaraderie with Suzanne's friends in Bordeaux. And the prices in Paris staggered me. I returned alone to Estepona by way of the old Spanish city of Toledo – a marvelous place. One of the streets I walked through was so narrow I could stretch out my arms and touch the wall on both sides.

By the time Mary joined me in Estepona Feb. 23, I had become quite familiar with the town and had come to love it. There were things to do here. I joined the American Club, attracted by its stacks of English paperback books and its bar, staffed by volunteers and offering cheap drinks, with a dependable supply of dedicated and convivial drinkers. And the club sponsored quiz nights like the Personality Pub's in Cyprus (though not so raucous), and occasional special parties and outings. It had several hundred members, mostly expatriate British who outnumbered the Americans by far. I seemed to be the only boat-person in the group.

And, after much hesitation, I started sitting in at the weekly practice sessions of the Estepona Town Band. I didn't play at their concerts, but the members seemed happy to see me at rehearsals. None of them spoke more than a word or two of English, so far as I could tell, and I couldn't always follow the conductor's instructions. But musical notes look the same in any language. And the printed directions are often in Italian, which gave us all the same handicap.

I had the only slide trombone. The rest of the section all had valve trombones, rather like elongated trumpets. The band had about 50 members, mostly men, and they were good musicians. The rehearsals tended to be relaxed and playful, with a considerable amount of joking and dilly-dallying. But on concert nights the members were uniformed and attentive, and they played very well.

The setting for the weekly concerts was lovely: the musicians sat in an octagonal bandstand built atop a stone municipal building at one end of a cobblestone town square. Along one side of the square were huge pine trees overlooking the old town below, and on the other was a large stone church with a magnificent bell tower. Several hundred folding chairs would be set out in the square, and usually there were very few left empty. At regular intervals during concerts the old bell tower would peal out with its own musical selection, but nobody minded.

This old section of town was truly beautiful. Many of the streets and little squares were lined with orange trees, sometimes in fruit and sometimes in fragrant flower, and every café and bar had chairs and tables set out on the sidewalk. Somehow the town had managed to avoid the crush of heavy traffic and high-rise construction that was engulfing most of the Costa del Sol.

I made some good friends at the marina – Sid and Doreen Fisher on the big ketch OLD PECULIAR next to me (he an expert on Hemingway, the two of them potters, farmers and former editors of a weekly newspaper in the wilds of the Hebrides); John Callaghan, a British retired teacher now laboring to rebuild the big sloop DOMINGO with the help of Tony, an Esteponian always accompanied by the most frantic ball-chasing dog in the world. And at the American Club there was Rosie, a tiny former ballet dancer, the dynamo who ran the Social Committee, and her husband Tony, a retired entertainer who was always on stage.

I had a lot of good times in Estepona, but there were plenty of lonely moments too. I was looking forward to having company. When Mary arrived we did a six-day unofficial bus tour that included five historic cities in Spain, each with its own character, and then a trip by bus, train and plane to Wurzburg, Germany. There we visited Robert and Gudrun, our safari friends from Kenya, and their new daughter, now 2 years old.

Meanwhile the hunt for crew was on again. Through a neighbor yachtie who ran a business in nearby Gibraltar we met a young backpacking couple: Neil Williams of Scotland and Mette Haarr of Denmark. Neil was an avid windsurfer with some boat-sailing experience: that sounded good. Mette was a big good-looking blonde with a guitar. She had no sailing experience, but she promised to learn fast.

Both had jobs in Gibraltar; Mette a barmaid and Neil a cook, and they wanted to keep working as long as possible. Mary and I wanted to visit Morocco, tantalizingly visible just across the strait, before resuming the main voyage. So we arranged to pick up our new crew members in Gibraltar after we two had seen Morocco.

Log entries began April 11, 1995, when we left Estepona, to the cheers of Sid and Doreen:

> *Despite the name Costa del Sol, today is gray – even had a brief spatter of much-needed rain. Wind very light from NE. Rolling heavily now & feeling queasy.*

4:30 p.m.:

> *Arrived at Marina Smir (Morocco) & found it almost totally empty. About five sailboats, maybe 15 big power boats, & almost nothing else. A staff of 3 women at the marina office w. almost nothing to do. We were directed to a Med-style berth*

on the other side, far from the showers & toilets. Many empty stores alongside – at least two restaurants open, one w. a tuxedo-clad maitre d' vainly trying to rustle up some patrons.

April 15:

Have been windbound here for 2 days w. a strong ESE wind raising hell. BIG breaking waves at the harbor entrance. Wednesday we took a taxi to old city of Tetuan – toured the intricate Medina w. a guide. Endured the hard sell from a rug merchant, did not buy.

Yesterday (Good Friday) we took a bus to the town of M'Diq, close by. Walked around in the wind, had lunch. Mary bought a small rug from a genial merchant. Today did nothing but endure the wind, which shows no sign of letting up. Boat seems secure w. many lines, but moving around a lot. Spray bursting heavily over harbor wall, ¼ of a mile away. We're moored bow-to, broadside to the wind. Not comfortable.

April 16:

Cab to Tetuan & bus to ancient city of Fes. Arrived 8 p.m. & stayed in seedy hotel. (We had selected it from our guidebook because it was listed as three-star. We thought we'd splurge for once and have some real luxury. It turned out to be probably the worst place we'd experienced. Almost nothing worked. And we were pursued so tightly by one would-be guide that we had to sneak out a side door next morning to avoid him.)

We went to the train station to check on travel to Tangier, and there we met Hassan, an ebullient ex-soldier who proudly showed us his official guide's badge issued by the government and seemed burly enough to stave off the ever-hovering hustlers. With Hassan herding us like a mother hen (he actually introduced us now and then as "my mother and father", or "my chickens"), we toured the incredible Medina of Fes, a hidden inner city with a labyrinth of narrow passageways.

Without Hassan we were sure we'd never have found our way out of the place. I gave him my Red Sox baseball cap, and Mary promised to send him some American T-shirts, when we left him in the train station that afternoon.

April 19, 20 and 21:

Windbound, still. We had plenty of time to explore Marina Smir, which seemed to be a monument to great expectations that failed. It was a huge development, ringed with handsome apartment buildings half-completed (with no apparent work continuing), and elaborate shops, bars and restaurants, most of them unfinished and unoccupied.

(Later, we heard rumors that the whole operation involved money-laundering by "the Russian Mafia." We left the place, at last, feeling as mystified as when we first arrived.)

April 22:

Wind light SW, scattered showers. Tacked/motorsailed across the strait – wind picked up & was fairly choppy but held course W of Europa Point & entered the bay. Were halted by a British patrol boat, which told us rather sternly to haul down our Spanish courtesy flag (we'd forgotten it was still up), and replace it with the British. Found Queensway Quay Marina, radioed in & entered to a good bow-on berth between STEADFAST, a U.S. boat w. all-Austrian crew, and BALDO, a small Italian boat. Nice friendly people on each side.

May 2:

Still here in Gibraltar, hoping to leave tomorrow, but it's gusty E wind and blowing gale-force in the strait. Neil & Mette, our new crew, have moved aboard & are ready to go. We plan now to go to the Canaries, then on to W. Africa, & eventually the Cape Verde Is.

Saw as much as we wanted to – maybe more – of Gibraltar during this wait for weather. I learned how to negotiate my bike through the narrow car-clogged streets. We visited the many restaurants and British pubs (including both Neil's and Mette's places), took the cable car to the top of the Rock and its semi-tame apes and basked in the spectacular views, jostled with thousands of tourists in the jammed duty-free shops.

Inspired by the many buskers on the streets – a very poor Elvis imitation was enormously popular – Mette and I had a try at it. We sat on a sidewalk bench at a busy corner, put Mette's cowboy hat on the pavement in front of us, and started playing, Mette on guitar and me alternating between trombone and harmonica. (Mary and Neil watched discreetly and anonymously from across the street, trying to keep faces straight.)

I soon learned that eye contact was the clue. Those who marched on past without looking at us were hopeless. Those who looked or lingered were at least possible patrons, though many left us nothing. One old lady stopped, requested a number of songs, listened with apparent enjoyment and then walked off leaving the hat untouched. Surprisingly, kids seemed to be the most generous. In addition to a few coins, we collected several small bags of peanuts, candy and crackers. Maybe we looked hungry.

We quit after about two hours and found we had earned somewhere a total of around $1.50 U.S. in American, British, Spanish and Gibraltar currency, plus the eatables. Without doubt, Elvis did a hell of a lot better.

CHAPTER 26

Islands

All the Canaries, blowing in to the Cape Verdes.

1995

May 7:

> *Through the strait – Have rounded Cape Espartel @ NW corner of Morocco &*
> *now proceeding slowly down the African coastline heading SW, in general direction*
> *of the Canaries. Have weathered wind & rain so far; ran engine most of the day to*
> *keep clear of shipping lanes. Now under midget jib, staysail & reefed miz, finally*
> *turned off engine. Passed some colorful blue fishing boats just before dark.*

May 8, 11:15 p.m.:

> *Boat has hardly moved in last 5 hours. A pigeon (green band on one leg) asleep*
> *in cockpit. A half-moon & a lot of stars out – a bright night. New crew working*
> *out very well. (Two hours on & six off – what luxury!)*

May 9, 9 a.m.:

> *A quiet night w. little wind . . . Lots of stars & quite cold. Pigeon sat quietly at*
> *stern (shitting copiously, as we later learned), then at daybreak flew down into*

the cabin w. a great beating of wings. Stayed indoors several hours (more guano to mop up), then allowed itself to be shooed outside. Flew round the boat several times, but always returned. Now back in cockpit – seems to like us. Saw hundreds of crabs this morning – 3-4 inches diam. & light brown color – swimming along quite happily in water 400 feet deep.

May 10:

120 miles since noon yesterday – a good 24-hour run. Pigeon was missing but now back w. us, looking disconsolate & shitting steadily.

May 11, Noon:

135 miles in past 24 hrs. – best run so far this trip. So far today we've seen porpoises, a turtle, a whale spouting in the distance, and now a real European turtle dove, perched on the lifeline & looking at us, quite unafraid. Looks exactly like the carved model Mary gave me. I call this a significant & very favorable omen.

7:40 p.m.:

A day for wildlife – have now seen 3 turtles and, half an hour ago, a small whale (20-25 feet, maybe) jumped out of the water four times. Neil saw it first & called us out. We think it was either a pygmy sperm whale or a short-finned pilot whale (but our book says the latter rarely breaches.) The turtle dove is still with us, hunkered down on the cabin top.

May 12, 4 a.m.:

Trailed long length of 5/8-inch anchor line in attempt to make steering easier. Helped a little, I think. Dislodged the turtle dove in the process & he flew off. Hope he made it. Took water in cockpit 2-3 times. Rolling heavily – rough sailing.

May 13, 8 a.m.:

About three miles from Arrecife, Lanzarote I. Another rough nite, most of it under staysail alone & dragging about 150 feet of anchor line. Still averaged about 5 knots! Island shows many volcanic cones. Strong trade wind & waves seem to persist right up to the shore.

Arrived in Puerto de Naos, Lanzarote, & berthed bow-on in a rather primitive marina (no toilets & no showers) at 1,250 pesos per night. Town looks grimy & landscape seems to be mostly cinders. Had almost no pesetas, & no place open to change money on a Sat. afternoon. Borrowed some local money from John of California, on a neighbor boat at the marina. Walked into town, bought a few groceries at a big new supermarket, then had 2 beers & a fish dinner at a local cafe – very good. Spent almost all our Spanish money.

** 684 miles, Gibraltar to Lanzarote – 6 days, average speed 4.7 knots. (Pretty good, considering that we were becalmed for hours on two different nights . . . At one point, with only a double-reefed main & staysail, we did 24 miles in 3 hours.)

Arrecife seemed strange: very neat, but mostly cinders and gravel. We took a little island tour on a local bus and found big cones of cinders all over the place. Seemed pretty bleak to me. But there were nice little restaurants – just across the harbor two fish cafes side by side, so much alike that we couldn't remember which one we had already tried. They were both excellent.

May 16, 9 p.m.:

Arrived Gran Tarajal in the dark – found it much smaller, more rocky and a lot more rolly than imagined. Harbor quite uninviting; finally got the benighted Danforth to hold on the third try. Had a very late macaroni dinner.

May 17, 10 a.m.:

Away without going ashore, heading for Puerto de Mogan, Gran Canaria.

We spent three nights at Mogan and took two bus trips through mountainous scenery in the southern part of Gran Canaria. The coastline was spectacular and the marina was beautiful but rather expensive – about $22 U.S. per day.

It was here that Mette told us she would be leaving. She had made friends with people on a French boat heading for Europe and wanted to return home with them, she said. I felt some dismay at this, but Mary didn't seem too sad. She maintained that Mette really hadn't done her share of the work, letting Neil take over her chores.

The guidebook says the acceleration zone (a kind of wind tunnel effect between certain neighboring islands) can be difficult between the high islands of Gran Canaria and Tenerife. Mette's French yacht, heading out for Europe, tackled this spot under full sail, somehow lost its rudder and had to limp back to Puerto de Mogan for repairs. Mette had to fly home. We failed to conquer the zone on our first attempt and retreated to Playa de Tararte, a little indentation close by. There was a bar/restaurant and some campers and fishermen there. We swam, then rowed in for a beer. The beach was composed of millions of baseball-sized rocks, and when we tried to jump out of the dinghy they rolled under our feet and all three of us went sprawling in the surf. We sat on the patio of the bar and drank beer beyond closing time – the proprietor finally announced that he was going home and asked us to close up the place when we were through. We did so. Pretty hospitable, I thought.

Next day we lowered sail and had another go at the acceleration zone. We could actually see a white line of small breakers marking its leading edge as we approached, but we passed through this time with little difficulty.

May 23:

> *Sailed around southern tip of Tenerife to Puerto de Colon, where we were turned away because place was full. Continued on about two miles to a little bay with a big ketch. They were on a mooring & cast off just as we approached. We latched onto it & were preparing to stay the night when a big British catamaran came up & told us politely it was theirs. Mary was mightily embarrassed. But they told us to tie on behind, gave us three beers each (we gave them a bottle of wine), & directed us to another mooring nearby. We went there & stayed the night, looking at hippy cave-dwellings along the cliffs & old lava flows on shore. A beautiful spot.*

Next day, beginning to despair of finding an open marina anywhere on Tenerife, we followed the northwest coast another 10 miles or so to Los Gigantes, described in our guide as a tourist town with a marina "at the southern extremity of enormous cliffs which reflect incoming swell . . . very prone to surge."

The marina management was not very prone to accept us, saying they were full. But finally they said OK – for one night only. We tied up alongside a big concrete wall and immediately started fighting off the surge, which rolled in regularly and threatened to grind up our starboard side. Finally we rowed the dinghy out into the channel and set an anchor out there to hold us away from the wall.

We stayed well beyond our one-day allotment. Mary was to return to Rhode Island in a week, so we tried to see as much of Tenerife as possible before she said goodbye for three-plus months. We took a bus trip to Puerto de la Cruz, a pretty town, and then on to Pico de Tiede, the big dormant volcano that is more than 12,000 feet high. There are big extremes of vegetation on this island: dry lava fields and banana plantations in the south, green trees & grass and thousands of flowers in the north, pine forests on the slopes of the big volcano.

Now it was just Neil and me, heading for Isla de Palma, reportedly the prettiest of the Canaries. We didn't like the looks of the anchorages there at either Santa Cruz or Naos, and wound up at Tazacorte, our last chance at finding a place on the island. This was a small harbor surrounded by black rocks, crammed full of boats. With considerable difficulty we anchored fore and aft and watched big breaking swells come right around the corner of the breakwater, just a few yards away. Rough as hell & much too close quarters, I thought. There were people riding surfboards on the swells, so close I could have hit them with a rock. We walked into the little town, past a huge swordfish being dismembered at the slippery dinghy landing, and had two nervous beers. We stayed another night, gritting our teeth.

June 3, 7 p.m.:

> *Arrived at Valle Gran Rey (Vueltas), island of LaGomera, & tied up to a huge rough wall w. some difficulty. A French yacht at our bow and a small boat at our stern – we threatening both of them as we surged back & forth in the swell. To my horror, I saw our bowsprit actually poking into the inflatable dinghy on the French yacht – a little more and we would have speared it like a marshmallow on a stick. We struggled w. long spring lines & warps & bumpers & tires and put out a side anchor, but continued to surge all night. I got very little sleep.*

Next day I decided we should move down to the very end of the narrow little harbor and try to squeeze between some yachts moored stern-to there. They looked a lot quieter.

We detached ourselves from the huge wall, nearly hitting the boats at either end of us, then had to struggle to raise the anchor leading out from the side as the wind caught us. Finally freeing ourselves, we chugged down to the harbor end, managed to get turned around in the narrow space and then caught a neighbor boat's mooring line in our propeller as we tried to squeeze in backward. I jumped overboard and managed to get us unwound, apparently without damage. Of course, this last fiasco had to occur under the gaze of neighboring skippers, already safely moored on each side of us. They seemed to take it in stride. Anyhow, we were at last away from that godawful wall.

June 5:

> *Bus to San Sebastian & back – two hours each way w. many switchback turns around spectacular views. More beautiful stone walls than I've ever seen before. Banana plantations, palm trees, lush green rain forest in the national park high above. Back in harbor we met Wally, an odd American-German lady who has a daughter living in Dorcester, Mass. Wally hailed our boat from shore, having noticed our BOSTON name board. We kept running into her in town, and I had a feeling that she would have liked to be more friendly. I let this pass.*

June 10:

> *Departed Gomera with little difficulty after a pleasant week. Rather sorry to leave. Bound for Hierro, if it's OK there. If not, we'll press on to the Cape Verdes.*

8:30 p.m.:

> *Arrived at Pta. de la Restinga, Hierro. Small and rocky, w. four yachts anchored fore & aft, including the French boat whose dinghy we almost speared in Gomera, and LA VENTURA, Jimmy Cornell's boat, last seen next to us in the Port Mogan marina. The couple on board, Jeanine of N.Z. & Gunter of Germany, formerly Australia, had us over for drinks, snacks & coffee. Nice people.*
>
> *I'm worried about our boat, of course – we're about 50 feet from rough lava rocks, with a big swell & two spectacular blowholes spouting white spray. Pretty windy in the morning, but anchors holding OK. Will stay here one more night, I think: pressing our luck?*

We stayed another night and were invited to a fine dinner party on the ketch APSARA, manned by a French couple and their 6-month-old baby. There were six couples as guests – two French, one Dutch, one Australian and us.

The guidebook describes Hierro as "the smallest, most remote, tranquil and unspoilt" of the main Canaries, and notes: "Until the establishment of the Greenwich Meridian, Punta Orchilla at the western tip of El Hierro was taken to be Longitude 000 degrees, and for centuries was the western limit of the known world." It certainly was one of the trickiest anchorages I'd seen, but it truly was a memorable spot

We left Hierro June 12 with light following winds. I felt proud that we had visited all seven of the main Canaries. By noon the next day we had covered only 66 miles, not a great start on the 800-mile trek to the Cape Verde Islands off West Africa.

June 13:

> *Caught a beautiful 4-pound dorado on my home-made lure! (two strips of red cloth draped over a small cork "body" with double hook attached). Trolling at maybe 3 knots – most remarkable to catch anything going so slow.*

June 14:

> *Almost flat calm. About all you can say is we're going in the right direction. Two birds, a pigeon w. leg bands & a small black-and-white swallow, which needed at least an hour to work up enough nerve to land on the boat, joined us yesterday. Pigeon is still with us, but swallow disappeared when I washed down the deck. After slatting around all afternoon, finally doused jib & started engine. Chugged very close past a big old turtle just floating on the surface. Pigeon still with us. Saw at least four turtles during the day. This is an endangered species?*

June 15:

Our fourth straight day of almost no wind. At one point yesterday a bit of rope that had dropped overboard actually wound up ahead of us – apparently we were going backward. Am re-reading Thoreau. A ship crossed our stern an hour ago, first since Hierro. Pigeon is eating leftover couscous & drinking out of tin can (and shitting over everything).

June 16, 9 a.m.:

Another night of almost no wind. Pigeon was absent all night & I thought he'd flown, but he appeared around 7 a.m., looking ruffled & grumpy. I gave him some rice kernels, served in a roach-trap can, & he devoured them, then deliberately flipped the can upside down w. his beak. Arrogant little bugger. Gave him another serving, despite his bad manners.

Noon:

50 miles. We finally have a good NE breeze; doing 4 knots. Ship's company in much better spirits. Started fishing again.

June 18, noon:

Good wind for last 24 hrs., but it's calming now. Pigeon still with us, & eating dry rice w. relish.

June 19, Noon:

115 miles, again. Wind came up pretty strong & held all night – strenuous sailing. I appreciate how much more work is involved when there's only one crew. Experimented w. square sail made of old 8 x 12 canvas hung on bamboo whisker pole. Worked well, but eyelets pulled out – sewed in some reinforcing patches & put it up again today. Finally doused it for fear it would blow out. So I think I'll get one made. Will have to be of strong stuff.

June 20, 8 a.m.:

Three porpoises joined us as I scrubbed up pigeon shit from that miserable bird. Feeding him may have been a big mistake, but I couldn't let him starve. Porpoises hanging right under the bowsprit, twisting sideways to look up at me – big old guys with gray patches on their flanks.

June 21, 0005 a.m.:

> *So far a good night. I find I can lie on my back in the cockpit & steer backwards, using the North Star as a guide. Every now & then a huge glowing blob of phosphorescence goes sailing off astern, apparently provoked by the propeller dragging through the water (even though the engine is not running). Now & then I see a big underwater light flash off to the side. Fish?*

8:30 a.m.:

> *Land ho! Ilha de Santo Antao in the Cape Verdes sighted, just off to starboard & about 30 miles away. A big central peak over 5,000 feet high. We're heading for Ilha de Sao Vicente, slightly to the SE. We'll pass between the two islands (Santo Antao and Sao Vicente) to get to Porto Grande and Mindelo, our destination. May be there by mid-afternoon.*

> *Pigeon still here, despite plenty of land to look at. He refuses to look – just stands on one leg and stares at me.*

It was a dramatic arrival. The wind picked up stronger and stronger, ripping the jib all to hell as we approached the harbor ("among the finest in the eastern Atlantic," said our cruising guide), and as we entered it was howling. We got the engine going to head into it, maneuvered & dropped the big plow anchor, which immediately dragged. Then we dropped the small Danforth and it dragged too. Dragging both anchors, we tried to fight our way up to a big ship mooring buoy, and twice were blown away at the last minute.

Finally two guys came out in a rowboat. With the rowboat alongside and its oars banging us unmercifully, we managed to pass them a long anchor line and they struggled with it up to the ship mooring. In the meantime, our anchor chain had slipped and carried away one of our pulpit supports. The guys got the line attached to the buoy & returned, hand over hand. They climbed aboard & then here came the French boat, first met in Gomera and then in Hierro. We rigged bumpers alongside and, after three attempts, we got them tied up beside us.

Then our helpers (by now numbering three – a newcomer had somehow paddled out to us on a surfboard) carried out another line from the French boat to the mooring buoy. All this while the wind steadily increased. We were getting gusts stronger than any I'd experienced – 60? 70? I know I could hardly stand up in it. We had to close the portholes to keep out the spray – in the harbor! I was mighty grateful for the two guys who rowed out: we gave them $10 apiece, plus an old foul-weather jacket for one and a new baseball cap for the other. They seemed pleased. Orlando, the rescuer who arrived by paddleboard, was paid by the French folks, who seemed equally grateful.

And somewhere along the line our pigeon fled the scene. Wise bird.

June 22:

Wind has calmed to a gentle breeze – we & Frenchies waiting gingerly while still buffeted by occasional gusts. Am trying to figure out whether yesterday's gale was common or unusual. Town looks small & dusty but inviting. The town & all the black faces remind me of the Caribbean. Wish I'd seen the pigeon take his leave. He was with us 9 days – longer than some crew I've had.

** 796 miles & 10 days, Hierro (Canaries) to Mindelo.(Cape Verdes). About 16 engine hours. Only three ships sighted en route.

We were on the island of Sao Vicente, anchored in Porto Grande Bay, looking at Mindelo, second largest city in the Cape Verde Archipelago. We stayed there nine days, and toward the end of our visit I noted:

Orlando & Caesar, our two "boat boys", will stick in my mind. Orlando, 38, small and eager, always thinking ahead – "You remember Orlando, now" – and Caesar, serious and shy with a really nice smile. Orlando usually barefoot (he seemed able to walk on anything, including broken glass), Caesar better dressed w. a cap and strangely-new yellow leather work boots. Beach at Mindelo infested w. small boys (6-12?) who seemed completely uncontrolled – at one point about 10 of them almost turned me over in the dinghy, just horsing around in the water & having a hell of a time as I tried to row in. Boat boys apparently necessary to "watch the dinghy" – keep the kids from stealing oars, etc. Rather a pain.

Otherwise the natives very friendly, always smiling & seemingly happy though dirt-poor. A lot of activity in Mindelo: cars, trucks, taxis & buses, fishermen, even a uniformed lady traffic cop on duty at the main intersection in town (but there are no traffic signal lights). Seems that it hardly ever rains. Downtown has rows of none-too-healthy palm trees & one other kind (acacia?), but you see no greenery outside of town. Kept meaning to take a short bus tour but I never did.

My overall impression of Mindelo was of deep poverty: a lot of people really scratching just to get by. And things were not improving, apparently – our guidebook had said the Club Nautico at the dinghy beach had "a small bar, cold showers and safe storage for dinghies," but in fact the place was abandoned and littered with trash.

Neil, with his white skin and blonde hair, seemed a big hit with the local girls. I saw plenty of pretty obvious overtures made in his direction, but I never saw him respond. He really was rather shy.

We presented cash and clothes to Orlando and Caesar the night before we left. I felt a particular kinship with Orlando – 38 years old and greeting yachts by hand: still paddling out on an old chewed-up surfboard, but always cheerful, always willing and always available. There really wasn't a whole lot of opportunity in Mindelo for somebody like Orlando. But he was doing his best.

July 1, 7:30 a.m.:

> *Hauled up all three (!) anchors & departed in good style. Strong trade wind from E, with TURTLE DOVE just holding the 115-degree course & taking quite a beating in the process – big waves, gusty winds, much spray & an occasional partial wave hitting us. Not fun. I had my jacket on & after one wave hit me I put up my hood, only to find the hood half-full of seawater. So got soaked again.*

> *No respite till we were maybe 2 miles off Sao Nicolau (next big island, southeast of Sao Vicente), where we finally found a lee. All this doesn't augur too well for the remaining 400+ miles to Dakar, since that is also on our 115-degree course. Our hope is that the wind will swing a little more N as we near W Africa & make things a bit easier.*

It was 9 p.m. and very dark when we reached Sao Nicolau and we had to feel our way in, most cautiously. We stayed two nights, and Neil met two young guys who took him to a festival/disco the second night. I watched a huge swordfish being cut up on the boat-launching ramp and considered trying to buy a piece for dinner, but the size of the critter intimidated me. I swear it was 10 feet long, and cutting it up was a bloody business.

We took off July 3, heading for Ilha Boavista, the next and final stop in the Cape Verdes. But we couldn't make it in one tack and decided to head straight for Dakar, about 450 miles away.

July 4, noon:

> *Today will be a big day at home. We had to alter course a bit to steer around the rock Ba Joao Valente, charted as less than 2 meters underwater with breaking seas – the only obstacle for 40 miles. We never saw it.*

July 5, Noon:

> *90 miles since last noon – A most welcome wind shift came in abruptly around 5 a.m. So suddenly we are heading for Dakar, maybe even a little north of it. Hot, wet & muggy. Halyards all have a light coating of yellow-red dust. I wonder if our lungs have the same. (The guidebook says this dust is carried by the harmattan – a hot, dry wind coming from the interior of Africa, carrying dust as far as 600 miles off the coast.)*

July 6, 10 a.m.:

Neil's 23rd birthday – we'll celebrate tonight with a special dinner (canned sausage & mashed potato).

Wind picked up strong last night & by 9 p.m. we were down to jib only. Have had to keep everything closed up, trying to keep out red dust, and it's horribly dark & muggy down here: everything feels half wet, including this log book. Yesterday I split off part of one of the caps on my front teeth – so much for the great $5,000 dental work at home last fall.

July 8, Noon:

85 miles in past 24 hrs. Wind from S last night – gradually worked around to north. NE Trades don't seem very reliable here. Looks like we won't make Dakar before dark. 47 miles to go.

CHAPTER 27

Africa, West

Dakar, Containerville, River Gambia, Mary P. in/out /in.

1995

The Cap Vert light is a brilliant welcoming beacon. We were 15 miles away when we spotted it at 9 p.m. July 9. We doused the jib and jogged slowly southwest under main alone, rounding the cape that shelters the big harbor of Dakar. There we hesitated a little, waiting for light enough to recognize infamous Goree Island, where thousands of slaves were held to be shipped across the Atlantic. Now we could see the anchorage and about 50 anchored yachts.

As we motored in we were overtaken by native fishing boats, long and low in the water w. distinctive upswept ends – big dugout pirogues, 50-70 feet long, carrying half a dozen men and propelled by big outboards. Waiting on shore was a colorful solid mass of people ready to buy fish, at 7 a.m. on a Sunday morning.

*** 491 miles and 6 days from Sao Nicolau, Cape Verdes, to Dakar, Senegal, West Africa. Engine hours about 14. Saw lots of fish; caught none.*

Dakar, capital of Senegal, has a population close to 2 million, very African and very French at the same time. We anchored at the Cercle de la Voile de Dakar Yacht Club, a kind of do-it-yourself enterprise operated by its members. Like any modern yacht club it had its own haulout apparatus, but this was an ungainly wooden cradle on wheels that could be hauled up on the beach by hand at peak high tide. The club had a launch service also, but the launch was an ancient skiff powered by a decrepit outboard with an equally decrepit native operator. He was a friendly old guy; with his big dark glasses he was a dead ringer for Ray Charles.

The club had a long rickety dock and a simple kitchen with a refrigerator offering limited space to club members. Surprisingly, it also had a squash court, which doubled as a sail loft when nobody was playing squash. There was a do-it-yourself laundry and a lady sailmaker who lived on her own boat in the harbor. And there was a very comfortable bar, with good prices for drinks and a fine view. The club was in a little suburb several miles from central Dakar. There were several shops nearby, one of them a good-sized meat market that sold marvelous steak. Close by in the other direction was a little native village where we could usually buy bread and fish and, sometimes, canned juice. There were several good restaurants here also. You could catch a big city bus into Dakar, though the buses usually required a long wait and were always jammed. But the passengers were cheerful and helpful with directions and were glad to offer an arm for support at a particularly tight curve.

Dakar is a big busy city and it is proudly, overwhelmingly black: the businessmen in their dapper suits and two-tone shoes, the beautiful women in their elegant dresses and bright turbans, the policemen, the old folks, the school kids, the shoppers and the hustlers. Some of the hustlers had developed the art of being obnoxious to a real science. One provoked me so much (I was waiting for a bus and couldn't get away from him) by telling me over and over, in perfect English, "You just don't like black people!" that I finally bellowed out, "It's not that I don't like black people – I don't like *YOU!*") This got a laugh from some fellow bystanders.

But some of the hustlers would have melted hearts of stone. One young guy moved along the sidewalk kneeling on a little handcart, propelling himself with his knuckles like Porgy. He was a handsome young man with thick shoulders and muscled arms, but from the waist down he was a twisted ruin: polio. I learned that polio was still an active scourge in Africa. I saw this fellow almost every time I went into the city, and I never saw him without a big smile on his face.

In U.S. cities it sometimes seemed to me that black people carried themselves with a kind of self-consciousness, as if they were very conscious of their minority status. Not so in Dakar – this was *their* city and *their* country. *Fine with us if you wish to visit,* they seemed to say, *but you're here with our permission and under our approval.* As in Nairobi, the place was vibrant with life. Streets were crowded with shoppers and teeming with vendors offering everything imaginable – I saw one middle-aged man patrolling the sidewalk carrying ironing boards for sale. This city has to be one of the world's top spots for outdoor café-sitting and people-watching.

Neil and I hung out at the yacht club for 10 days, enjoying the bar and the conviviality. We made friends with David Seed of England, a young mechanic who was slowly rebuilding one of the world's smallest ocean-going yachts: the 16-foot GALLIETTE II, Wayfarer No. 1307. David proudly told us the boat was Number 46464 on the British Small Ships Register.

We were to see more of David after our initial departure for the Gambia, as it turned out.

July 19, 9:30 a.m.:

> Started off, after many goodbyes in the yacht club last night, in very light wind under jib, when wind failed. Tried to start engine: Nada. Managed to creep back to harbor under sail & re-anchor.

Luckily, we located our friend Dave immediately. He found that one positive connector in the engine's wiring harness was corroded away completely. But as he reconnected it he bumped a heavy galvanized steel elbow that was part of the engine exhaust system. The elbow collapsed into a pile of rusty dust. It was completely rotted out and apparently had been staying in one piece out of pure habit. This wasn't just an ordinary steel elbow – it had a short piece of smaller pipe welded to it, to carry cooling seawater out with the exhaust gases in the larger pipe. We were not going to find something like this ready-made, and ordering a new part from Westerbeke in the U.S. might take forever. So we spent the next day and a half traveling by taxi to auto junkyards and scrap heaps in Dakar, collecting parts, cutting them to fit and finally having them welded together into something approximating the busted part. It looked pretty ugly, but it seemed to work when we tried it.

I hoped this jerry-built contraption would hold together, at least until Mary Pagano could bring out a new part from the U.S. when she met us in the Gambia.

We left on a Friday – a day that sailors believe is extremely bad luck. It's said that this superstition was so annoying to British naval authorities that they deliberately laid the keel of a new ship on a Friday, had the vessel launched on a Friday, and sent her off on her maiden voyage on a Friday – all in an attempt to torpedo the superstition. Trouble was, the ship was never heard from again.

I had decided, though, that we could leave on Friday, so long as the projected voyage would be less than 100 miles. The Gambia, somewhere around 80 miles away, fitted nicely into this little exception.

July 22:

> Well, here we are (illegally?) in Oyster Creek, the Gambia, midway between Banjul & Bahau. Had a pleasant sail all night – at first light found ourselves off Buoy #1, at entrance to River Gambia, & spent a good part of the day tacking, & finally motoring, to Banjul City. The anchorage in Banjul, where you're supposed to stop to visit Customs, looked really uninviting with wrecked half-sunken ships all over

the place, & it was pouring rain, so we decided to take our yellow Quarantine flag on up into Oyster Creek.

Tried to follow our typewritten directions to the creek entrance & got ourselves stuck on a mud bank. Anchored, explored in the dinghy looking for deeper water & finally worked our way off. Followed a power boat into the beautiful creek, lined w. mangroves bearing yellow flowers, & motored our way up it with no difficulty; depths varied from 6 to 20 feet. Many many birds – Mary will love this place.

** 2,925 miles, Gibraltar to Oyster Creek.

July 23:

Now have discovered that Monday July 24 is a public holiday. Beginning to wonder if we'll ever clear into Gambia officially. This settlement at Oyster Creek is really funky. Buildings are mostly old containers off ships, and about half the boats here are half-sunken. Met Mr. Ceesey (recommended in our copy of the typewritten sailor's guide to Dakar & Banjul), & John Cox (recommended by mechanic David in Dakar, who said Cox helped nurse him back to health after a bad siege with malaria.)

Mr. Ceesey, barefoot, wearing shorts and a bright yellow undershirt, was waiting at the beach on our first visit ashore. He greeted us warmly and reeled off a list of services he could provide: water delivery, trash disposal, yacht tending and repair, trips to Banjul or Serekunda (Oyster Creek was halfway between the two.) Ceesey seemed to be the unofficial mayor of the place, which I decided to call Containerville.

John Cox, who showed up shortly afterward, apparently was the only white person living in the area. He was a craggy old Scotsman who had come to the Gambia years ago to run the city shipyard, married a native woman and raised a family, and just stayed on. Cox was the proud designer, builder and owner (and, on rare occasions, the skipper) of a ferro-cement racing sloop, a rather odd-looking vessel prominently moored in the creek just off Containerville. It looked as if it would barely float, but we were told it was quite speedy.

We also met two resident boat people: Paul, a young Englishman who caught barracuda and sold them to local hotels, and a rather unfriendly German man whose name I never did learn. There were several other yachts moored in the creek, but they were currently unoccupied and under the care of Lamin, a young native guy who became a good friend.

Baba Touray, the earnest young proprietor of the Harbour Cafe, was to become an even better friend. His rather grandly named place of business was a container that he had converted into a bar and restaurant offering beer, soda and fried egg sandwiches. Baba had outfitted the container with a door, windows, an awning and an outdoor table with four chairs. (When Mary Pagano arrived later, she hustled him off to a big commercial nursery to buy plants for the "patio".)

Neil and I took a bus into Banjul and finally managed to clear in officially. The Customs men insisted on inspecting the boat in person, so we all returned to Oyster Creek (I was touched by their concern for my pocketbook – I had offered to pay for a taxi, but they insisted on going by bus), borrowed a bigger skiff at Containerville to accommodate everybody, and inspected TURTLE DOVE at her anchorage.

One of the many nice things about the Gambia was that English was the native tongue. This was a considerable relief after days of wrestling with the French spoken in Dakar. We spent three days in Oyster Creek, buying groceries in Banjul, meeting the numerous inhabitants of Containerville, and checking the engine for the next leg. We hoped to go up the River Gambia as far as possible, where we might see wild crocodiles and hippos.

When we started we successfully negotiated the creek in strong winds and heavy rain and cautiously turned upriver at a point called Half Die. Our typewritten guide calls this spot "probably the worst possible introduction to the Gambia" and continues:

> It derives its name from a cholera epidemic in 1869 when literally half of the population did die. Things have improved since then, but the area still has a reputation for being a hotbed of rogues and thieves. While anchoring there, keep a keen eye on security; some boats have been robbed while their crew were on board asleep. It can also be very uncomfortable, especially with wind against the tide.

July 28:

> Arrived Mandori Creek, our guide-writer's favorite spot on the lower river, with Neil swinging the lead as we entered w. little difficulty: we had about 8 feet at the shallowest spot. Did not see all the eagles, pelicans, etc., promised by our guidebook, but did see some big herons. Went in a short distance w. many big mangroves & silently waving fiddler crabs on the bank on each side (are they talking to each other?) & anchored in about 20 feet. It's deep, even though the creek is pretty narrow.

> Installed outboard on dinghy & motored several miles upstream, then killed motor & drifted farther up w. incoming tide to listen to the birds & lots of odd calls & noises. Back on the boat we then had a heavy rainstorm – pranced around naked in the cool rain. It felt wonderful. Filled two 5-gal. jugs in no time, which just about filled the water tank, and had two pails left over for washing. A lovely rainstorm.

> Played trombone a bit; first time since Gibraltar. Then along came two old guys wearing orange stocking caps & paddling a really ancient-looking dugout with a big net piled into it. We all said hello, but they didn't stop paddling toward the

creek outlet. Now I wonder if we'll find the net strung across the outlet when we try to leave tomorrow morning.

July 29:

A very quiet, and almost bugless, night. Forgot to light lantern, but no matter – we were the only humans for miles around, apparently. No net at entrance, praise be.

Worked our way around the curves (river becoming more narrow now, w. considerable mud banks on one or both sides), & arrived at "village" of Balingo (two visible buildings, four cows & a number of pirogues & people) around 3 p.m. Crossed the channel & anchored about half a mile off, intending to dinghy to the village. But storm clouds were gathering & soon we had another lashing of wind & rain. Anchor held, & again we filled the water tank, with extra to spare. So it's still raining & we sit here looking at Balingo across a half-mile of choppy water. It's OK – we plan to go tomorrow.

There are fishing pirogues moored all over the river – whole fleets of them riding the current. (These are narrow dugout hulls with a long pole lashed crossways and a float on each end, to provide stability.) Are there nets connected between them? We haven't found out yet.

Upriver about 2 miles we can see the white-and-yellow Yalitenda Ferry, a key link on the highway connecting Ziguinchor with Dakar.

July 30:

Awoke at 8, and around 10 we dinghy-motored across the river to Balingo, where we were greeted w. great dignity by an elderly man who spoke a little English. He escorted us to a village compound (thatched huts, roosters & goats & cows & donkeys & corn & lots of little kids staring at us) where a lady sold us three "pancakes," (rather like the fried "doughboys" at home) for 1 Dalasi (10 cents) each, & I took pictures of the kids, for an additional 2 Dalasi. Then we walked a short distance up the red dirt road to Farafenni, greeting & being greeted by everybody. Countryside very lush w. deep-green grass, trees, cornfields, animals, friendly folk. Seemed positively idyllic. We hung around a while, then motored back to TURTLE DOVE ("The Ship", several natives called it).

Passed Elephant Island, choked with huge mangrove trees, saw four big white and black hawklike birds that looked very much like American eagles. (Think they were African fish eagles.) Threaded our way past the moored pirogues, which seem to be everywhere & now are strung pretty well across the entire river. Finally started motoring between them, rather than trying to steer around the end of the line. No apparent problem – if they are connected to fish nets the nets are deep enough not to be an obstacle.

Finally anchored just S of Sea Horse I. (where Portuguese explorers saw hippos & called them sea horses) just before sunset.

July 31, 2:15 p.m.:

Just threaded our way through a fishing raft made up of 20 pirogues & a host of other floating objects, strung completely across the river between Sea Horse I. & the mainland. Waited till 1 p.m. to start, but still we'll have two hours or more of strong contrary tidal current. While waiting, I rowed to the island & up the inner channel a short distance – very pretty & peaceful. Saw only some curlew-like birds that have a strange cry. Yesterday we saw a no. of pelicans, my favorites.

4 p.m.:

Didn't get very far. South of & within sight of Kau-Ur the engine overheated & we pulled over & anchored. First it looked like a serious oil leak – there was black oil in the bilge. But the dipstick still showed a sufficient level of oil. Then discovered a broken hose clamp & a lack of fresh-water coolant. Replaced hose clamp & figured all OK. By that time it was around 7 p.m., so we stayed there overnight. A pretty spot, but very hot & buggy. It poured rain during the night, so had to close things up even further.

Aug. 1, 8 p.m.:

Arose early, trying to catch most of a favorable tide. Started engine & ran it awhile – all seemed OK. Had just pulled up anchor when engine overheated again. Re-anchored, waited not long enough for engine to cool & got sprayed w. hot coolant when opened filler cap: no damage. Put a second hose clamp on offending spot & tried again. This time seemed OK. But in the meantime discovered a very wobbly pulley wheel on the saltwater pump. Looked as if the bearings are shot. Left anyway & so far things seem OK. Progressing cautiously.

Aug. 2, 8:30 a.m.:

Girding up my loins to tackle The Wobbly Pump. Yesterday we apparently resolved The Water Leak (but not The Oil Leak, which drips oil slowly but steadily while the engine runs). Found my Westerbeke repair kit for the saltwater pump, and it includes a new bearing. I think the old one has given out. So I must tackle it.

Yesterday we anchored just at the entrance to the shallow northern section of the river, passing just west of the village of Kudang, & took the dinghy up the shallow section on a hippo hunt. Didn't seem very shallow & we saw no hippos, but we did see a small troupe of monkeys running through the reeds along the riverbank.

It was incredibly hot in the sun, & the cockpit of TURTLE DOVE is infested w. small houseflies which buzz around furiously all day long. They don't bite but they make a hell of a noise. TURTLE DOVE also now has some large black slow-crawling beetles, & some very big ants. Don't know how they got aboard. Boat is becoming an entomologist's dream (or nightmare?)

* 25 miles, Sea Horse I. to Deer Is.

6 p.m.:

Spent most of the day wrestling w. the G-D pump; finally gave up trying to rebuild it. The old bearing was torn up – 5 lonesome little steel balls fell out as we took it apart, but we could NOT get the stainless steel rim off to fit it onto the new bearing. And my kit does not include a new rim. So: no water pump, and thus no engine. We'll turn around here & try to sail back, using favorable tides and the little outboard (1½ horsepower) on the dinghy, lashed alongside when necessary. Should be interesting, to say the least. It's about 130 miles back to Oyster Creek, as the crow.

Aug. 3, 1 p.m.:

Waited all morning for tide to turn. Wind light & right on the nose: not very favorable conditions for this great epic. Finally got started & tacked (Neil estimated 100 times), heading down the river. Despite our poor pointing ability we did well, aided by the current. Finally stopped, almost in darkness, just as current went slack, just south of peanut factory at Kau-Ur. Never did use the mighty Yamaha.

Aug. 4:

Anchored about 6 miles upstream of the Yalitenda Ferry after an interesting day. Sailed against the current with a favorable wind about half the day; then, as the current changed, the wind direction changed too, and we had to tack. We tacked along merrily in the downstream current, coming very close to the mangroves along the bank on each side. But at one tack, when I pushed the helm over She Didn't

Answer. We slowly plowed right into the trees, with a hell of a great crashing & snapping of branches. Poor Neil was out on the bowsprit, trying to fend off, but he had to flee as the branches crashed in on him. There we were, stuck in the forest, but, amazingly, still afloat. We dropped all the sails & Neil tried to push us off from the trees while I started the outboard to tow us out, backward. We came out easily, drifting downstream in the current & festooned w. leaves and broken twigs. No damage, apparently. We raised sail (somewhat shakily) & proceeded on our way. But we started our tacking maneuver a little farther away from the banks after that.

Neil said he had seen the current actually running between the trees, carrying us straight into the mangroves when we crashed. He said the final score for the encounter should be BOWSPRIT 1; MANGROVES 0.

Aug. 5:

Ran the mighty Yamaha w. dinghy lashed alongside. It barely moved us through the water but it allowed us to steer the boat. Stopped to buy a barracuda from two fishermen. Then motored past the Yalitenda Ferry at 3 p.m. It was packed with passengers.

Aug. 6:

Finally anchored off Muta Point (Kemoto Pt. Hotel) after a hell of a lot of backing & filling. Were met at the landing by a host of men & little kids. The kids walked w. us (holding our hands) through a rather large village, with them importantly pointing out every well, water tap, big tree, wash house, etc., up to the hotel, which was clearly fenced off from the natives.

Found the place beautifully decorated w. carvings & dark local wood they call mahogany, much heavier and darker than the mahogany I know. Had two Beck's Beers & chatted w. the native barman & the asst. manager. A white English lady came in to have a soft drink & make radio telephone calls: she the boss of a tropical disease research station about 20K away. Phone won't work there, she said. Returned to TURTLE DOVE w. the usual retinue of small boys. One had carefully written out his address, & I promised to send a postcard to: Essa Touray, c/o Lamin Semateh/ Kemoto Hotel/P.O. Box 2785/ Banjul, the Gambia/West Africa.

Aug. 8:

Departed after a brief visit to the village of Albreda, near Jufirreh, setting of Alex Hailey's novel "Roots". Sat at the Rising Sun Restaurant next to enormous Cotton tree sheltering hundreds of chattering yellow & black birds & their nests. Would like to return to this spot: it's quite nice despite the bad rep. Encountered only one pain in the ass, an indefatigable hustler. Then anchored (unwillingly) in 6 feet of water about 1 1/2 mile east of the entrance to Oyster Creek. We must wait for the wind to calm down before we can proceed with the mighty Yamaha.

* Sailed about 30 miles – 18 as the crow.

Aug. 9:

Well, we're back at Containerville. Up at 6:30 & underway at 7. (Several powerboats stopped last night to offer help, but we said we were waiting for morning.) Had light wind on the beam to start, & a favorable current most of the way; just crept along but did all right. Place seems just the same.

** 185 miles, Oyster Creek to Deer I., River Gambia, & return.

I remained at Oyster Creek for a little over a month, waiting for Mary Pagano (and a new water pump) to join me. Neil stayed for the first week and then left to return to Scotland. I last saw him climbing into a crowded Dakar-bound "bush taxi", wearing his heavy backpack and clutching his guitar, carefully wrapped in a black plastic bag. I lent him $500 to get home and was sorry to see him go. He was a good reliable crewman and he didn't complain. He had sailed a lot of miles on TURTLE DOVE

I became friendly with the gang at Containerville, a motley crew of young guys and a few women who hung around smoking, drinking beer, cooking dinner over a perpetual campfire, now and then looking for the odd job. The gang had several dogs: my favorite was Fidel, a rangy tan female (despite her name) who was very smart and liked riding in a dinghy.

With only one plane in its fleet, Gambia Airways couldn't have been any smaller. I had a ticket for the Sept. 12 flight from Serekunda to Dakar to meet Mary, and was assured that the plane would fly that day. But when I got to the tiny "International" airport the flight was canceled. I rushed by cab to the airline office in Banjul, got my money back, charged back out to the airport by taxi, found an Air Senegal plane just about to leave for Dakar, and (somewhat breathless) got a seat.

I reached Dakar in time to rent a room in a tourist hotel about two miles from the Dakar Airport. It was a lucky find: the little hotel was quiet and charming. It overlooked the ocean and an enormous beach sprinkled with big native fishing boats, vigorous soccer games, horses and wagons, little food stands in tents pitched on the sand, native families swimming in the surf and strolling in the warmth of a setting sun. There was activity everywhere.

Mary's plane arrived at 10 that night, and she was immediately hit hard by the heat and humidity of West Africa in mid-September. In the airport we fought off the most determined hustlers I'd ever seen, secured a cab and went direct to our non-air-conditioned hotel. Our room was just bearable with the help of a single fan, and we stayed at the hotel for two days, strolling the beach while Mary tried to get accustomed to the heat. It didn't happen.

Early on Sept. 15 we clambered into a "bush taxi", a well-worn van packed with luggage and passengers, for a bumpy five-hour ride to the Gambia. The road was paved but honeycombed with huge potholes – in many places it was a lot smoother where there was no paving left at all. And every 10 or 12 miles we had to stop at a roadblock manned by surly-looking soldiers who demanded to see our passports. By the time we reached Banjul, after crossing the River Gambia on a jam-packed ferryboat, Mary was close to collapse from the heat. We limped into a downtown restaurant and the lady proprietor prescribed a large drink of cold water and lime, laced with both salt and sugar. It seemed to help a bit.

We still had one more cab ride to reach Containerville, and it was full dark when we got there. I could see the usual campfire blazing, its light flickering across the dark faces gathered around in silence as they watched us feeling our way down the winding dirt road. The usual pack of dogs started growling and I felt apprehensive.

"It's Jack!" I called out. "We're here!"

Out of the dark came a familiar voice: "Is this MUM? Welcome!"

Either Baba or Lamin, I thought. It was all right. They were glad to see us.

Two days later, Mary was still sick and I was having trouble with my right eye: I was sure I had a foreign object stuck in there somewhere. Paul and John Cox, who had taken Mary under their wing immediately, recommended that we see Dr. Peters at the medical clinic in Serekunda. We went there Monday morning, but by then Mary was already saying she wanted to go home. Dr. Peters said I had conjunctivitis and prescribed an ointment for my eye. They did lab tests on Mary, found a slightly elevated white blood count and prescribed antibiotics. She decided to wait out the 48 hours Peters thought might be needed for her to feel better.

By next day, both Mary's eyes looked bad. We returned to Dr. Peters and he prescribed a different eye ointment for her. Thursday morning, Sept. 21, Mary said she must go home. We took the bus to Serekunda to call Sabena Air in Dakar, were told to go to the Sabena office in Banjul, took the bus to Banjul & learned that the Sabena office was in Serekunda after all. Back to Serekunda on the bus, then a cab to Sabena on Pipeline Road. Changed Mary's return ticket for a flight out in two days.

Friday we had a brief outing with the outboard and dinghy up Oyster Creek and into a pretty little side creek. Next day we took the bus to Banjul Airport and Mary left on the 4:30 p.m. flight to Dakar. She had been in the Gambia only 8 days.

Four days later Mary sent me a FAX from home. Her doctor had said the ointment Dr. Peters gave her was outlawed in the U.S. 15 years ago because it causes swelling in the eyeball and, rarely, leukemia. The letter concluded, "So, my leaving was a darn lucky thing."

My conjunctivitis slowly disappeared. Almost everybody had it, even the man who sold me the eye ointment in the Banjul pharmacy. Natives called it "Apollo," because the first outbreak had occurred at the time of the first Apollo spacecraft launch. Apparently some saw a mysterious connection between the two.

Mary returned about a month later and we agreed to undertake another river trip. We would go up the Gambia and cross into the River Bandiala, go upstream another 20 miles to a point where we could cross into the Diamboss River. From there we would head downstream to enter the River Saloum and follow it back to the sea. That would leave us about 60 miles of ocean sailing to return to the yacht club in Dakar. Mary would leave and I would head out from Dakar for the trip back across the Atlantic to the Caribbean.

My typewritten guide to the Gambia did add a cautionary note, however:

> *Remember that the whole coast from here down to Guinea Bissau is constantly changing from the effects of mangrove growth and river sediment. It is therefore always possible to hit mud or sand banks which are not charted. In some places you will find that the river has changed, or an island appeared or disappeared.*

Turned out to be true.

Nov. 7:

> *A frustrating day yesterday, trying to get into the main Diomboss River. Motored up the Bandiala with little difficulty (2 shallow spots), looking for a shell island at the entrance. Tried various directions & kept running into mudbanks – were actually on the mud at least three times but got off each time. Finally anchored, put outboard on dinghy & motored around w. sounding pole, looking for a way out. Found deep water along a long sandbank, but could not figure how to get past the bank. Finally raised anchor & moved over to a spot near the bank in 22-26 feet of water & stayed the night, still no nearer the Diomboss.*
>
> *We'll stay here today, but it looks like we'll have to go back the way we came. Apparently the only way out.*

At dusk we were visited by guys in a pirogue who wanted cigarettes. They left peaceably when we didn't have any, but the encounter left us feeling a tad uneasy. The only other sign of life was a big monkey, moving slowly along the sandbank gathering oysters that grew on the little mangrove bushes. Apparently he had figured out a way to open those hard crusty shells. After he left I rowed over and picked some myself. The oysters were small but very tasty. (Mary said she felt sorry for the monkey because I was stealing his oysters.)

Nov. 8:

Now recovering from the cost of a meal (about $63 U.S.!) at the El Paradiso Hotel, where we stopped on our way back down the river. We had beer, a very good mixed salad, cooked veg. & gravy, & pigeon – good, but pretty bony & hard to get at the meat. Almost totally exhausted our supply of Senegalese money to pay for it.

(Later we finally realized why we had waited a long time for our dinner, while listening to repeated booming sounds coming from the woods around the hotel. Apparently the hotel staff was out hunting, to provide for the big pigeon dinner.)

Nov. 9:

Down the Bandiala River & out the sparsely-marked entrance, then NW up the shallow coastline to the well-marked entrance to the Saloum River. Now anchored near the village of Djifere, opposite the Campement de Djifere hotel. Rowed ashore & bought 3 beers, which exhausted our Senegalese money after last night's debacle.

* 44 miles motoring.

Nov. 10, 8:40 a.m.:

We felt very comfortable in Djifere as we hiked down its neat little dirt streets, past shops and compounds of thatched huts. Some had centerpieces of flowers and almost everybody said hello. Several people called to us and invited us to sit with them on their front porches. We did so, though we couldn't do much but smile at each other.

We managed to exchange two U.S. $10 bills, which gave us a little bit of local cash. There were a host of beautifully-painted pirogues on the beach. Everybody seemed connected with fishing and there was a big plant (we thought maybe for freezing fish) at the end of town, perilously close to the end of a long sandspit which the ocean had cut through in a storm several years ago. We spoke to several people about taking the passage through and were assured it was fine. It would save us about 16 miles on the route to Dakar, so we decided to try it.

Nov. 13:

Back in Dakar again: it took us two days & two nights to go a little over 60 miles from Djifere to here. I must try very hard after this to avoid bucking the trade wind. We had no problem negotiating the pass (12 feet deep in the opening where

*once was land), but then we had strong wind, dead on the nose, and big choppy
waves all the way.*

*Reached vicinity of Goree I. around 1 a.m. & had trouble finding it in the dark. In
the process, Mary seemed bent on steering directly for a large fishing boat heading
out with many bright lights. I grabbed the tiller & swerved away from it, but the
skipper of the fishing boat had some words for us (in French, of course). Both of
us were tired & cranky. We dawdled around till there was enough light at 7 to
see anchored yachts at the club.*

David Seed, my trusty young diesel mechanic, had departed for somewhere in
West Africa in his tiny yacht. But I was able to recruit two young French sailors who
helped me fix our oil leak: it turned out to be mostly a matter of loose fittings on a
new oil filter. I started making preparations for the next leg: back across the Atlantic to
Barbados in the Caribbean. The crew would be my old sailing buddy, Paul Harrigan,
and his friend, David Small.

Mary, preparing to head back to Rhode Island, was not looking forward to being
besieged again by the relentless hustlers at the Dakar Airport, especially the guy in the
wheelchair who had harassed her when she waited there alone for me to show up. He
was there again on her departure day, but this time the two of us chased him away.

Once again we said goodbye. Outside, the lurking cab drivers were even more
persistent than the hustlers indoors, and they weren't confined to wheelchairs. They
literally pounced on me when I emerged from the airport, pulling me in various
directions toward their waiting cabs. I pushed them off, picked the closest cab and
piled in, breathless, only to discover that I was in the worst-looking jalopy in the
parking lot. We lurched away, traveled less than a mile and then pulled over to the
side of a very dark highway. The driver kept assuring me that all was OK, but it didn't
help much.

Within a minute, another car pulled in behind us and my driver indicated I should
change vehicles. I did so, with considerable misgivings. To my surprise, this was a
new car, and it was positively luxurious. Off we went, without a word from my new
driver, direct to the yacht club. I never did learn the reason for the switch.

I had to return to the airport to collect Paul and Dave a few days later, but this
time I vowed there would be no more wrestling matches with cab drivers: I arranged
with a local man to do the driving both ways. My two new crewmen tottered out
through the Arrival gates, lugging their bags and looking totally bewildered by the
bedlam swarming around them (including the guy in the wheelchair, once again).
They were the center of a first-class feeding frenzy and were pretty close to speechless
when I reached them. We hustled toward our waiting jalopy and our driver helped
us beat off the swarm. Paul and Dave swore they'd never seen anything like it. To
add to their confusion, on the way back to the club our car was pulled over by two

guys in police uniforms who questioned us and then sent us on our way. We never learned why they stopped us.

We were working on a fairly tight schedule – both my crew wanted to be home by Jan. 1, and Barbados was about 2,500 miles away, as the crow. If we averaged 100 miles a day that meant at least 25 days to get there, and they still had to connect to Rhode Island after that. There was no way we could leave before Dec. 5, which would leave us no leeway at all. Well, so be it, I thought. We would just have to do a little bit better than the average.

Dave and Paul didn't see very much of Senegal – or Dakar either, for that matter. We spent most of their only full day in Africa at a local supermarket, collecting supplies for three men for seven weeks at sea. We did pretty well, though the canned meat selection was sparse. (We bought a number of cans labeled "sardine pate", as close as we could translate the French. Turned out to be a mistake.)

Back at the club, we paid a local kid to help us lug everything (including six heavy jerrycans of water) out the long rickety dock, into the rickety launch and finally into TURTLE DOVE. Then we spent a few more hours getting everything, and ourselves, assigned space in the boat. Then a late dinner ashore, a couple drinks at the club bar (the members were staging an elaborate pot-luck dinner that we did not attend), and it was bedtime: their second and last night in West Africa.

We left next day, *at the crack of noon*, as sailors say.

CHAPTER 28

Atlantic

Dakar to Barbados with Paul, Dave and dead flying fish.

1995

Dec. 5:

Crew Paul Harrigan and David Small – Barbados-bound. YAY!

Said goodbye to Dakar with a good NE wind, maybe Force 4, and bright sun – will be full moon tonight. Took a brief side-sail across the big harbor to see hundreds of brightly-dressed villagers waiting at the shoreline for the fishing boats to come in – the same scene that greeted Neil & me when we first arrived here. At least Paul and Dave got a tiny look at life in Africa.

Dec. 7 (Pearl Harbor Day):

Been experimenting w. square sail – so far not a big success. Wind slightly off the quarter & it not working well. Harrigan hit in head by flying fish while steering last night. Tonight wind eased a bit, & seas flatter – we sailing under jib & staysail only, & still making 4-5 knots. Har. quotes friend Eric of Pleasant St. Wharf as saying his brother-in-law did this route in seas so calm that they dined every night on a table in the cockpit. Hard to believe.

David's sore right leg, which he arrived with, is getting more painful. This is worrisome. Told him we'd stop in Cape Verdes if necessary, but we'd probably have to leave him there for treatment.

Dec. 8, Noon:

132 miles – We are bookin'!

Dave elects to stay on boat & not seek medical help in Cape Verdes. Says he's feeling some better. Hope it's the right decision. I'm glad – didn't really want to stop there. (But I did worry, whenever I watched him carefully preparing himself for sleeping, propping himself up with bedrolls, etc. I knew he was hurting.)

Dec. 10, Noon:

143 miles – Another great run. Harrigan hit twice by flying fish during one shift. (!) I collected four dead ones from the deck this morning & am planning to bombard him w. them tonite, if I can sneak up on him. Trade wind very strong and constant. Have been talking politics & politicians all morning.

Dec. 11:

Har survived my fish attack last night. At approx. 12:15 a.m., after he had started his shift, I crawled back to the companionway, selected a defunct fish from the bag of four I had concealed in the engine room, and fired it just past his nose as he sat at the tiller, gazing dreamily off to port. "Jesus CHRIST!" he yelled while I tried to stifle myself. Then I fired a second fish, which hit his arm & landed on the cockpit floor. Since it never moved and was obviously dead, he realized what was happening & threw it back at me. The game was up at that point, & the remaining fish never got used. A pretty successful gag, though.

Dec. 13, 3 a.m.:

We seem to have lost the trade wind, at least temporarily. Much slatting & banging of gear, accompanied by groans & curses from crew. No ships sighted for several days.

Noon:

* 986 miles from Dakar to date.

Dec. 14:

At last we have clear skies & bright sunshine! Seems like the trade wind is back with us. The halfway point is approaching – we should reach it tomorrow. A committee of 3 is planning the ceremonies.

Harrigan and I discussed ways to deal with bureaucrats. I told him that in listing Occupation in Immigration offices, I sometimes write "Retired Oral Hypodontist." Har suggested "Retired Raconteur," or – even better – "Retired Straight Man in Two-Man Comedy Team." We amuse ourselves in this fashion.

Dec. 16:

22 miles to halfway point. Almost becalmed for some hours; then dark clouds & a big wind shift from SE to N, followed by heavy rain. Collected about 12 gals. water. Could have had much more, but ran out of containers.

Dec. 17:

Celebrated crossing the halfway point last evening by having sips of Grand Marnier & opening Ellen's Bon Voyage present to Har (about 3 days before the specified Two Weeks at Sea). Turned out to be a bunch of little Snickers bars, much to the delight of all.

Midnight:

Broke the recent fishing jinx w. a 6-lb. dorado that grabbed my red-and-white surface lure. Made a fine dinner, along w. noodles w. cheese & onion sauce. Many many bright stars & few clouds tonight. Still no ships seen. GPS says 1,078 miles to Barbados.

Dec. 19, 3:30 a.m.:

Just spoke w. a Greek supertanker, which altered course & passed us red-to-red (port to port, like cars on the highway). He's bound for Nigeria, then Taiwan. Wished us good weather & a good voyage. Our first ship sighted in at least a week. Wind almost non-existent for past few hours. Millions of stars overhead.

9 p.m.:

Talked w. another tanker: this one bound for St. Croix w. 50,000 tons of aviation gas. Crew of 70 Filipinos, 7 Danish officers, Maersk Line. To arrive St. Croix Dec.

22. Speed 16 knots. Exchanged good wishes for a Merry Christmas. He turned on his radar to see us (why wasn't it already on, I wondered), and said we showed up clearly. Friendly guy who spoke English well.

Dec. 20:

* 1,614 miles from Dakar.

At about 6:15 p.m., Paul & Dave saw the back & tail of a big whale as it came to the surface & then sounded, about 100 yards away. I was down below cooking fish chowder & missed it. Chowder was good, though.

Dec. 23, 6 a.m.:

Around 9 last night saw a most peculiar star or planet in SE: approx. bearing 130 degrees, elev. 35. It was brilliant, twinkling, with bright red, white & blue colors. (A U.S. UFO?) To the naked eye the colors were elusive, but through binoculars they were bright & distinct. Kept its place & moved steadily across the skies with all the other stars. Seemed to lose most of its colors as the night progressed.

Noon:

104 miles. Fought & lost 2 big dorado during the afternoon – no fish dinner this night. Now we complain because the fish we hook are too big!

* 1,912 miles to date.

11:45 p.m.:

Boat rolling heavily as we charge along through the dark doing 6 knots, maybe more. Wind just about dead astern, from the E (as always, it seems). Once again there are millions of stars above. Tonight we did not see the multicolored one that dazzled us last night.

Dec. 24:

117 miles. A good run in good weather, albeit w. considerable rolling. Much talk about arrival in Barbados: what we'll see there (is there a marina or not?), whether there will be time to do anything, etc. Crew in good mood after a good day's run.

Dec. 25, 3 a.m.:

Began Christmas Day with all hands mustered to put 2d reef in main as trade wind piped up. Boat charging along, rolling wildly, under millions of stars & no moon. Dave hung up a Christmas stocking & Santa provided a few modest goodies: an onion, an orange & a bag of hard candy, plus a can of the ever-popular sardine pate. A different Christmas, for sure: my first at sea.

Noon:

118 miles, another good run. Weather is amazingly consistent. Started fishing early today (for Christmas fish?).

Dec. 26, 9 a.m.:

No Xmas fish yesterday (holiday dinner was canned meatballs, canned corn & rice), but a good day, nevertheless. Wind was light; sun bright. Heard a few Xmas carols on Radio Antilles ("The Big RA," they call it), our first radio program from the New World.

Dec. 27:

Beginning to feel a little nostalgic about this trip already – and it ain't even over yet.

Dec. 28, 3:30 a.m.:

A night of heavy rolling w. moderate following wind but occasional cross-seas that set the mainsail to thrashing. Finally put 1 reef in to try to quiet it down. Meanwhile the mizzen sits there quietly. Pretty soon we'll be on the "Approach to Barbados" chart. Meanwhile, departure day draws ever closer. Will be sorry to see these two leave.

Two pools going: first, when we arrive (Jack says 5 p.m. Friday, Paul 6 p.m. Friday, Dave 10 a.m. Sat.); second, first to sight land (winner gets free dinner but must buy dinner for other two if his sighting is a false alarm.)

Dec. 29:

Sailed briskly up to Carlisle Bay, Barbados, all night & reached it about 8 a.m. Dropped sails & tried to start engine w/out success. Re-raised sails & tacked in, finally finding an anchoring spot. Were rather close to another yacht so threw dinghy in & rowed the big Danforth out & dropped it, to move us over a little. Next day we made radio calls to locate Customs & Immigration, which turned out to be at the commercial harbor two miles away (with 6 huge ships there, including Queen Elizabeth II). Got permission not to bring TURTLE DOVE there (would have been virtually impossible), but were told to go there by dinghy: 3 of us in a 7 ½-foot boat for about two miles in considerable chop. Had to bail constantly, and Har had a wet ass by the time we got there. (Turned out that all three of us could have traveled there by cab – the authorities never left their office.) Completed the bureaucratic bullshit, made phone calls, got local cash & settled in.

* (In the hubbub of arrival, we forgot to decide on a winner for either pool.)
*** 2,584 miles sailed, 24 days, Dakar to Barbados.

CHAPTER 29

Islands Again

Barbados, Schamar's, Ange and Cuban sniffer dog.

We dined that night at The Boatyard, a swinging place on the beach facing the anchorage. From the water it was a pretty scene, but there was a heavy swell coming in that almost swamped us when we dinghied in. Folks on the verandah were having fun betting on whether incoming dinghies would make it with dry asses.

Next morning we unloaded Paul and David's gear from the inflatable dinghy, hovering just outside the breaking waves. Dave (dubbed "The Deep Man") climbed into the water and waded in with big duffels on his head. We had a few beers and took a cab to the airport, where I said goodbye. Suddenly the boat seemed awfully empty and I decided to get busy on a project: getting the engine started. When my attempts got nowhere I appealed for help from Jean-Luis, skipper of a neighboring Swiss boat. He offered to recharge my starting battery with the generator on his boat. But after a lot of effort this too was unsuccessful. It was back to the drawing board – and by now it was New Year's Eve.

HAPPY NEW YEAR 1996!

I had a celebratory drink at The Boatyard, but I felt very much alone among the revelers and left early. At midnight I was jolted awake by what sounded like a 1,000-amp band breaking into *Auld Lang Syne*, with red parachute flares fired off from anchored boats all around me. Alone in my boat, I had some very mixed feelings.

I'm approaching the end of a long saga, I thought. *I wonder what I'll be doing in this new year.*

The new year started at 9 next morning when Jean-Luis arrived with his tool box. Three hours later he had carefully cleaned all the connections and terminals and had installed an old starter motor I had carried as a spare all the way from New Zealand. To my surprise, it worked. A major hurdle cleared.

Now I was awaiting two new crewmen: my Numbers 2 and 3 sons, Chris and James, were to arrive in five days. (The original plan had been for Mary Pagano to meet me in Barbados and continue on from there, but Chris persuaded her to delay her arrival until the boat reached St. Lucia, where he and James would be leaving. She agreed to change her plane ticket to accommodate them.)

I didn't much like Barbados – it seemed too flat and too touristy, but it wasn't a difficult wait. I did some shopping and some boat maintenance, had drinks at The Boatyard every evening, and every morning I could watch for the arrival of The Horseman. He and his beautiful horse would wade out together through the gentle surf for a morning swim: the horse would paddle sedately out into the harbor, towing his master by his tail, both of them seeming to enjoy the outing thoroughly. Once back ashore the man would towel the horse dry, climb aboard bareback and head for home. Watching this was a good way to start the day.

Chris and James arrived Jan. 5. We did a final shopping, loaded everything through the surf, (James was "The Deep Man" this time), and said goodbye to Barbados the next day.

Jan. 7:

> *Anchored near the reef in Tobago Cays – maybe 50 other sailboats here. Have I crossed my earlier line, thus completing my circumnavigation? Either yes, or very close to it; we sailed right by Union I. this time, and I was there before. So I'll declare the circumnavigation complete. YAY!*

> ** 125 miles, Barbados to Tobago Cays.*

Jan. 8 (my 67th birthday):

> *Anchored (after minor dragging, tried it again & put out a second anchor) in Bequia Harbor. For sure this completes the circle – I've anchored right here in this harbor before. It was July 28 & 29, 1990 – arrived here with 16-year-old J.J. Binder as crew.*

Now we were resuming a familiar route, though the stopping points and crew members weren't always the same. I said goodbye to Chris and James in St. Lucia, where Mary Pagano rejoined me to visit St. Vincent, Martinique, Dominica, The Saints islands of Guadeloupe, Antigua, Nevis and St. Kitts, St. Eustatius, St. Croix and Puerto Rico. In Boqueron we were relieved to see the perpetual pool game still underway in Schamar's Bar, with some of the same players.

Mary left, to return to her pets in Rhode Island, and oldest son Andy joined me once again. We took off in late May for Luperon in the Dominican Republic, then pressed on (with some apprehension) for the forbidden island of Cuba.

Crossing the Mona Passage we broke a chainplate anchoring the main stay to the mainmast, but managed to jury-rig a repair job in Cuba. There we met a lot of polite soldiers, had an expensive meal as the only guests in a government-run hotel, and spent several days in a heavy-duty marina near Varadero Beach. Three officials cleared us in there but we had 14 uniformed men, plus a sniffer dog, examining us on board when we wanted to leave. The country and the people were wonderful, but we felt so frustrated by the oppressive bureaucracy that we decided to skip Havana altogether.

We sailed to Bimini in the Bahamas and then north up the Gulf Stream, to land at last on the U.S. mainland near Savannah, Georgia. From there it was easygoing up the good old Inland Waterway. But the worst weather of the entire voyage still awaited us. Hurricane Bertha was on its way.

CHAPTER 30

Bertha

Ange and me and a hurricane.

1996

July 9:

Here we are in Wrightsville Beach on the North Carolina coastline, right in Hurricane Alley. This harbor is almost completely landlocked. There are relatively few boats anchored here, at least so far, so we're not so likely to be damaged by another boat. There's a low fixed bridge at one end and a long row of docks on one side, but about half the harbor is bordered by marshland, relatively soft. This looks like a pretty good spot. And we're here. We've decided to stay.

July 10:

All sail covers tied down tightly, inflatable dinghy & floorboards & radar detector brought inside so they won't go flying. So far, only 7 sailboats here – we have plenty of room. A lone Englishman (Peter) on COQUETTE and a lone Clevelander (strangely enough, also named Pete) on ANTIC, are our closest neighbors. Don't know if there are people on the other boats.

July 11:

> *We now have all four anchors out: no more anchors & no more line. Radio says mandatory evacuation of Wrightsville Beach. Coast Guardsmen stopped by earlier to take down our names & addresses & phones (to notify next of kin?), just nodded when we said we were staying on board.*

July 12:

> *Storm now about 175 miles away, moving steadily toward us. Wind strong & heavy rain spattering down at intervals. Tide unnaturally high. Landfall of the storm now expected near Myrtle Beach, maybe 75 miles away, around noon. This is a Class I hurricane, which I gather means rather low-grade and no-account. Plenty for me, though.*

7:35 a.m.:

> *This whole process is so unbelievably slow – & meanwhile the wind howls louder & louder, the entire boat shaking as the masts vibrate. Rather scary.*

In late afternoon Bertha arrived at last: first the north side of the storm, where all four anchors dragged and we had to motor in gear to try to hold our position. The surface of the water was a stinging driving mist about 10 feet high that you couldn't look at because it hurt your face, the wind was shrieking through the rigging, the rubber dinghy attached to Pete's boat nearby was turning flips 12 feet in the air like a kid's kite gone crazy, big hunks of roofing were blowing off the houses on each side of the anchorage.

Then came the eye of the storm: a brief few moments of light wind & drizzle while we tried to tie everything down once again, & then the southern half, which seemed just as horrendous. Our anchor lines tangled as the wind shifted 180 degrees, and at least one didn't seem to be holding at all. We kept on motoring, trying to keep the bow up into the wind while we watched Pete's boat swinging perilously close to the fixed bridge as darkness fell.

And it was *very* dark. The authorities had evacuated everybody and turned off the power, so we couldn't see much of anything on shore. We couldn't tell whether we were drifting or holding still. This was a development we hadn't anticipated. We tried to take half-hour shifts outside, but both of us were on deck much of the time, one watching the tangled anchor lines to make sure we didn't overrun them. At times it seemed we were bound to drag down onto the bridge, but we didn't.

Around 1 a.m. we realized that we could take the engine out of gear & still hold our position, but we were so shell-shocked that we didn't actually stop the engine until almost an hour later. By 2 the sky was full of stars and the wind was a modest 15-20.

First thing in the morning two guys came by in a skiff and offered to phone home for us – they said we weren't permitted to go ashore yet. They wouldn't take any money for the call.

CHAPTER 31

Homeward Bound

Mary P., Harrigan and the same old mooring.

July 14:

Went aground in Bogue Inlet & had to get towed off. The grounding was a combination of circumstances: (1) A crucial green channel buoy was missing (courtesy of Bertha, I guess), (2) Two Coast Guard boats from New Jersey were coming toward us & they were outside the channel too, forcing us even farther out, and (3) We misread a marker ahead, thinking it was red when it was really green.

Anyway, apparently no harm done. We sat there for an hour, occasionally bumping in the turbulent tidal current & the wake from other boats. Talked with 3 different Coast Guard boats (the two originals, plus a rubber one that came by); all said they could not/would not pull us off. But they called the towboat, and it pulled us off handily. I was rather pissed at this, since it was mostly the Coast Guard's boat-handling that put us aground, but what could you do? So: now we are here in Beaufort in this lovely anchorage between the town on one side and the long skinny island w. wild horses on the other.

July 16:

> *Ange plans to leave tomorrow. I phoned Mary Pagano; she said she'd be arriving soon and told me she had been so worried that she called the Marine base at Camp Lejeune and asked them to take us in for shelter during the hurricane. They respectfully declined.*

July 19:

> *Departed Beaufort, just Mary & me, & soon afterward ran aground TWICE within a half-hour while trying to negotiate the route back into the main ICW channel. But got off unassisted both times & proceeded.*

July 21:

> *Up early, called Harrigan, who will take plane to Norfolk tomorrow. Negotiated tricky Currituck Sound, w. wide expanse of shallow water and long narrow 10-foot dredged channel leading through it. Finally reached a little anchorage at mouth of Blackwater Creek, just south of Pungo Ferry, where we could see that the swing bridge of 8 years ago is now replaced by a new 65-foot-clearance fixed bridge. Saw mother raccoon & baby swimming bravely across the channel.*

July 23:

> *Met Harrigan at Waterside Marina, Norfolk, yesterday afternoon, departed today. Glad to see him – he's a great shipmate, despite having one unusable leg in a brace. (Mary looked at me with my bad hip, and herself with two bad knees, and observed that there were only two half-decent legs between all three of us.)*

July 25:

> *Just passed a partly-deflated plastic balloon, pink & green & blue, saying "HAPPY BIRTHDAY." Much talk about the mysterious crash of a TWA airliner in this area the night before Mary flew to North Carolina. Wondered if we might see floating wreckage, or even a body. Did not.*

July 28:

> *Pulled up our two anchors in Great Salt Pond w/out difficulty & left Block I. Had a good evening ashore last night w. beer & dinner, were back on the boat & asleep before full dark.*

At 9 a.m. We were motoring over a calm sea on a beautiful clear day, Point Judith clearly visible ahead. We entered Narragansett Bay and there were George and Mike, old friends, sailing out on their venerable yawl AMPELISCA. "Where have you been?" George yelled as we passed each other.

I don't usually come up with the quick rejoinder, but this time I had one. "*AFRICA*!" I yelled.

The wind came up from the south as we entered the bay. We passed under the new Jamestown Bridge wing & wing, and in good old Greenwich Bay we met a welcoming committee: my son Chris and his wife Deb in their new inflatable dinghy. They escorted us into quiet Apponaug Cove at 4 p.m.

At Harrigan's house, overlooking the cove, we were joined by Chris & Deb, Paul's girlfriend Linda, my son James, Dave Small, who had sailed with us from Dakar, and his wife Earlene, Mary's son Mike and his wife Sue and their two kids. We had champagne and beer and pizza and gazed out into the cove to see TURTLE DOVE resting quietly at her old mooring.

She looked as if she had been there right along.

**** 46,758 miles and seven years, ten months and seven days, from Apponaug, Warwick, R. I., U.S.A., to Apponaug, Warwick, R.I., USA.

THE END

Edwards Brothers Malloy
Thorofare, NJ USA
July 8, 2013